PLAYER-KING
AND
ADVERSARY

Two Faces of Play

in Shakespeare

EILEEN JORGE ALLMAN

LOUISIANA STATE UNIVERSITY PRESS
BATON ROUGE AND LONDON

Designer: Albert Crochet
Type face: VIP Caledonia
Typesetter: LSU Press
Printer and Binder: Thompson-Shore, Inc.

Quotations from *The Riverside Shakespeare* are reprinted
with the permission of the Houghton Mifflin Company.

LIBRARY OF CONGRESS CATALOGING IN PUBLICATION DATA

Allman, Eileen Jorge, 1940-
    Player-king and adversary.

    Includes bibliographical references and index.
    1. Shakespeare, William, 1564-1616—Criticism and
interpretation.   2.   Role playing in literature.
3.   Play in literature.   I.   Title.
PR3069.R59A4   822.3'3   79-15365
ISBN 0-8071-0592-9

*To
Jack and Jennifer*

Contents

Acknowledgments

⚓During the evolution of this book from its origins as a paper on *Measure for Measure* in 1964 to its present publication, I have acquired many professional and personal debts. For the gifts of inspiration and knowledge that made the original paper possible, I am indebted to Leonard Lief and Mary Marshall, my Shakespeare teachers. For overseeing the development of that idea through various stages into a dissertation, I am deeply grateful to my friend Peter Mortenson, who directed it, and to Joseph E. Bryant, Jr., and Arthur Hoffman, rigorous and supportive critics. To the Louisiana State University Press and its readers and staff, I owe an eternity of good words.

When I consider other kinds of debts, I think over and over of my students, whose sense and humanity have kept me committed to education and to people. I wish I could name them all here individually. And I think as well of my husband, John Allman, who took time away from his poetry to help me read, reread, and proofread this book. That debt I shall soon be repaying in kind.

PLAYER-KING
AND
ADVERSARY

CHAPTER I

Introduction

✑ "All the world's a stage." This phrase, although a cultural commonplace, effectively summarizes a set of beliefs at the heart of Shakespeare's plays. Men and women exit and enter life and its stages, putting on and off costumes that suit roles acted or discarded. Parent-child, king-subject, husband-wife, criminal-victim—each role defines another; but beneath the mutual isolation of those roles, all are players. All, at various times, are aware that they are playing. And all, in varying degrees, approach the full meaning of play, which is not merely to act out an established role pattern, but to create from available patterns a new situation and then to stage and act it.

Shakespeare's works recognize the universality of human play; indeed, they assert it as the appropriate medium for exploring, defining, and educating human nature. This emphasis is hardly remarkable for a man so immersed in the art of the theater. For a period of approximately twenty years, Shakespeare committed himself to it as actor, producer, and playwright. In the course of those two decades, his average rate of composition was two plays per year; and he probably appeared in seven times that number as a performer.[1] His most intimate friends and enemies were his fellow actors and playwrights. This dense saturation of Shakespeare's life with plots and plays, characters and players, must at times have blurred the distinction between the world he played to and the world he played in.

1. This approximation was arrived at by using the figures on the average repertory of an Elizabethan leading actor in Bernard Beckerman's *Shakespeare at the Globe, 1599–1609* (New York: Macmillan, 1962), 9.

In Sonnet 111, for example, Shakespeare comments on the consuming nature of his craft: "And almost thence my nature is subdu'd / To what it works in, like the dyer's hand" (6–7).[2] In deploring his loss, Shakespeare expresses the human nostalgia for permanence in a mutable world, a nostalgia echoed by his fellow player Ben Jonson in his *Discoveries:* "*I have* considered, our whole life is like a *Play:* wherein every man, forgetfull of himselfe, is in travaile with expression of another. Nay, wee so insist in imitating others, as wee cannot (when it is necessary) returne to our selves: like Children, that imitate the vices of *Stammerers* so long, till at last they become such; and make the habit to another nature, as it is never forgotten."[3] Both Shakespeare and Jonson lament the loss of the "I" who becomes the other, yet they admit that they cannot preserve that "I" unchanged in time.

Play itself, then—"eterne in mutabilitie" like Spenser's Adonis—accurately describes and imitates the course of human life in a sublunary world. Where truth shapes only to fragment again, play is also a way of connecting pieces. For example, a man who lives the role of businessman absorbs the principles of merchandising so well that they become second nature. He will use metaphors of business to explain other aspects of life, perhaps demanding productivity in his schools, or evaluating his emotions in terms of profit and loss, or viewing his children as prized possessions. These metaphors and the scenes they produce as they are acted out express the partial truths of his limited role. When the world becomes a stage rather than a store, however, that single role of player embraces the possibility of all other roles and their truths. Shakespeare, with all the accouterments of the theatrical world at

2. All citations from Shakespeare are to G. Blakemore Evans (ed.), *The Riverside Shakespeare* (Boston: Houghton Mifflin, 1974).

3. C. H. Herford, Percy and Evelyn Simpson (eds.), *Ben Jonson* (11 vols.; Oxford: Clarendon Press, 1954), VIII, 597.

his disposal—stage, actors, plots, costumes, scenery—could keep a universe of partial truths in motion, giving to each its local habitation and name. He could also create patterns from those colliding worlds, and he could grant a creative ability to the pattern-makers within his drama in order to give it the self-generating quality of life.

God's creation of humanity in His image and free of will is the theological premise behind Shakespeare's creation of these figures: human history and Shakespearean plot are created from within by the characters themselves, even though those characters' creators shape their ultimate ends. Therefore, when Shakespeare's play world is brought before an audience as public performance, it serves as a mirror held up to its viewers' natures as well. United through the playwright are players acting within the drama and players acting outside the drama, both within the purview of a divinity who is at once playwright and audience.[4] We have Thomas Heywood's affirmation of the principle:

> The world's a Theater, the earth a Stage,
> Which God, and nature doth with Actors fill,
>   ... our play's begun,
> When we are borne, and to the world first enter,
> And all finde *Exits* when their parts are done.
> If then the world a Theater present,
> As by the roundnesse it appeares most fit,
> Built with starre-galleries of hye ascent,
> In which *Iehoue* doth as spectator sit.
> And chiefe determiner to applaud the best,
> And their indeuours crowne with more then merit.

4. Jackson I. Cope, *The Theater and the Dream: From Metaphor to Form in Renaissance Drama* (Baltimore: Johns Hopkins University Press, 1973), 19, 100, discusses the neo-Platonic "perspectives" of God as both "omnivoyant" and "the sum total of each viewpoint, of every viewpoint"; and of humanity as "[knowing] himself through seeing and being seen—as spectator and spectacle, as audience and actor at once."

> But by their euill actions doomes the rest,
> To end disgrac't whilst others praise inherit.
> He that denyes then Theaters should be,
> He may as well deny a world to me.[5]

All the world's a stage, and even the stage has a world within it where characters play to their audience of characters.[6]

In Shakespeare's plays, the pattern-makers within the play are of two generic types, types that I call Player-King and Adversary. They are, as the terms suggest, antagonists, their battleground the middle earth of the thrust stage. Each has his own understanding of play, and each has his own motives for

5. Thomas Heywood, "The Author to his Booke," *An Apology for Actors* (1612; reprint ed., New York: Garland, 1973), 13–14.

6. Anne Righter, *Shakespeare and the Idea of the Play* (London: Chatto & Windus, 1962), after studying dramatic occurrences of the Renaissance concept, "all the world's a stage," finds in Shakespeare an uncommon preoccupation with the metaphor. Righter presents a hypothetical progression in Shakespeare's relationship with the stage from a deliberate separation of drama from audience in the early comedies, through disillusionment with theater as witnessed in the tragedies and dark comedies, to a complete blurring of that distinction between drama and audience in the late comedies. Throughout, Righter values the clear separation as a mark of what she views as the progression of theatrical art from the religious to the secular. Like E. K. Chambers, in *The Elizabethan Stage* (4 vols.; Oxford: Clarendon Press, 1923), on whose work her idea of progression is based, and unlike Glynne Wickham, in *Early English Stages, 1300–1660* (2 vols.; London and New York: Routledge and Kegan Paul and Columbia University Press, 1963), who casts serious doubt on that earlier concept, Righter assumes that medieval drama, in which the audience served as part of the community of actors, had to die before an artistic, classically-oriented drama could evolve. Robert Egan, *Drama within Drama: Shakespeare's Sense of His Art* (New York: Columbia University Press, 1972), 12, opposes Righter's concept of evolution, discussing Shakespeare's establishing a relationship between play and audience by "[defining] drama as a dynamic element within the play's world . . . [and establishing] a cognate place for the play itself in the world of its audience." Egan, however, limits his scope to three late plays—*King Lear, The Winter's Tale,* and *The Tempest*—on the grounds that drama in the early plays is "something essentially unreal" (p. 8). I do not share either view. Shakespeare had at his disposal all the acting and playwriting techniques of his theatrical tradition. At any time, for reasons related to plot and genre, he could either widen the separation between audience and drama, as in *Troilus and Cressida,* or emphasize the separation in order to heal it, as he does in *Henry V.* James Calderwood, in fact, in *Shakespearean Metadrama* (Minneapolis: University of Minnesota Press, 1971), 5, concentrates on the early Shakespeare, asserting that the plays are as much about themselves as they are about other issues. He has also commented on the use of interior dramatists as reflections of Shakespeare the dramatist (pp. 15–16).

using it on himself and his fellow characters. The Player-King, in his generic form, is the complete player—actor, producer, and poet-playwright. Rarely, however, does he begin his drama in such perfect form; he is instead created, seemingly self-created, within the drama by an educational process performed before the audience. Because he is a character who can lead his society—both within and outside his formal drama—toward communal harmony, his learning experience must be shared by his two audiences.

From Player-King to Player-King, that education follows a similar pattern. It begins with a psychic shock that isolates him from faith in his identity—Richard II loses his name; Portia lives imprisoned in a casket; Hal mistrusts his stolen title; Vincentio doubts his ability to rule; Prospero forfeits his estate. Friends, names, and possessions—Everyman's Fellowship, Kindred and Cousin, and Goods—betray him as he comes to understand the inevitability of their dissolution. With the shock that extricates him from pride in the self and its possessions comes the realization that any specific role is a limiting pressure on a person's capacity to understand the nature of human variability and so to deal justly and effectively with other people. The future Player-King therefore becomes a social cipher, accepting the essential anonymity of life as he disguises himself, shifts his perspective, and absorbs more of life's partial truths. He comes to view himself as potentially everyone and no one—that is, as the quintessential human being.

If it becomes possible for him to complete his pattern by returning to the role he abandoned or lost, he brings to it an understanding of human nature and a method of teaching—play. At this point, the Player-King uses play to act out his own understanding, to playwrite the education of his fellow characters by having them act out their limited vision within the confines of his plot, and to educate his external audience through those enactments. The Player-King, therefore, in his full cycle, changes his identity from the fixed name of his given social role to the cipher of anonymity, the "crooked figure [that] may / Attest in little place a million" that *Henry V*'s Chorus cites (Prologue. 15–16), becoming at last a combination of the named and the anonymous. His social vision, which he enacts in his last phase, is harmony, the blending of individual notes into an inclusive and complex pattern. With varying degrees of successful completion, Richard II, Henry V, Duke Vincentio, Hamlet, Coriolanus, and Prospero all follow the path of the Player-King.[7]

His dark opposite, the Adversary, limits all existence to the boundaries of self. In his use of play, he parodies, although often unconsciously, the Player-King. Rather than risk the loss of self in an effort to comprehend truths and, through them, truth, he plays to bring the world into forced obedience to himself. The Adversary's aim is always to crush the world into his own image. Iago's "In following [Othello], I follow but myself" (I. i. 58) is a generic statement of his purpose; and "Were I the Moor, I would not be Iago" (I. i. 57) is an announcement of his limitation, frequently expressed as a set of mutually exclusive alternatives, as it is here.

7. Righter, *Shakespeare and the Idea of the Play*, uses the term Player-King to mean an artificial dream king, one who has lost his actual rule. I am using it to mean the opposite, because in play or artifice lies the Platonic reality that material rule can only concretize. James Winny, *The Player King: A Theme of Shakespeare's Histories* (New York: Barnes & Noble, 1968), 46, gives titular significance to the term but defines it vaguely, using it to refer to all the kings in the history plays who try but are unable to achieve the identity of king in all its meaning: "In each of the later Histories the king is forced to come to terms with the nature of the royal identity which he has tried to assume, and to recognise a disparity between his ideal of majesty and his personal ability to fill the role assigned to him. The costume is laid out and the part rehearsed, but the performance falls short in respects which both actor and audience acknowledge. The player is not the king." Again, my use of the term differs markedly. In my definition, the Player-King is a ruling figure who succeeds in fusing the ideal of majesty and his playing of the role because he understands the nature of play, uniting himself through it with that ideal and acting it out publicly to his community.

The Adversary is a proficient technician and a shrewd competitor. He can analyze another person's strategies and devise a counterplot in the split second it takes him to receive and program the data. His observations are reflex-quick, chiefly because his aim—control—is unswervingly single. Since he always knows what he wants, he need not spend any time on the fruitful, if seemingly confused, meanderings of the searching mind. Because his total wisdom resides in his personal desire to win, he is cut off from the Player-King's form of visionary play, a fact that makes the Adversary a dangerous enemy of civic peace and individual salvation. His play causes the destruction and chaos that result from his narcissistic separation of himself from his human and natural communities for the sole purpose of asserting control over them. He is the man who has no music in him. The Adversaries in the Shakespeare canon include Bullingbrook, Falstaff, Angelo, Pandarus, Claudius, Macbeth, Iago, and Edmund, but their consciousness of the powers of darkness behind the evil they choose to create varies in intensity from one to another.[8]

The result of the conflict that arises between these opposing figures takes form as genre. When the Player-King achieves a victory, the genre that evolves, despite tonal variations and temporary threats, is comedy. Shakespeare acknowledges the force of self that leads to tragedy as well, however, in the Adversaries' local victories for destruction. The lines of individual development of Player-King and Adversary and the

8. Sidney R. Homan's discussion of Iago in "Iago's Aesthetics: *Othello* and Shakespeare's Portrait of an Artist," *Shakespeare Studies*, V (1969), 142, exposes the negative image of the artist in the Renaissance who was often seen as "a seducer, a demonic charlatan." Homan refers, too, to Madeleine Doran's emphasis on the artist's self-love as one suspicious aspect of his nature in *Endeavors of Art: A Study of Form in Elizabethan Drama* (Madison: University of Wisconsin Press, 1964). Doran states that we get "a whiff in him of devilish brimstone" (p. 58). Inspiration, a form of frenzy, must be checked by the human discipline of reason. In the Player-King's educational process, we have a progression toward the workable, moral, and human play form, whereas the Adversary plays out only the frenzy of self-love.

dynamics of their conflict—their plots and counterplots—are the internal plot-making force of the formal drama. The plot evolves as the characters' own plans of action, their separate truths with their separate motives colliding on stage.

Renaissance Play Theory

🎭 The figure of the Player-King emerges naturally from a tradition Shakespeare could have absorbed from a number of sources: medieval drama, Renaissance educational philosophy, working contemporary artists. From the medieval drama, he inherited a way of viewing play as an occasion of instruction for actors and audience. This use of play prevailed beyond the avowedly doctrinal drama into the occasional plays prompted, for example, by feasts, jousts, or visiting monarchs. Glynne Wickham cites the instance of Richard II's return to London in 1392 after a disagreement over a denied loan had led him to abandon his court there for York. On his return, among the speeches and pageants shown him was one in which St. John the Baptist, patron saint of the Merchant Taylors' Company (of which Richard was an honorary member), stood in a pageant forest pointing to a sign reading "*agnus et ecce Dei.*" Wickham describes the happenings as follows: "The King and Queen were each given an engraved tablet by an angel who 'descended from the high roof' to present them. The scripture given to the King reminded him that as forgiveness most became Christ on the Cross, so that quality would most become Richard in his relations with his subjects. The Queen's tablet told her that as Esther mediated between the wrath of Ahasuerus and his subjects so she too should mediate between the King and the citizens when the need arose."[9] On the next day,

9. Wickham, *Early English Stages*, I, 70–71. See also David M. Bergeron, *English Civic Pageantry, 1558–1642* (Columbia: University of South Carolina Press, 1971), for descriptions of Elizabethan, Jacobean, and Caroline progresses and pageants. Bergeron attests to their essentially didactic intent.

when visited by the London municipal representatives, Richard and his queen acted in precisely the manner suggested by the pageant. Theatrically, the citizens of London were an outer audience observing their king; he in turn was watching the play before him.[10] Richard, therefore, was simultaneously player and audience, the crucial link in the dramatic chain. As audience, Richard absorbed the lesson of the play before him. As player, he was free to abandon the royal role that had led him to be harsh and unyielding and to approach the problem freshly through another consciousness. In assigning to their monarchs specific roles to act, the citizens of London availed themselves of the most direct means of affecting their king's behavior towards them. On this occasion, they cast him in the role of a merciful, compassionate Christ.

This complex exchange of roles among playwright, actor, and audience occurs strikingly in the Brome *Abraham and Isaac*.[11] In it, a human playwright depicts God, the playwright of human history, using Abraham as his surrogate to act out the conflict and agony of His sacrifice. Like Richard and his audience, both God and Abraham learn from their play: Abraham comprehends the unspeakable pain of God's sacrifice, and God the worthiness of humankind. Their mutual understanding results in an exchange of gifts as Abraham sacrifices a lamb and God promises to multiply his seed. In writing the play, the human playwright is creating a way for his audience to echo this mutual learning experience. Playwright-audience and character-surrogate learn from each other, and the audi-

10. Dieter Mehl, "Forms and Functions of the Play within a Play," *Renaissance Drama*, VIII (1965), 43–44, notes this focus on the audience within the play rather than on the play within the play in *Sir Thomas More*. Robert J. Nelson, *Play Within a Play: The Dramatist's Conception of His Art* (New Haven: Yale University Press, 1958), 30–31, explores the way this focus moves in Shakespeare, with the real audience often being asked not to respond like the audience on stage—for example, to identify with Hamlet rather than with Claudius.

11. Osborn Waterhouse (ed.), *The Non-Cycle Mystery Plays*, Early English Text Society, extra series, CIV (London: Kegan Paul, Trench, Trübner, 1909).

ence learns from their learning. Shakespeare often creates similar interchanges—with Hal and Francis, for example, or Prospero and Caliban.

The direct connection between play and education was an important aspect of the theories and practices of Renaissance schoolmasters. At Eton, under headmaster Nicholas Udall, playwriting, acting, and staging were part of the curriculum; Udall himself probably borrowed the technique from his own education at Winchester. According to one of his pupils, William Malim, Latin plays helped the pupils learn their grammar and pronunciation; English plays provided "subtlety and humour."[12] Udall, as both headmaster and playwright, combined education and playing in a way that became common in sixteenth-century England and emerged prominently in the body and writings of Richard Mulcaster, yet another of his pupils. Sir James Whitelocke's testimony affirms Mulcaster's emphasis on producing plays: "yeerly he presented sum playes to the court, in whiche his scholers wear only actors, and I on among them, and by that meanes taughte them good behaviour and audacitye."[13] Mulcaster had some apt pupils—Thomas Lodge, Thomas Kyd, and Edmund Spenser, to name a few. He may also have turned out Thomas Jenkins, who, as T. W. Baldwin suggests, was probably Shakespeare's teacher at the King's Free Grammar School at Stratford.[14] If so, this connection between education and drama was made for Shakespeare himself in his own early schooling. Since the educators traditionally functioned as playwrights, playwrights could assume that the corollary was true and function as educators. Aubrey, reporting

12. T. H. Vail Motter, *The School Drama in England* (1929; reprint ed., Port Washington, N.Y.: Kennikat Press, 1968), 87.

13. Sir James Whitelocke, *Liber Familicus*, ed. John Bruce (Westminster: The Camden Society, 1858), 12. These schoolmasters were also notorious for less humane methods of education—they were merciless floggers.

14. T. W. Baldwin, *William Shakspere's Small Latine and Lesse Greeke* (2 vols.; Urbana: University of Illinois Press, 1944), I, 478–79.

William Beeston's statement that Shakespeare was a country schoolmaster during the "lost years," offers us some tantalizing food for thought.

The playwright, who works with his entire community, is, of course, a far cry from the headmaster-playwright. His style of education must be more artistically conscious, his skill standing, as Sidney says in *The Defence of Poesie*, "in that *Idea*, or fore conceit of the worke, and not in the work it selfe." The "Artificer's" skill resides in finding the form capable of reaching his audience and inspiring its members to imitate the good; it is a kind of mediation between the world of the imagination and the world of the flesh:

> And that the Poet hath that *Idea*, is manifest, by delivering them foorth in such excellencie as he had imagined them: which delivering foorth, also is not wholly imaginative, as we are wont to say by them that build Castles in the aire: but so farre substancially it worketh, not onely to make a *Cyrus*, which had bene but a particular excellency as nature might have done, but to bestow a *Cyrus* upon the world to make many *Cyrusses*, if they will learne aright, why and how that maker made him.[15]

Sidney measures effectiveness in art by its ability to inspire imitation. The playwright, discovering the "Idea" that will form his work, can create a breathing, talking Cyrus for his audience.[16] Moreover, if he forms his work around players who are playing within the drama, he can make his audience understand that Cyrus is merely an actor playing Cyrus, that a member of the audience is an actor playing a member of the

15. Albert Feuillerat (ed.), *The Prose Works of Sir Philip Sidney* (4 vols.; Cambridge: Cambridge University Press, 1923), III, 8.
16. Thomas Heywood's defense, *An Apology for Actors*, also concentrates on art's ability to inspire imitation. Heywood states that the sight of actors playing such figures as Hector, Troilus, Pompey, Caesar, and Hannibal would make the viewer an Alexander (pp. 20–21). He cites the ancient Greeks as using "moralized mysteries" "to plant humanity and manners in the hearts of the multitude" (p. 27) and ends by praising Edward Alleyn, a great actor and a good man, as the living proof that actors are not all degenerate (pp. 42–43).

audience, and that we may all therefore be Cyrusses if we choose to assume the role. A Player-King can generate an audience, perhaps even a culture of Player-Kings if the playwright's "Idea" produces a work with far-reaching influence.

The Adversary, however, whose aim is to destroy such imitable forms of goodness, has as strong a tradition behind him as the Player-King. In fact, it is the same tradition. Since the principle of bringing body, mind, and spirit into coordination by having a person play out his lessons—whether the subject is Latin grammar or moral uprightness—is integral to Renaissance thought, the Adversary can use play to spread evil by teaching its postures and words. Satan, too, was a player, and his response to the angelic will to serve was self-service. Separating, darkening, untuning, uncreating, Satan offers Adam and Eve and their progeny roles that either reverse the divine will or mire it in separate selves. He creates an illusion of power that his followers can draw on by enacting the parodic rituals of divine worship called black magic.

Shakespeare makes his ultimate Player-King, Prospero, a white magician. But Prospero took over his island from Sycorax. The Player-King, a playwright and a white magician, discovers through his loss and renewal of self a body of power existing beneath the world's surface of names and things, a body of power he can reach in play. That power can serve its original purpose—as a channel of communication between the human and the divine—or it can be diverted, if only temporarily, into a circle of irresponsible, egoistic power. And so play must be used carefully, for if all the world's a stage, there is a dark audience beyond the human, an audience one must be chary of inviting into the action.[17]

17. See Edgar Wind's discussion of the neo-Platonic difficulty in keeping "mystery" from including not only ritual and poetry but magic as well in *Pagan Mysteries in the Renaissance* (New York: Norton, 1968), 1–17. For a full critical discussion of the relationship between magic and play, see Kirby Farrell, *Shakespeare's Creation: The Language of Magic and Play* (Amherst: University of Massachusetts Press, 1975).

The self-appointed watchdogs of England's spiritual health, the Puritans, accepted the burden of warning the country against allowing the performance of plays. John Northbrooke's *A Treatise wherein Dicing, Dauncing, Vaine playes, or Enterluds . . . are reproved* and Stephen Gosson's *The Schoole of Abuse*—famous because it occasioned Sidney's *Defence*—began an antitheater campaign that culminated in 1633 with William Prynne's *Histriomastix*. The intemperate Prynne not only attacks plays as lies and players as "the very dregs of men" but also interprets such events as the plagues, the burning of the Globe and the Fortune, and the apparition of a devil raised during Edward Alleyn's famous performance of *Doctor Faustus* as God's judgment on England. And Prynne certainly refutes the claim that acting is educational in any positive way. Because the student is asked to take on another station, habit, or even sex, Prynne maintains that he is being educated in hypocrisy, obscenity, and effeminacy.[18]

Nor was this exposure of the dangers involved in acting restricted to extreme and literal minds. In the Induction to John Marston's *Antonio and Mellida*, the boy actor who is to play Antonio worries about having to portray an Amazon: "Ay, but when use hath taught me action to hit the right point of a lady's part, I shall grow ignorant, when I must turn young prince again, how but to truss my hose." In that sentiment, the actor reaches out to both Prynne and Jonson, whose remarks on stammerers echo the reluctant Amazon's.[19]

If metaphors are manipulated into action not merely through ignorance, but intentionally by the Adversary's malevolent

---

18. John Northbrooke, *A Treatise wherein Dicing, Dauncing, Vaine playes or Enterluds . . . are reproved* (?1577; reprint ed., New York: Garland, 1974); Stephen Gosson, *The Schoole of Abuse* (1579; reprint ed., New York: Garland, 1973); William Prynne, *Histriomastix* (1633; reprint ed., New York: Garland, 1974), 133, 556–61, 167.

19. John Marston, *Antonio and Mellida*, ed. G. K. Hunter (Lincoln: University of Nebraska Press, 1965), ll. 77–79. See, too, Jonson's "Epitaph on S. P. a child of Q. El. Chappel," Herford and Simpson (eds.), *Ben Jonson*, VIII, 77.

force, the destruction possible can be checked only by an equal but benign force. The universe may ultimately work its way to goodness, but the local human devastation can be considerable. The Renaissance attitude toward play, then, is ambivalent. Play is a force that molds our minds and behavior for good or ill, that allows us to reach beyond ourselves into a dangerously powerful, possibly forbidden sphere of energy, and that reconnects us to absolute forces who use us for their own actualization.

Modern Play Theory

ᚤ The Renaissance understanding of play, reaching as it does into metaphysics, psychology, and criticism, carries a heavy weight of Christian meaning. Modern play theory, which has created a climate for appreciating Shakespeare and his world more fully, is as metaphysical, psychological, and literary, but not as specifically theological. The result is a body of contemporary thought at once more speculative and more utilitarian than Renaissance theories and practices, but nonetheless capable of comprehending the Player-King and the dynamics of his education. All the world is still a stage.

In the area of metaphysics, Johan Huizinga's *Homo Ludens* has provided fertile new ground for the ongoing attempt to define human and cosmic nature, describe their activities, and relate them to one another.[20] In a collection of essays devoted to pursuing Huizinga's ideas further into their relevance to philosophy and literature, Eugen Fink discusses human play as the link between humanity and the cosmos, finding in play the spiritual search for atonement with a force or pattern we perceive as more powerful than but of the same nature as ourselves:

> Play is such a phenomenon that by its very nature is endowed with the character of symbolic representation. Is this to say that play

20. Johan Huizinga, *Homo Ludens* (Boston: Beacon Press, 1950).

can become the symbolic theatrical enactment of the universe, the speculative metaphor of the world? This bold thought has actually been formulated before. In the dawn of European philosophy Heraclitus says: "The course of the world is a playing child moving figures on a board—the child as absolute ruler of the universe" (Diels, Fragment 52). And after twenty-five centuries of philosophy Nietzsche says: "Becoming and dissolution, building and destruction without moral implication, in eternal innocence, are to be found *in* the world only in the play of the artist and of the child"—"the world *is* the play of Zeus" (in *Philosophy in the Tragic Era of the Greeks*).[21]

Life is a play of cosmic magnitude in which a person can symbolically enact the creation, life, and destruction of the universe in his own play patterns. He is simultaneously the creator and object of those patterns: as creator, he becomes one with the pattern-maker, feeling the power of the ascent to the "Idea" that Sidney speaks of; as object, he is himself still a microcosm in the Renaissance sense, doomed to suffer death as well as to create life.

Modern philosophers concur with some of the principles of Renaissance play; modern psychologists use play both theoretically and clinically in ways that resemble Renaissance educators and dramatists. Child psychologists, for example, have found that children use play to release unacceptable impulses, reverse roles usually taken, mirror growth, express problems, and experiment with solutions. "Through dramatic play these children are attempting to expand the horizons of the self, to break through the rigid and confining limits which circumstances have imposed on them."[22] A child's mental health depends on his overcoming the crippling paralysis of rules, problems, and guilts. Play grants him the immediate escape from a constricting world, the means of exploring new realms

21. Eugen Fink, "The Oasis of Happiness: Toward an Ontology of Play," *Game, Play, Literature* (New Haven: Eastern Press, 1968), 29.
22. Ruth E. Hartley, Lawrence K. Frank, and Robert M. Goldenson, *Understanding Children's Play* (New York: Columbia University Press, 1952), 27–40, 38.

of experience, and the passage back to his point of origin. It allows him to follow the educational process of the Player-King. Play therapy, as exemplified in Virginia Axline's *Dibs in Search of Self*, is capable of miraculously transforming a completely withdrawn child into a functioning, self-aware human being.[23]

Child psychologists, like Renaissance educators, provide truths applicable to the adult mind. Achieving and maintaining mental health through play is certainly not restricted to children, although it is most natural to their age and situation. Any person who clings to one role throughout his life, thus denying his human need to play, finds first that his body will rebel, usually in the form of psychosomatic illness, and second that his mind will cease to function clearly and perhaps even rationally. In a psychology column of a newspaper, Dr. Alfred Messer tells the story of a general who enjoyed going home to hunt with an old guide who still called him "boy": "Being able to shift to a different role from time to time is one of the major factors in recouping or recharging after emotional stress and fatigue. . . . The individual's capacity to shift to different roles is one measure of his emotional health." Dr. Eric Berne's work on transactional analysis, *Games People Play*, uses the terms of play to describe human behavior patterns. Like child psychologists, he reveals the seriousness of games, some of which end in suicide, as he logically follows through to its conclusion the long-standing therapy practice of having a person act out and thereby break through his neurotic limitations.[24]

In modern criticism, Kenneth Burke uses the terms of play to describe the psychological aspects of art, including the body's art of "dancing out" the mind's attitudes. He sees art as

23. Virginia M. Axline, *Dibs in Search of Self: Personality Development in Play Therapy* (Boston: Houghton Mifflin, 1964).

24. Eric Berne, *Games People Play: The Psychology of Human Relationships* (New York: Grove, 1964).

a strategy for making public and thereby releasing the artist's private burden. In viewing a work as its creator's psychodrama, a temporary release from neurosis, Burke limits himself to the psychomedical approach to art.[25] If, however, we add play's metaphysical function, art becomes not merely the functional adaptation of a man to his problems, which is a type of what Plato and Prynne call a lie, but also a form of atonement with divinity and humanity. This belief in both the metaphysical and psychological functions of art, which becomes a force for morality in the human community, is closest to Sidney's critical theory.

Modern play theory recognizes the Adversary's iconoclastic power as well, but only glancingly. The Adversary exists potentially in Nietzsche's insistence on true playing as "without moral implication," in Burke's view of the artist releasing himself from his burden by giving it to others, and in the growing contemporary awareness of amulets, astrology, and cults. Yet modern play theory emphasizes the benign power of the Player-King who, in both modern and Renaissance theory, personifies two related functions of play: first, the spiritual, the private release from a limiting human role into its ultimate source, the experience of knowing by becoming the pattern-making force in the universe; second, the psychological and physical, the exploration of potential and actual roles and the expression of the self's difficulties in acting them out. Play is both an emancipating, visionary experience and a didactic performance of that vision.

Shakespeare's Player-King is both a visionary and a performer. He is Sidney's Poet, who transcends his immediate time and space to find the "Idea" that will create imitable good. He is a provider of that "symbolic theatrical enactment of the universe, the speculative metaphor of the world" that

25. Kenneth Burke, *The Philosophy of Literary Form: Studies in Symbolic Action* (New York: Vintage Books, 1957).

Fink traces through the history of philosophy. He uses his body to dance out his mind's attitudes, becoming his audience's medium between the mutable and the permanent. He contains the Adversary's power, ultimately shedding light on that dark purveyor of chaos.

If the Player-King and the creator he mirrors are to bring the members of their audience into harmony with themselves, the formal drama must move out of its confines. By forcing on the audience the recognition that all the world's a stage, Shakespeare pulls down the barriers between the drama and its spectators. He is Jonson's "true Artificer": "An other Age, or juster men, will acknowledge the vertues of his studies. . . . How he doth raigne in mens affections; how invade, and breake in upon them; and makes their minds like the thing he writes."[26] This invasion of other selves and other designs is the source of relaxation and escape an audience seeks upon entering the theater. It is also the educational base of Shakespeare's world of play.

26. Herford and Simpson (eds.), *Ben Jonson*, VIII, 587–88.

CHAPTER II

History Enacted: The Emergence
of a Player-King

❧ Shakespeare's exploration of the ties between leadership and community, both historical and dramatic, carried him through the writing of two tetralogies encompassing eighty-six years of English history. Having recorded corruption prolifically engendering itself in the political upheavals of *1, 2, 3, Henry VI* and *Richard III*, he turns to the power vacuum that occasioned it—Richard II's defeat and death, and Henry IV's struggle to hold his destiny back from the vortex of his sin. There, between the sin and its expiation, hemmed in by violence on either side, son of Henry IV, the usurper, and father of Henry VI, the victim of usurpation, resides Henry V—the ideal king. Shakespeare renders Henry V's mysterious success humanly intelligible by showing him undergoing the educational process of the Player-King stage by stage over the course of three plays. In contrast to his predecessors and followers, who blocked orderly movement and communication in both their countries and their plays, Henry V is a leader with the ability to pattern motion and open channels. He can penetrate the surface of names and things, explore the vestigial connections of the prelapsarian world, express them in metaphor, and enact them in play. In Tudor history, he is a luminous interval between two darknesses; in Shakespearean dramaturgy, he is the culmination of the history plays' decade of search for a Player-King.

Richard II: The Paralysis of Mode

❧ In the history of Richard II's reign, Shakespeare faces two failures of leadership. A weak, corrupt king is forced to relinquish power by a forceful, decisive challenger. The historical sources explain ideologically why a seemingly beneficial act will end in national destruction. The king's body, consecrated in the coronation ceremony, is assumed into the spiritual significance of his role; the sanctity of the kingship is inviolable and cannot be broken without stern, expiatory punishment for the sacrilege.[1] History's ambiguous treatment of the two cousins, each guilty of crimes against the kingship, is resolved in Shakespeare's search for the point where ideology touches human character, a search given its magnetic poles of action in his creation of two incomplete versions of the Player-King and the Adversary. Richard, as anointed king, will not fulfill in play his potential vision, and Bullingbrook, an Adversary with a thirst for order, cannot shake off the anxiety he suffers for seizing power and destroying his enemy. To exhibit fully the lacks of each character as man and leader, Shakespeare involves them in two separate actions: the first a competitive game of power with England as prize; the second a noncompetitive search for selfhood and salvation. Each man has the opportunity to play two significantly different roles in one drama— Beggar and King. And each performs in closely paralleled circumstances the measure of his success and failure against the other.

Structurally, the play's complexity results from Shakespeare's splitting the tragic rise-and-fall pattern in two and giving each king half. Yet despite its complexity, the structure, built from within by the players Bullingbrook and Richard, is singularly monotonous, almost motionless. Richard is king: he presides over his court and country as judge and general; he

1. Ernst H. Kantorowicz, *The King's Two Bodies* (Princeton: Princeton University Press, 1957). See also Maynard Mack, Jr., *Killing the King: Three Studies in Shakespeare's Tragic Structure* (New Haven: Yale University Press, 1973). For my discussion of the tetralogy as an ultimately successful search for the ideal king, I am indebted in a general way to the works of E. M. W. Tillyard, *Shakespeare's History Plays* (London: Chatto & Windus, 1944); Derek Traversi, *Shakespeare from "Richard II" to "Henry V"* (Stanford: Stanford University Press, 1957); and John Dover Wilson, *The Fortunes of Falstaff* (Cambridge: Cambridge University Press, 1943).

watches the gauge challenge between his cousin Bullingbrook and his noble Mowbray; he passes sentences of exile on them; he moves against the Irish rebels. In all these actions, Richard is unsuccessful. Bullingbrook becomes King Henry IV: he oversees the gauge challenges involving his cousin Aumerle and his court of nobles; he passes sentences of exile and death on his cousin Richard; he fights against English rebels. In all these actions, he is victorious.

Yet the difference between victory and defeat is not as significant as the paralyzing repetition of events. Bullingbrook, trapped on the throne of his former opponent, has inherited Richard's problem—the endlessly repeating conflict between those who possess power over the material world and those who desire it. He can maintain control where Richard failed, but he cannot change his country's agonistic mode of play.[2] He cannot bring fruit to a land grown barren beneath him; he cannot heal the gash of rebellion or create harmony where schism prevails. *Richard II*'s structure, therefore, folds back on itself. Harmonious growth, rooted in enacted vision rather than blind action, eludes the corrupted body politic. For the players' inner audience—the England within the play that they rule— the tension of repressive authority produces uncanny shivers and ominous forewarnings. Despite the desperate activity of move and countermove, no redemptive change emerges to free the characters within the play from their immobility.

Richard II: The King Is Not Himself[3]

 The play's first actor in the role of king is the hereditary heir to the throne. Richard II bases his reign on the mistaken

2. Leonard F. Dean, "*Richard II*: The State and the Image of the Theater," *Publications of the Modern Language Association*, LXVII (1952), 211–18, places the theatrical metaphors of *Richard II* in the light of the theater-state comparisons drawn by More and Machiavelli. He notes the "dualism of the theatrical state" (p. 218) under both Richard and Henry IV, who use guile in their ceremonial performances, and the resolution of that dualism under Henry V.

3. The title is also used by Michael Quinn in " 'The King Is Not Himself': The Personal Tragedy of Richard II," *Studies in Philology*, LVI (1959), 169–86.

idea that he can separate his role from his name, that is, his physical actions from the magnetic efficacy of the title he believes will render him personally invincible. Because a universe of power watches over it, he assumes that kingship can take care of itself even though he rejects the selflessness required of a communal leader and pursues hedonism to its mortal depths. Yet even the meaning of the coronation of a king, a ritual play strongly rooted in universal mystery, will perish if the life in that belief is moribund. Unless play enacts the connections between the name and its source, the name becomes only an imitation of itself. All metaphor, unacted, comes to a halt and petrifies; even the name of king, reduced to a vessel empty of divine energy, becomes a pawn in the political power struggle.

Compared to the Player-King, who wills his being into the perpetual enactment of metaphor, Richard is an Audience-King, enjoying the activity before him as if it were a spectacle he had no part in. The Player-King's selfhood resides in his kingship; but Richard is only a specter in symbolic regalia, a frozen idol. Using his title as an escape from responsible action, he counteracts the universal pattern on which its efficacy rests. A king's realm acts out his will, but England under Richard is at a dead halt. He has extended his personal paralysis as king outward to his community in the form of a repressive tyranny over action. Richard's deadening hand moves only to impede and stop, never to set in motion, while England, struggling in the grip of his divided being, faces the choice of death or rebellion. This result of Richard's perverse play world—personal and communal division and stagnation—is apparent in the court when the drama opens. As Richard continues to rely futilely on his name to control the other names in the country, assuming that they alone will govern the flesh they mark, the unnatural separation of name from act immobilizes the land and speaks for rebellion as health.[4]

4. See Calderwood, *Shakespearean Metadrama*, 149–86, for a provocative dis-

Richard's inability to maintain this unnatural separation appears first as he presides over the challenge of Bullingbrook to Mowbray. The hurling of insults and gauges—violence of language and gesture—reveals the strength in the temporarily displaced hostility and foreshadows the power behind the final upheaval. Yet Richard, sitting as audience rather than as judge or participant, deludes himself into believing he can stop the challenge short of definitive action. Luxuriating in the spectacle of words and posturing, Richard foolishly goads the antagonists further, baiting them like animals pitted for his entertainment:

> What doth our cousin lay to Mowbray's charge?
> It must be great that can inherit us
> So much as of a thought of ill in him. (I. i. 84–86)

> How high a pitch his resolution soars!
> Thomas of Norfolk, what say'st thou to this? (I. i. 109–10)

Characteristically, he then attempts to halt the hostility short of combat.

Not surprisingly, neither Bullingbrook nor Mowbray will obey. Richard, faced with the refusal of those he should govern to abide by his ruling and so confronted by the impotence of his kingship, shields himself from the discovery by donning a merely verbal disguise of power, thereby reinforcing his personal division:

> We were not born to sue, but to command,
> Which since we cannot do to make you friends,
> Be ready, as your lives shall answer it,
> At Coventry upon Saint Lambert's Day. (I. i. 196–99)

Thus, despite Richard's attempts to prevent the play of challenge from reaching its resolution, movement invades his realm and, with it, a successful beginning to the attack and overthrow

---

cussion of the relationship between word and act in *Richard II*. Calderwood notes that "as royal dramatist Richard specializes in modes of both verbal and actional incompletion" (p. 162).

of his nominal power. In response to movement, Richard's strategy of paralysis becomes defensiveness. The halting of the joust at Coventry is only an extension of the same tactic. Typically waiting until the last possible moment before dropping his staff, Richard allows the desire for movement an opportunity to feel its strength before he—temporarily—deactivates it.[5]

Yet Richard's unwillingness to act does not preclude an understanding of metaphoric correspondence; he has the imagination and language of the Player-King.[6] He explains why he threw down his staff:

> for we think the eagle-winged pride
> Of sky-aspiring and ambitious thoughts,
> With rival-hating envy, set on you
> To wake our peace, which in our country's cradle
> Draws the sweet infant breath of gentle sleep;
> Which so rous'd up with boist'rous untun'd drums,
> With harsh-resounding trumpets' dreadful bray,
> And grating shock of wrathful iron arms,
> Might from our quiet confines fright fair peace,
> And make us wade even in our kinred's blood.
>   (I. iii. 129–38)

5. Winny, *The Player King*, 48, 50, sees Richard's substitution of verbal action for physical action as part of his "complete absorption in the identity of king," which makes him shy away from reality in favor of self-deluding fantasy. Yet Richard the man is not absorbed into the title; he instead separates the two and allows them to pursue different courses.

6. Derek Traversi, *An Approach to Shakespeare* (2 vols.; Garden City, N.Y.: Anchor Books, 1969), I, 159–78, discusses Richard's language as artifice, and so a sign of his weakness and his exhibitionism. This view leads Traversi to see Richard's death as pathetic rather than tragic. His language, however, seems rather a frustrated royal power, which he understands, can express, but will not act out. Wolfgang Clemen, *The Development of Shakespeare's Imagery* (Cambridge: Harvard University Press, 1951), points out the essential qualities of Richard's character: "Poet, actor, dreamer, passive spectator—all these qualities unavoidably lead him to revel in imagery whenever he speaks. Instead of deciding, he interprets the situation by means of elaborate similes; instead of turning to action, he prefers to reflect upon his own state" (p. 55). Clemen adds that Richard "possesses a fine insight into what could be called the inherent symbolism of a situation" (p. 57), which leads him, when he does act, to appropriate symbolic acts for his deposition.

In his comment, Richard falls instinctively into metaphor, a habit of mind that will bear dramatic fruit only when he is no longer king. His speech, first, makes clear political sense: whoever loses the joust might command a faction strong enough to pursue revenge, which in such elevated circles means civil war. The speech is, second, a threat in its implication that the spirit of war, once aroused, will devour relative as well as stranger. Third and most important, it expresses the implicit awareness that acting out war's hostility in a miniature form like the joust creates the danger of arousing the corresponding hostility of actual war. Richard's language demonstrates an understanding that within the universe, held together by ties of metaphor, activity is created by playing out those metaphors. Further, his language fits harmoniously into the patterns he sees. His syntax is hypotactic, inclusive yet controlled; his diction is richly varied; his governing unit is metaphor: Richard's speech reflects both variety and order. He chooses, however, to use that intuitive understanding negatively to cease action rather than to produce it. Ironically, Richard expresses the Player-King's awareness at the very moment he is willfully neglecting the responsibility it entails of personally playing out that awareness and thereby guiding his subjects to positive action.

As a result of his consistent, tyrannical repression of motion, Richard's realm has suffered an unnatural inversion. Acts, gestures, postures, isolated from their metaphysical connections, finally force the word back on itself. Words begin to express only an inner direction, a self-conscious awareness of their separate existence, which is the beginning of verbal paralysis—silence. Mowbray, touchingly describing the desolation of wordlessness that he sees in exile, suggests the full function of language, without which there is no life, feeling, or action, but merely ignorance, slavery, poverty, and death. In brief, he describes the fate of England under Richard. John of Gaunt is forced to use words against his son because Richard forces him to speak in the role of judge rather than father. Bullingbrook warrants his father's reprimand because he turns his silence on those who bid him good-bye. Aumerle parades his parting "Farewell" to Bullingbrook before Richard, priding himself on the deception of his brevity, seemingly caused by sorrow but actually by contempt. The tension produced by Richard's inaction and his willful perversion of words, both from the feelings that prompt them and from the acts they generate, builds to fatal proportions. Subduing one crisis, he merely instigates another. To avoid the joust, he passes sentences of exile on the combatants. Yet the term *exile* becomes ominously ambiguous when all England seems to follow Bullingbrook to the shores of the land. On him, England has rested its hopes of the instigating movement that will free the country from Richard's paralysis. The play's first action, a challenge, is incomplete in itself, but its expression of the violence threatening to erupt is a token of the future that only Richard ignores.

John of Gaunt, old and dying, whose son takes the potential motion of the English into exile, becomes in his last moments the voice of his country's frustrated will to act—a voice first of warning and last of doom. He remains the only spokesman for the full meaning of the king's name, a lone voice raised for the principle of active correspondence among natural, political, and cosmic orders. To Richard, he is an irritant; at Coventry he reminded the king of the limitations placed on all human power:

> Thy word is current with him [time] for my death,
> But dead, thy kingdom cannot buy my breath. (I. iii. 231–32)

Since Coventry, Richard's condition has worsened with now even the kingdom divided, its fruit no longer naturally harvested by its monarch.

With the play that connects the body politic to the other

orders of the universe left unacted, the infinite richness of metaphor reverts to material poverty. Vanity, the love of the world's finite gifts, as Gaunt observes, is a cormorant that preys on itself at last (II. i. 38–39). Richard descends from kings who traveled to Jerusalem to connect their royalty to the spiritual king from whom they inherit, yet he hastens to abrogate all connections between himself and the spirituality that inheres in his name. The encounter between Richard and Gaunt, therefore, begins as it will end, with a discussion of names. The dying man gives Richard a lecture on the relevance of a man's name to his actions, displaying his sense of metaphor by punning elaborately on his own name, Gaunt. Richard's contemptuous response allows his uncle to press home his point: I, like England, am Gaunt, and you, who are King of Gaunt, will die with the land you starve. The end of Richard's irresponsible refusal to act out his name will be the loss of land, people, and finally the name from which they are inseparable.

Gaunt completes the rebellion against Richard by naming him in terms of his actions, thus combining what Richard has torn apart and laying the groundwork for future action: "Landlord of England art thou now, not king" (II. i. 113). A king rules a spiritual community as the heart of the law that holds it together; a landlord, however, is subject to law, a mere possessor of salable goods. Gaunt touches the nerve, and Richard, with almost insane spite, rushes to seize and sell illegally this disruptive family's estate with his uncle scarcely dead. Despite his uncle's admonitions, Richard still believes that the magic will never leave him even though he has separated himself from his human community, sold the land he rules as guardian, and finally, manifesting total divisiveness, broken the law that exists in his name.[7]

Gaunt unlocked the tongues of the country by renaming

7. R. J. Dorius has noted this doubleness of Richard's attitude in "A Little More Than a Little," *Shakespeare Quarterly*, XI (1960), 13–26.

Richard, thus rejoining the broken connection between the name and its enactment. Hereafter the finite name he bequeaths him reverberates in the doubts of his country. Northumberland observes: "The King is not himself" (II. i. 241). Willoughby answers: "The King's grown bankrout, like a broken man" (II. i. 257). Rallying the forces of opposition against Richard, Northumberland verbalizes the state from which they rebel:

> If then we shall shake off our slavish yoke,
> Imp out our drooping country's broken wing,
> Redeem from broking pawn the blemish'd crown,
> Wipe off the dust that hides our sceptre's gilt,
> And make high majesty look like itself,
> Away with me in post to Ravenspurgh. (II. i. 291–96)

The country's ascending motion impeded, the crown's value translated into money, the spiritual glitter of the scepter's gold hidden by material imperfection—all find their way into Northumberland's plea for action. The rebellion's aim—to make majesty look like itself—rejects Richard's separation of the name and the man. Freed by Gaunt's curse, the rebels seek a king who will act like a king.

They seek the actor Bullingbrook, a man with the Adversary's capacity to serve a cause by serving himself. Bullingbrook has no interest in the spirituality of the king's name except as it provides the motive for absolute obedience. Power is the end of his striving:

> How long a time lies in one little word!
> Four lagging winters and four wanton springs
> End in a word: such is the breath of kings. (I. iii. 213–15)

The physical world supplies Bullingbrook with the material and the goal of his enterprise—followers, soldiers, arms; his medium is his ability to play the role of commander convincingly enough for the rebellion to believe that he could indeed

make majesty look like itself. In fact, he is a beggar, deprived
of name and title, but he gathers around him enough material
force to make any audience believe him the ruling power. The
illegal and unjust loss of name and estate, carefully manipulated, is the weight to balance his illegal seizure of another
name and a larger estate. Gambling against his original dis-
possession in the toss for power, Bullingbrook reveals what
will emerge as his characteristic mode of perception—the clear
division of any problem into mutually exclusive alternatives.
Linguistically, that perception expresses itself in a syntax governed by either/or: for example, either the kingship or death.

The ability to act and to manipulate others into his play exists in Bullingbrook without the revelation of metaphor. His
contempt for poetry, which builds bridges between alternatives, appears clearly in his rejection of the imaginative faculty.
When, after the sentence of exile has been passed, Gaunt suggests that he use his imagination to find a better reason for
flight, or to transform the flowers in his path to ladies and his
solitary footsteps into a dance, Bullingbrook replies:

> O, who can hold a fire in his hand
> By thinking on the frosty Caucasus?
> Or cloy the hungry edge of appetite
> By bare imagination of a feast?
> Or wallow naked in December snow
> By thinking on fantastic summer's heat?
> O no, the apprehension of the good
> Gives but the greater feeling to the worse. (I. iii. 294–301)

In the either/or confrontation between the real and the imagined, he sides with the real. The imagination is only the coward's faculty of escape from a world which Bullingbrook
believes he can seize by force like an unprotected jewel.[8] He

8. Winny, *The Player King*, 71, sees Bullingbrook's rejection of this offered fantasy as his unsentimental attachment to reality. Reality, however, must be defined in
terms of the ideals it manifests. Winny's comment is no compliment to Bullingbrook.

knows what he wants, and he understands his opponent's weaknesses well enough to attain it. His grasp of human motive is limited, like the Adversary's, to personal ambition, but it exceeds by far Richard's poor capacity for interpreting even overt action as it concerns his well-being.

Bullingbrook, then, demonstrates the Adversary's forte in his cleverly plotted attainment of power. Even the deceitful gesture and the lying word contain the promise of productive change to a country that has been rendered motionless and mute. Bullingbrook easily persuades Northumberland that he is humble and grateful, York that his claim to his own lands is his sole objective. To Northumberland: "Of much less value is my company / Than your good words" (II. iii. 19–20). York, to whom he has knelt, he twice calls "my gracious uncle" (II. iii. 85, 106). Successfully deceitful, Bullingbrook convinces his followers that he wants what each of them wants: a king attendant to his nobles, or the end of favoritism, or the prevalence of justice in the realm. Even York will lend his honorable face to an enterprise launched against the "caterpillars of the commonwealth" (II. iii. 166). Most of all, however, Bullingbrook attracts his followers by the movement he embodies. He has arrived on the shores of England; he marches through the frustrated country; he gathers force and momentum along the way as people flock to him. From exile to the heart of England, the ruined castle that houses a king, Bullingbrook progresses, a principle of action in the paralyzed land.[9]

Flint Castle: The Death of Ceremony

Before the mode of the drama can shift its key from the king's inclusive yet unfulfilled language and its national consequences to the Adversary's either/or style, the community's structure of belief, linked through ritual play to the universe's

9. *Ibid.*, 69.

metaphoric pattern, must dissolve. Ceremonial ritual, the last refinement of play, is the first play form to lose efficacy when the human community no longer touches its divine source of vitality. The death of creative play and the hypertrophy of its corrupt imitation under Richard were the first blow to the ceremony that consecrated him as king. Richard's reaction to the pressure of rebellion will occasion the second and the third, his verbal and finally physical descent from the kingship. As the crisis of power moves towards its culmination in the changing of actors, the pattern of the drama becomes a rapidly shifting alternate structure, focusing in turn on the moving Bullingbrook and the cornered Richard. The alternation describes the beginning of Bullingbrook's mode taking hold on the drama's form, on the country's communal life, and on his opponent, whose divided identity as a human figure and a ceremonial figure is forced into the syntax of alternatives.

The drama focuses first on Bullingbrook's aggression. With a strong and prestigious army gathered around his core of motion, he manages in his first enterprise not only to expose Richard's weakness and to eliminate two great enemies, Bushy and Greene, but also to begin his ascent by linguistically equalizing his position and Richard's:

> You have misled a prince, a royal king,
> A happy gentleman in blood and lineaments. . . .
> Myself, a prince by fortune of my birth,
> Near to the King in blood. . . .
> [you have left no sign]
> Save men's opinions and my living blood,
> To show the world I am a gentleman.
>   (III. i. 8–9, 16–17, 26–27)

The crucial step in his desire to own the breath of a king is to use language to elevate his titular state to Richard's. The titles "prince," "king," and "gentleman" attach themselves to both of them as he subtly denies the sanctity of the king's position while seemingly affirming it in the same terms he uses to affirm his own. In his words and in the thought they mirror, he recognizes a chasm between the origin and nature of the power he covets and the means he must use to attain it. In order to become king, he must feign reverence to the community's beliefs while working to destroy and supplant the central embodiment of them. He must sanctify ceremony for himself while denying its effects for Richard. Bullingbrook manages to appear as a unifying force through his use of equivocation; yet in separating what he says from what he means and does, Bullingbrook recreates the paralyzing split between the word and the act.

With Richard, the will's imprisonment in language resulted in passivity and stagnation. With Bullingbrook, the will freely creates surface activity, but language, the link between perception and action, is dissimulating and drastically limited in range. When Bullingbrook is stage managing—giving orders, setting scenes, commanding gestures and intonations—he employs brief paratactic units, reflecting his will's movement along a series of actions arranged linearly towards a clearly defined end:

> Uncle, you say the Queen is at your house,
> For God's sake fairly let her be entreated.
> Tell her I send to her my kind commends;
> Take special care my greetings be delivered. (III. i. 36–39)

When he is acting, however, his syntax is the rigid either/or, a narrow evaluation of the world into two possibilities.[10] In this syntax, muffled under layers of equivocating diction that unites only the surface of deep division, he will address his

---

10. Jo Ann Davis, "Henry IV: From Satirist to Satiric Butt," *Aeolian Harps*, ed. Donna G. Fricke and Douglas C. Fricke (Bowling Green, Ohio: Bowling Green University Press, 1976), 86, views Bullingbrook's role in this play as satirist and remarks on his own choice of play roles as director and producer rather than leading man.

demands to Richard. Since perceptual limitation can only lead
to a limitation on the kind of action possible in the realm, Bullingbrook is destined to lead England back into the dearth of
expression that becomes silence and paralysis. While he provides the sensation of awakened motion, the country feels
hope return. But by the end of the drama, the poverty of mind
that reveals itself in his language will again immobilize the
land.

The drama then turns to Richard. Under Bullingbrook's now
dominant mode, Richard's predicament, long a fault beneath
the surface, is forced to light: either he is the man or he is the
king, either the flesh or the name. Well-meaning followers and
damaging news prompt him to oscillate between expressions
of optimism and despair. First he asserts his belief in the magic
of his ceremonial title: "Is not the king's name twenty thousand names? / Arm, arm, my name!" (III. ii. 85–86). Then he
rejects it entirely for his fate as the man hiding within the
crown:

> for within the hollow crown
> That rounds the mortal temples of a king
> Keeps Death his court, and there the antic sits,
> Scoffing his state and grinning at his pomp,
> Allowing him a breath, a little scene,
> To monarchize, be fear'd, and kill with looks,
> Infusing him with self and vain conceit,
> As if this flesh which walls about our life
> Were brass impregnable; and humor'd thus,
> Comes at the last and with a little pin
> Bores thorough his castle wall, and farewell king!
>   (III. ii. 160–70)

As he swings helplessly from extreme to extreme, Richard allows the death of the king to invade his richly figured imagination, and once there it is attended by all the associations he
has before suppressed—his now awakened remembrance of

the kings whose sad stories it is imperative to relate. The man who considered himself divine in his role as supreme audience on earth discovers that he was an actor all along, observed in his turn by Death, the devourer of all vanities—a body, a country, a name. Shaken by the assault on his understanding of the world, he cooperates with Bullingbrook in annihilating the ceremonial acts that sanctify a king:

> throw away respect,
> Tradition, form, and ceremonious duty,
> For you have but mistook me all this while.
> I live with bread like you, feel want,
> Taste grief, need friends: subjected thus,
> How can you say to me I am a king? (III. ii. 172–77)

Confronted by what he can no longer shrug off even with a verbal disguise of omnipotence—the knowledge that his kingship is doomed despite his right, his title, his consecration—Richard discharges his followers and moves to Flint Castle to await the attack. The consequence of his inaction, which began with passivity and descended to defensiveness, is finally total paralysis of will—despair.[11]

With ceremony refuted, the next step can occur; in language, which is the origin of act, Richard and Bullingbrook move to exchange postures of power. The transfer occurs in two parallel speeches. Bullingbrook stands before Flint Castle, at last in the presence of his opponent, his party hastening to raze Richard's title:

> *North.* The news is very fair and good, my lord:
>   Richard not far from hence hath hid his head.
> *York.* It would beseem the Lord Northumberland
>   To say King Richard. (III. iii. 5–8)

Despite York's pointed comment, with its implications that "Lord" is attached to the same chain that ends in "King," the

---

11. Traversi, *An Approach to Shakespeare*, I, 168.

blasphemous movement proceeds. Bullingbrook sets the stage for his speech, occupying the ground and covering it with his army in sight of Richard's weak height on the battlements of an undefended, decrepit castle.

The equivocation that screens his activity from challenge dominates his speech as he stages the final destruction of Richard's power.[12] Ambassadorial diction loosely disguises rigid, legal syntax:

> Noble lord,
> Go to the rude ribs of that ancient castle;
> Through brazen trumpet send the breath of parley
> Into his ruin'd ears, and thus deliver:
> Henry Bullingbrook
> On both his knees doth kiss King Richard's hand,
> And sends allegiance and true faith of heart
> To his most royal person; hither come
> Even at his feet to lay my arms and power,
> Provided that my banishment repeal'd
> And lands restor'd again be freely granted. (III. iii. 31–41)

Bullingbrook, conscious of the impression he needs to create on his audience, allows Richard to retain his title; he establishes his ascendancy more subtly by giving precedent and authoritative reference to his own name, recovered despite Richard's illegal seizure. Words clash against words, "ruin'd ears" against "most royal person," "allegiance and true faith of heart" against "brazen trumpet." The diction, dominated by formal titles and ceremonial terms of address, establishes the tone of piety, but the characteristic Bullingbrook either/or, here in the form of "Provided that / If not," melts the compliment:

> If not, I'll use the advantage of my power,
> And lay the summer's dust with show'rs of blood
> Rain'd from the wounds of slaughtered Englishmen,

12. *Ibid.*, 169.

> The which, how far off from the mind of Bullingbrook
> It is, such crimson tempest should bedrench
> The fresh green lap of fair King Richard's land,
> My stooping duty tenderly shall show. (III. iii. 42–48)

Carefully juxtaposed are two verbal acts—one a ritual gesture of deference to the communal belief in a king's sanctity, kneeling; the other an act destructive to the basis of that belief, threatening war on the king and the land that is his manifestation:

> Go signify as much, while here we march
> Upon the grassy carpet of this plain.
> Let's march without the noise of threat'ning drum,
> That from this castle's tottered battlements
> Our fair appointments may be well perus'd.
> (III. iii. 49–53)

When Bullingbrook adds the directions for his army's maneuvers, he reinforces the double intention of his words in staged action. Both spheres of communication, language and act, split in two.

His language, however, reveals his leaning towards the Adversary's rebellious act, the description of which alone breaks the legal barrenness of his diction. That startling contrast of a red tempest drenching a green lap, again a study in duality, is the first clear picture to emerge in his speech. Aside from it, only one further image takes form:

> Methinks King Richard and myself should meet
> With no less terror than the elements
> Of fire and water, when their thund'ring shock
> At meeting tears the cloudy cheeks of heaven.
> Be he the fire, I'll be the yielding water;
> The rage be his, whilst on the earth I rain
> My waters—on the earth, and not on him.
> March on, and mark King Richard how he looks.
> (III. iii. 54–61)

The ambiguous image he chooses serves to confuse the distinction between himself and his prey. It adds connotations of fertility to his warlike stance while giving Richard the role of the raging, destructive element. But the softening of his own physically threatening posture is undercut by his mention of rain, which restores to consciousness his earlier talk of crimson tempests and showers of blood. Successfully confusing the appearance of the issue by simultaneously revealing his intentions and casting doubt on them, Bullingbrook creates the proper climate for the power vacuum. He short-circuits the relationship between words and the actions they describe, finally achieving the epitome of equivocation by denying the full effect of his image—"on the earth, and not on him." All he need do to become king is maintain the dissimulating language of justice and reverence to cover his seizure of power.

As Bullingbrook tightens his control over the two strands of his newly forming political structure—mock piety and power worship—Richard discovers the full extent of his own split identity:

> O that I were as great
> As is my grief, or lesser than my name!
> Or that I could forget what I have been!
> Or not remember what I must be now!
> (III. iii. 136–39)

Caught in a crisis when the king must be himself or be king no longer, forced to bridge the gap he created, Richard discovers his impotence and the only way now possible to overcome it. Since he is not greater than his grief, he must become lesser than his name. The two polarities, in whose magnetic field Richard has maintained himself in stasis, are no longer his to control. Bullingbrook balances the duality of the realm, and Richard must move towards one of his two halves. In response to Bullingbrook's pressure, he verbalizes his demise, finally

unblocking his will and enacting metaphor by becoming a
man, a titleless beggar.

Richard begins speaking like the puppet he has become,
awaiting orders from his master:

> What must the King do now? Must he submit?
> The King shall do it. Must he be depos'd?
> The King shall be contented. Must he lose
> The name of king? a'God's name let it go.
> (III. iii. 143–46)

Ironically Richard uses his name to demonstrate its weakness
before he resigns his right to rule his land in the one name that
reigns supreme over his. Willingly giving up the name and the
awesome burden he could never bear and can no longer believe in, Richard pursues a new life with range and imagination:

> I'll give my jewels for a set of beads,
> My gorgeous palace for a hermitage,
> My gay apparel for an almsman's gown,
> My figur'd goblets for a dish of wood,
> My sceptre for a palmer's walking-staff,
> My subjects for a pair of carved saints,
> And my large kingdom for a little grave,
> A little little grave, an obscure grave.
> (III. iii. 147–54)

Verbalizing his metamorphosis, Richard begins to set in motion the process of change, beginning with the word and ending with the act. For the first time, he seeks to play out the
connections he has previously isolated in language.

He desires to see the actual representation of his demise:

> Or I'll be buried in the king's high way,
> Some way of common trade, where subjects' feet
> May hourly trample on their sovereign's head;
> For on my heart they tread now whilst I live,
> And buried once, why not upon my head?
> (III. iii. 155–59)

From establishing the acts that correspond to the degradation he has undergone, Richard then moves deeper into the link between metaphor and act, creating fantastic conceits of echoing movements in the land:

> Aumerle, thou weep'st, my tender-hearted cousin!
> We'll make foul weather with despised tears;
> Our sighs and they shall lodge the summer corn,
> And make a dearth in this revolting land.
> Or shall we play the wantons with our woes
> And make some pretty match with shedding tears?
> As thus to drop them still upon one place,
> Till they have fretted us a pair of graves
> Within the earth, and, therein laid—there lies
> Two kinsmen digg'd their graves with weeping eyes.
> Would not this ill do well? Well, well, I see
> I talk but idlely, and you laugh at me. (III. iii. 160–71)

Yet the exploration of his speech, seeking the appropriate action to embody the metaphors that spring with ease to his disturbed mind, ends in failure. He seeks to break the paralysis and take action against his revolting land, but he succeeds only in accepting his defeat. Richard cannot so readily discover the mode of his own action, not by making his grief the weather, nor by digging a grave with tears.

By the end of his speech, he has capitulated to Bullingbrook's mode and given away with his own breath the title that made that breath omnipotent:

> Most mighty prince, my Lord Northumberland,
> What says King Bullingbrook? Will his Majesty
> Give Richard leave to live till Richard die?
> You make a leg, and Bullingbrook says ay.
> (III. iii. 172–75)

Richard cannot yet fulfill his language in any action other than the crystallization of his unkingly weakness. He awaited his orders, and now, in Northumberland's curtsy, he finds them.

Into the base court he descends, for the first time moving in accord with his understanding. Richard is no longer king. The movement needs only Bullingbrook to ascend to complete itself: "Up, cousin, up, your heart is up, I know, / Thus high at least, although your knee be low" (III. iii. 194–95). The power game has ended with Bullingbrook the victor.

Placed crucially at the end of the first game is the gardening scene, an object lesson both in reading the universe metaphorically and in fulfilling what is read in act.[13] The scene abstractly reflects the principle of cosmic unity that Gaunt had spoken for with its emphasis on the corresponding planes of reality that extend from the celestial to the abjectly physical. The old Adam-Gardener, declaiming the lesson that what you sow you reap, enacts his role in perfect accord with the principle of unity he sees in the most insignificant piece of earth. The garden is a center of orderly change, the earthly emblem of the fallen state. There death and renewal reveal in vegetative form the laws governing all life. The gardener accepts his domain as a circle of life obedient to the same principle that ties together the stars in the heavens or the people of a commonwealth. He sees his king's fall there; he sees the acts that could have prevented the fall; he sees the results of the fall.

Echoing and extending the prophecy of Gaunt, who likened vanity to an insatiable cormorant, the gardener predicts Richard's future:

> We at time of year
> Do wound the bark, the skin of our fruit-trees,
> Lest being over-proud in sap and blood,
> With too much riches it confound itself. (III. iv. 57–60)

Richard, the king whose riches are too great for his frame, has been wounded in order to bear. Without his name and cere-

---

13. Dean, "Richard II," 216, states that the garden scene "re-asserts the ideal of the state as Eden and the possibility of its approximation by an Adam-like king."

monial respect—with enough sap and blood let to allow him to control his rich gifts—he will prove worthier to be king than he was in the heady flush of power. In that wound lies the possibility of Richard's breaking through the barrier of his language into a mode of action that mirrors his inner state.

An Adam-Everyman, in intimate contact with the earth that nourishes and buries him, in humble attendance to the heavens that ordain his life's pattern, the gardener is no mere choric figure, but the epitome of poet and player: a Player-King in his own domain. What he sees as true in his garden world, he will fulfill in act:

> Here did she fall a tear, here in this place
> I'll set a bank of rue, sour herb of grace.
> Rue, even for ruth, here shortly shall be seen,
> In the remembrance of a weeping queen.
> (III. iv. 104–107)

The gardener has used his human ability to enact a truth in his own commonwealth. Placed thus between the demise of Richard and the ascent of Bullingbrook, the scene posits a simple rule of human life: no one can ignore the universe's metaphors as Bullingbrook does; no one can ignore the human responsibility to enact them as Richard did. The gardening scene is a statement on the past and a prediction of the future, a link between two uncannily similar reigns.

The confrontation at Flint Castle creates the vacuum between the end of one structural pattern and the beginning of its twin. On the one hand, it marks the end of hope and the opening awareness of futility; on the other, it prefaces the play's second and more fecund search—no longer for power but for self. Bullingbrook, crowned with his attainment, will soon begin to feel the trap closing over him as he cannot, with all his power, change the mode of action in the land. Richard, doomed to public oblivion, sees at least the first glimmers of a newly defined world where he will assert himself as a whole man with one last but redeeming act.

The Beggar and the King

The game of power has ended. The reign of England has slipped from Richard's grasp into Bullingbrook's; only the denuded consecration ceremony remains to formalize the ascension of a new king. By the end of the drama, both kings will recollect the story of King Cophetua—who could have commanded any love he wished yet fell in love with a beggar maid—because it contains an irony that resonates in their own history. The beggar has become king and the king a beggar. Who is the king? Who is the beggar? Two halves still maintain separate and hostile lives; the structure of power perpetuates its Janus aspect.

As soon as Bullingbrook assumes control of the land, the similarities between him and Richard materialize as strongly as their differences did earlier. Both rulers wield authority absolutely. Both attempt to bury the sins of the man in the aura of the name. In both reigns communication sickens while suspicion breeds. Because Bullingbrook is a more careful observer of men and motives and a more skillful actor, he maintains power more efficiently. But the mode of England is still fixed to the duality that rebellion manifests.[14] Although Richard's language attempted to heal the split, his actions would not complete his awareness. Bullingbrook's actions attempt to unify the country by destroying opposition, but his language, syntactically rooted in duality, sustains it. In this second half of the drama, when power is no longer the object of the game and selfhood becomes the only viable search, Bullingbrook confronts his subtle beggary as the events of his kingship are drawn ineluctably into the pattern of Richard's.

His reign begins with the legal challenge of a royal cousin, Aumerle. Bullingbrook, never vague in his statement of will,

14. Davis, "Henry IV," 84, 88, sees the last two acts as parodies of the earlier ones, with Henry caught in an old play he no longer directs.

avoids Richard's error of allowing events to move outside his control. While Richard permitted his cousin's argument to proceed before him in order to enjoy the spectacle, even though it was ultimately dangerous to him, Bullingbrook corners his cousin in a similar argument and uses a cross fire of accusations to discredit him. The opening charge is hurled at Aumerle by Bagot, who escaped the fate of his compeers; his obvious treachery in now currying for Bullingbrook casts a revealing shadow over his statements. Nor is the choice of Bagot lost on the assembled peers. One by one they manufacture instances of Aumerle's treachery to please the new king. Fitzwater supplies the court with a suitable imitation of Bullingbrook's equivocating style: "As I intend to thrive in this new world, / Aumerle is guilty of my true appeal" (IV. i. 78–79).

The patterns that emanate from the king have begun to spread. Bullingbrook produces from within him the either/or sides of conflict and gives them to his country to play out, thus keeping the clash of opposites acting outside him. In a brief eighty-five lines of this scene, forms of the word *lie* appear thirteen times, the related *false* an additional two. But at no time does the word, which denotes the existence of duality, touch Bullingbrook himself. He succeeds in manipulating the scene to its end before the issue reaches him by burying the supposed search for truth with a dead man, the exiled Mowbray. Richard's personal division paralyzed himself and by extension his country; Bullingbrook engages his country in compulsively repetitive action, but eventually the circularity of such movement will engulf him as well.

Richard's legal pronouncement, exiling his cousin before the crowds at the Coventry arena, is paralleled by the deposition scene Bullingbrook must stage for Richard to play before the court. The king's aim in both cases is to rid himself of a powerful enemy by insinuating guilt while avoiding full legal resolution; in both cases the king's failure occurs as a result of poor

timing. Richard foolishly allowed hostilities to mount and po-
larize his realm before he moved to suppress them. Bullingbrook impatiently tries to skip the full process of his legal-
seeming, bloodless usurpation and begin his own ascension in
act before he allows Richard *his* last scene in the play of power,
the abdication in act.

The sudden "In God's name I'll ascend the regal throne"
(IV. i. 113), following the news that Richard has destroyed his
royal power to give names by making "heir" the last name he
gives, triggers Carlisle's outrage on witnessing this mockery of
ceremony. The casual treatment of what the bishop recognizes
as divine—the coronation of a king—forces antagonism into
existence before Bullingbrook is ready for it. He stops short,
realizing that he must curb his stage managing until he is king
and chief player of the realm.

Entering the scene of power with Richard, but no longer on
him, are the tangible regalia of kingship. Both men stand barren of ceremony, with the crown, final symbol of kingship,
poised between them: Richard has nothing to lose, Bullingbrook everything. As a result, Richard can freely allow action
to flow from language, while Bullingbrook must guard his
words and actions from betraying his intolerable itch for power:

> Give me the crown. Here, cousin, seize the crown;
> Here, cousin,
> On this side my hand, and on that side thine. (IV. i. 181–83)

Seize it now as you seized it in fact, Richard clearly implies,
embarrassing and endangering Bullingbrook by throwing aside
the protective veil of equivocation under which he habitually
operates. Bullingbrook's reluctance to take the requested action shows through the repetition of "Here, cousin." Richard
begins to play out what the ceremony requires of him as well:

> Now mark me how I will undo myself:
> I give this heavy weight from off my head,

And this unwieldy sceptre from my hand,
The pride of kingly sway from out my heart;
With mine own tears I wash away my balm,
With mine own hands I give away my crown,
With mine own tongue deny my sacred state,
With mine own breath release all duteous oaths.
                                        (IV. i. 203–10)

With a growing awareness that his inability to make his flesh perform the acts of kingship, in fact, deposed him, Richard uses words, which were the fruitless vehicles of his shallow royalty, to unking himself. The tears—the sap that must be drawn off before the tree can bear—reverse Bullingbrook's elemental lie: the fruitful rain falls from the sufferer. The paralysis begins to leave Richard as he acts out his failure with the faculties that he could not move to prevent it.

When he rejects the stage action planned for him by Bullingbrook and Northumberland, refusing to read his crimes and demanding instead a mirror, Richard seizes control of the scene. Since only he can depose himself, he will show Bullingbrook that the act will be done according to his sense of order and decorum. He has removed his title and his name, and now he will know how these changes in form have altered him. He wants to see his face:

Give me that glass, and therein will I read.
No deeper wrinkles yet? Hath sorrow struck
So many blows upon this face of mine,
And made no deeper wounds? O flatt'ring glass,
Like to my followers in prosperity,
Thou dost beguile me! Was this face the face
That every day under his household roof
Did keep ten thousand men? Was this the face
That like the sun, did make beholders wink?
Is this the face which fac'd so many follies,
That was at last out-fac'd by Bullingbrook?
A brittle glory shineth in this face,

As brittle as the glory is the face,
   [*Dashes the glass against the ground.*]
For there it is, crack'd in an hundred shivers.
Mark, silent king, the moral of this sport,
How soon my sorrow hath destroy'd my face.
                              (IV. i. 276–91)

Pressing hard against the word *face* in an effort to make it yield
the action he needs to fulfill his feeling of being ravaged, Richard finally conquers his paralysis. He could not make "foul
weather" in his revolting land with tears and sighs (III. iii.
161–62), nor could he become "a mockery king of snow" (IV.
i. 260), but he can destroy his face. For the first time, he can
force one of his conceits into the realm of action.

Bullingbrook, the unpoetic "silent king," has wisely re-
frained from addressing Richard; but now, against better judgment, he is moved to correct the error he sees in Richard's
analysis of his state: "The shadow of your sorrow hath destroy'd / The shadow of your face" (IV. i. 292–93). Richard is
sardonically pleased. In his new openness to all possibilities,
he entertains the idea:

      Say that again.
   The shadow of my sorrow! Ha, let's see.
   'Tis very true, my grief lies all within,
   And these external manners of laments
   Are merely shadows to the unseen grief
   That swells with silence in the tortur'd soul.
   There lies the substance; and I thank thee, King,
   For thy great bounty, that not only giv'st
   Me cause to wail, but teachest me the way
   How to lament the cause. (IV. i. 293–302)

Although Bullingbrook means *shadow* to connote something
of negligible importance and no substance, Richard understands the lesson differently. He has discovered that all meaningful action originates in the inner life, not—as the sovereign

Richard had always assumed—in outer show. Bullingbrook has announced Richard's new direction—instead of working through the face to the grief, he will work from the grief to the face. The language must become part of a moving journey from the inner man to his fulfillment in action.[15]

As Richard metamorphoses from king, to prince, to retired sovereign, to "Fair Cousin," he discovers that a title itself is nothing more than an unproductive word, of no more efficacy than a face that has been outfaced. The revelation is liberating. It allows him the emotional daring to wrest control over his own abdication scene from Bullingbrook. Although still confused about his new role as beggar, Richard has at least asserted himself as a suffering man. Bullingbrook, on the other hand, has lost momentum. The sense of control has slipped out of his hands, and its loss beggars his kingship.

Richard's fate gradually moves offstage until his reemergence from the journey to his human center. With the queen, he demonstrates an affection never visible before for another person. He tries to convey his discovery by telling her to consider their lives as monarchs a dream "from which awak'd, the truth of what we are / Shows us but this" (V. i. 19–20). The next word of Richard is York's description of him following the new king in public procession, the poor performer who plays after the "well-graced actor" (V. ii. 24) and is greeted with contempt. Yet the dignity that Richard maintains under a barrage of dust shows the end of his passive swaying with the current and the growth of a core resistant to mutability.

At the same time, the debilitating repetition of events continues to haunt Bullingbrook. Aumerle, whom he has deprived of his title and renamed Rutland, forms a rebellion with other

15. Donald Reiman, "Appearance, Reality, and Moral Order in *Richard II*," *Modern Language Quarterly*, XXV (1964), 39–40, views the glass shattering and Bullingbrook's comment on it as Richard's awakening, the key to his change—he is "learning to distinguish in himself shadow from substance." Winny, *The Player King*, 65, on the contrary, calls Richard's argument a sign of his "triviality of mind."

friends of Richard. Like Bullingbrook himself under Richard, Aumerle rebels twice: once in symbol and once in earnest. Again, as in the gauge scene, there is the difference: this rebellion is doomed to failure. Yet the surface of events is frighteningly similar. Another father is forced to speak against his son, York doing his duty as a peer of the realm against his son just as Gaunt, as a judge, spoke against Bullingbrook. As the Duchess of York explains to the king, her husband's refusal to sue for his son is setting "the word itself against the word"— an accurate definition of the state of the realm. Even Bullingbrook himself begins to be caught up in the duality of his rule: he must play beggar for news of the son he should be able to command. When the Duchess of York adds her knee to an already excessive number of beggars, Bullingbrook verbalizes his perception of the duality that seems to be trapping him: the scene is turning into the Beggar and the King. For all his power, he is not free. Acknowledging the uncanniness of these twin images of events and trying to break the pattern, Bullingbrook assents to the Duchess' pleading: "I pardon him as God shall pardon me" (V. iii. 131). From the "silent king," the Duchess has demanded a word, and she receives it. At the same time, the words he had uttered about Richard's dangerous living presence are bearing fruit in Exton's decision to make them act. "Such is the breath of kings." Bullingbrook cannot keep himself removed from the mode his duality has forced on the land: in one breath an act of mercy; in the other an act of doom.

Richard's reappearance on the stage after his absence from the scenes in which Bullingbrook finds himself the shadow of the usurped king witnesses him recapitulating the stages of his educational process. He sits in an isolated cell of a dungeon prison, solitary and helpless, obliged by now outside forces to remain immobile. Yet that cell, as Richard has the imagination to understand, can be construed as a new dominion, as revelatory as the England he lost or the garden whose lessons he neglected. His successor in the same state rejected the mind's ability to govern the body; Bullingbrook could not hold fire in his hand by thinking on the frosty Caucasus. Richard learns that he can.

He rebuilds his world in accord with the experience he has undergone in life, from the inner state to the outer world. In the state of nullity, he finds his ability to be whole, a reflection in one man of a universal truth:

> I have been studying how I may compare
> This prison where I live unto the world;
> And for because the world is populous,
> And here is not a creature but myself,
> I cannot do it; yet I'll hammer it out. (V. v. 1–5)

The difficulty of his journey from nothing to everything does not daunt Richard's resolve to discover the meaning of what he has experienced. The only key to that meaning is in creation:

> My brain I'll prove the female to my soul,
> My soul the father, and these two beget
> A generation of still-breeding thoughts;
> And these same thoughts people this little world,
> In humors like the people of this world:
> For no thought is contented. (V. v. 6–11)

Thus Richard achieves a created replica of the scene of his ordeal. By the operation of the soul—the center of the nothing that mirrors everything—on the brain—the center of intellect, memory, and so experience—all the world is created in thoughts that move unimpeded towards acts.

In his play world, Richard places the characters he has come to know intimately: the innocent, the powerful, the ambitious, the suffering, the beggarly, the criminal. The thoughts and the characters they spin off fall into the pattern of opposition that marks the new world; they do "set the word itself / Against the word" (V. v. 13–14). The Duchess of York had perceived the clash in her husband's pleas against his son. Richard deepens the problem to the question of salvation, his divine thoughts cancelled out by doubts, and Christ's promises to the innocent by His threats to the wicked. In himself Richard finds both halves of the duality; he sees himself as a man split in two by the roles he has played, roles which he extends outward to those who have played them before him. His problems are everyone's problems: "Thus play I in one person many people, / And none contented" (V. v. 31–32). Containing the two halves in himself, he searches to resolve them into one harmonious unit:

> Sometimes am I king;
> Then treasons make me wish myself a beggar,
> And so I am. Then crushing penury
> Persuades me I was better when a king;
> Then am I king'd again, and by and by
> Think that I am unking'd by Bullingbrook,
> And straight am nothing. But what e'er I be,
> Nor I, nor any man that but man is,
> With nothing shall be pleas'd, till he be eas'd
> With being nothing. (V. v. 32–41)

The oppositions find their synecdoche in the roles of Beggar and King, both of which Richard has played and continues to play in his imagination. He alternates compulsively between them until he achieves at last the thought that enlightens his personal predicament and the human predicament he has adopted as his own. At the zero point, the plus and the minus dissolve into their origin. A man, whatever he is, cannot encompass his own state until he has discovered his origin in nothing. Alone in his cell, creating metaphors that tie his experiences together into a moving play, Richard has met his origin.[16]

16. Quinn, " 'The King Is Not Himself,' " 183, states that Richard's identification of himself as nothing is "a profession of faith in Hell," a nihilism that is "the logical

This revelation opens for him the experiential pain of knowing exactly why he failed as a king. Mysteriously, music begins to play, causing in Richard the pain that unharmonious sound engenders. He perceives the music as his symbolic failure, seeing in that correspondence the seed of many more. He is achieving the cosmic perception that the gardener exhibits when his disgust is aroused by "dangling apricocks," "too fast growing sprays," and "noisome weeds" (III. iv. 29, 34, 38). The music disordered and improperly timed leads Richard to see his relationship to time in light of the importance of keeping time to produce harmony: "I wasted time, and now doth time waste me" (V. v. 49). With Bullingbrook as his king, Richard has become time's physical manifestation, his thoughts minutes ticking away with sighs and marked by the hourly groans that strike against his heart. His passive state of maintaining himself as if he could not change—as if he were not prey to time and to its executioner, death—ends with his realization that he has been fulfilled as a human clock, a useful measure.[17] With that thought, the chain of passivity breaks, and Richard becomes impatient to act. The music maddens him with its constant reminder of his failure, although he blesses the giver.[18]

The arrival of his former groom allows Richard the opportu-

consequence of Richard's isolation of himself from his social context." Righter, *Shakespeare and the Idea of the Play*, 125, also establishes Richard's loss of identity, but sees him becoming "merely a Player King." Winny, too, in *The Player King*, 59, asserts that his "state of nothingness" is the "satisfaction of a perverse desire." In fact, however, Richard has begun the process of becoming the central man, the nexus of humankind. If, as Quinn notes, Richard "dies as Somebody" (p. 184), it is because he faced that nothing at the center of whirling, contradictory roles.

17. Reiman, "Appearance, Reality, and Moral Order in *Richard II*," 37.

18. As Dorius notes in "A Little More Than a Little," 18, Bullingbrook is a master of timing. After Richard smashed his own face, he became a mere clockface. Dorius, however, sees Richard's thoughts at Pomfret as breeding "only destruction," and Richard himself as a figure of Death (p. 21). On the other hand, Reiman, "Appearance, Reality, and Moral Order in *Richard II*," 43–45, views Richard's education in prison as facing "his own human limitations" and learning, through the music, to distinguish between motive and act. It is this newly gained self-knowledge that makes Richard a tragic figure. Bullingbrook, meanwhile, is shown unable to distinguish between motive and act with Exton, thus repeating Richard's substitution of "formal rhetoric and external symbolic action for sincerity."

nity to correct his error. While cursing Barbary, as he cursed his land for not rising up to devour the usurper, Richard again forgets that everything has its place in the scheme of harmony and demands instead that it obey his will. But he checks that distemper, asking forgiveness of the horse that plays his role by bearing a rider. That observation brings him from his state of nothingness, in which he can become everything, into the state where he can make distinctions. He knows what he is; now he discovers what he is not—"I was not made a horse, / And yet I bear a burthen like an ass, / Spurr'd, gall'd, and tir'd by jauncing Bullingbrook" (V. v. 92–94). This act of rejecting a role is the point at which Richard emerges from his metaphoric meditation into the realm of action. When death knocks at the door, Richard does not passively accept it: "Patience is stale, and I am weary of it" (V. v. 103). The man who could never take action as a king in the last moment raises a hand with energy sufficient to kill two of his murderers before he is overcome. Richard's death, tragic in the sense of wasted possibility and squandered wisdom, is yet glorious and strange, unprecedented by the character of the king who was not himself.[19] With no road open to him to effect his awareness, the newly created Player-King resigns the parts he struggled to unite to their separate spheres, his soul up on high, his flesh to the ground on which it dies.

Temporarily, the death of his opponent seems to release Bullingbrook from his prison of conflict and make him whole. It seems to make him king. In quick succession, he hears that his enemies have been defeated and executed. Against the good news, Bullingbrook magnanimously forgives Carlisle. Yet this act is immediately counterbalanced by the entrance of Exton with Richard's body, and Bullingbrook responds in character by double dealing with him:

19. Traversi, *An Approach to Shakespeare*, I, 177, considers Richard's murder "a pedestrian piece of melodrama." It seems instead the fitting end for a man who has finally made "words respond to feeling" (p. 176).

> They love not poison that do poison need,
> Nor do I thee. Though I did wish him dead,
> I hate the murtherer, love him murthered. (V. vi. 38–40)

Bullingbrook cannot escape the will of his actions to follow his divided perception and language. Richard learned from Bullingbrook to look within for the origin of what is without, but Bullingbrook has not absorbed Richard's lesson—that what one thinks and speaks concretizes itself in act. The play ends with Bullingbrook's stated belief that with an act of expiation he can cancel entirely an act of sin. He seems not to have observed that his forgiveness of Carlisle was followed sequentially by the news of Richard's murder. Certainly he does not accept that alternation as the pattern of action he has stamped on his reign.

Richard II does not produce a Player-King, but it has explained the origins and education of the type. Richard owns the play's words, Bullingbrook the acts; one leads to redemption, the other to futile repetition. Bullingbrook, who restricts his mind's reality to the glitter of worldly power, is narrow, guilty, and driven. Richard, who willingly or not abandons the limitations of his role and expands his consciousness to include all human possibility, dies heroically in a physical struggle against the principle of destruction. The leader who will fulfill the search for a Player-King must achieve Richard's understanding of universal metaphor and its power to create harmonious action without cutting off his road to the kingship. The Player-King must be able to return from the mortal danger of being nothing, live a life that heals duality and teaches others to be whole, and understand how to be a beggar as a king and a king as a beggar.

1 *Henry IV*: The Strawberry and the Nettle

Thou art so fat-witted with drinking of old sack, and unbuttoning thee after supper, and sleeping upon benches after noon, that thou hast forgotten to demand that truly which thou wouldest truly know. What a devil hast thou to do with the time of the day? unless hours were cups of sack, and minutes capons, and clocks the tongues of bawds, and dials the signs of leaping-houses, and the blessed sun himself a fair hot wench in flame-color'd taffata; I see no reason why thou shouldst be so superfluous to demand the time of the day. (I. ii. 2–12)

With language that shivers the morbid solemnity of King Henry's court, Prince Hal assumes the stage. The responsibility of power lies at a remove in the future, the sting of guilt one generation past. The danger in acting out a metaphor, no less than the permanent loss of self, Hal transforms into the energy of discovery. Richard, who held the metaphor back from its fulfillment in act, had to relinquish a king's name in order to gain a king's wisdom. But Hal is already a cipher—the nothing that Richard found at the root of the human ability to be satisfied with whatever something he might become. Richard was wounded in order to bear wisdom's fruit only in death. Hal willingly seeks his reduction to nothing, covering himself with the nettle that protects his growth until he has matured. As the center of attention for his father—who continues to generate the mode of England— and for his country—divided by its ruler into two antagonistic camps—Hal understands the need for retreat. He has successfully shrugged off the responsibilities of his given role as Prince of Wales along with his duties as son. His withdrawal is attributable in part to his youthful drive towards unsupervised experience, in part to the psychic shock of knowing that the titled role he will some day call himself is sullied by theft and murder.

The duality of Henry IV's perception—his either/or—has indeed become England's mode, its dominance marked by the pairing of characters within the play into rivals and doubles: the King and the Rebels, Henry IV and Falstaff, Hal and Hotspur. As with Richard and Bullingbrook, the rivals are two

halves of a whole, which united could effect harmony in the
human community. Each is the other's man. With the complex
entity split and polarized, a man must choose whether to destroy or encompass his rival, to effect further division through
spurious unity or to aspire to harmony. The Player-King's aim
is to encompass the rival: Richard allowed Bullingbrook's perception of the shadow world to correct and complete his own.
The Adversary's choice is to destroy the rival without internal-
izing his principle: Bullingbrook acknowledges the personal
danger of Richard's live presence and annihilates him. But in
destroying Richard, Bullingbrook does not eliminate the principle of duality that will recur in every opponent he unwillingly forces into existence. He treats the manifestation but not
the cause of disorder. Because he never encompassed Richard's half of the man that together they could be, Bullingbrook
remains incomplete, half a magnetic field perpetually creating
and destroying its stabilizing other half.

On Hal rests the burden of the new dualities of 1 *Henry IV*.
Dominated by the mode of his father, he has been given a
natural rival—Harry Hotspur, son and nephew of his father's
rivals. His father exists solely to maintain the rule and to influence its perpetuity through his son. But Hal, instead of adher-
ing to the mode his father sets, seeks cover and escape, fleeing
from the old and seeking a new mode in his guide, father,
teacher, and play friend, Falstaff, who bears enough similarities to the king to serve well as Henry IV's uncanny rival-dou-
ble. Through Falstaff, Hal will learn to overcome his father's
understanding of power and to attain a perception of life more
inclusive than either father singly has achieved.

The Two Fathers:
King of England, King of Eastcheap

King Henry IV—the usurper Bullingbrook and Hal's
father—remains the most influential actor in the realm. In his

person, he creates the world of his country and its subjects—
the art form that selects and limits words, gestures, and actions. He continues to maintain England within the firm limits
of either/or.[20] In his rise to power, he separated the means he
used from the end he attained, destroying the ceremony that
protected Richard and then reviving it to command loyalty to
his own throne. The split created there carries over into his
reign in the two aspects of a man burdened with inexpiable
sin: harsh authoritarianism and sentimental regret.[21] He fled
from destroying the mirror image of his treachery in Aumerle,
thereby reflecting a fear of his sin punishing him in his own
image. But he never allows the anxiety born of his guilt to
affect the politics of his realm.

A tired voice opens the play with a formal wish to move
from domestic conflict to the holy war that Henry sees as its
alternative; but fatigue transforms into steel before an enemy's
face:

> My blood hath been too cold and temperate,
> Unapt to stir at these indignities,
> And you have found me, for accordingly
> You tread upon my patience; but be sure
> I will from henceforth rather be myself,
> Mighty and to be fear'd, than my condition,
> Which hath been smooth as oil, soft as young down,
> And therefore lost that title of respect
> Which the proud soul ne'er pays but to the proud.
>
> (I. iii. 1–9)

Separating his "self" from his "condition," Henry yearns for

20. Winny, *The Player King*, 86–89, argues that the Bullingbrook of *Richard II* is
incompatible with the figure of Henry IV in *1 Henry IV*, that the two plays do not fit
together. Yet Bullingbrook's syntax and the mind it mirrors are the same in both
plays; in addition, the ambivalent emotions he feels in the last act of *Richard II* are
visibly dominant in the opening act of *1 Henry IV*.

21. Winny's assertion that Henry IV does not realize "the consequences of his
crime" until he is dying does not take into account the subtly pleading tone of his
first speech, nor does it give full weight to his desire to go to Jerusalem. *Ibid.*, 96.

the time when he can pull them together and "be myself," just as he longs for the holy war in Jerusalem to erase the blot of usurpation and murder. His impatience to ascend the throne and become king perpetuates itself in the form of a desperate anxiety to attain the always elusive satisfaction of feeling that he *is* a king. But the king is still not himself. Now it is the Percies, those omnipresent reminders of his slippery road to power, who seem the last block to stable peace for his kingdom and himself. In fact, however, in neither his personal nor public life can Henry's will fuse his divided perception.

Henry's weakness still exposes itself in his syntax; his limitations are a continuation of the linguistic narrowness he had exhibited as Bullingbrook:

> No more the thirsty entrance of this soil
> Shall daub her lips with her own children's blood,
> No more shall trenching war channel her fields,
> Nor bruise her flow'rets with the armed hoofs
> Of hostile paces. Those opposed eyes,
> Which, like the meteors of a troubled heaven,
> All of one nature, of one substance bred,
> Did lately meet in the intestine shock
> And furious close of civil butchery,
> Shall now, in mutual well-beseeming ranks,
> March all one way and be no more oppos'd
> Against acquaintance, kindred, and allies. (I. i. 5–16)

The steady cadences of Henry's heavily paralleled, wishful statement of the past and the future include an awareness of the unnatural division of rivals "of one substance bred," who force their country into acts of cannibalism and infanticide. Yet the division within his own language, his then/now split reinforced by the repeated "no more," makes the hope for harmony in the country fated to end unfulfilled.

Henry cannot change the mode that he has himself established, and, when confronted by the bare face of opposition,

the softer accents of his earlier speech revert to the abrupt
units of command, terminating in the naked edges of either/or:

> Thou dost belie him, Percy, thou dost belie him;
> He never did encounter with Glendower.
> I tell thee,
> He durst as well have met the devil alone
> As Owen Glendower for an enemy.
> Art thou not asham'd? But, sirrah, henceforth
> Let me not hear you speak of Mortimer.
> Send me your prisoners with the speediest means,
> Or you shall hear in such a kind from me
> As will displease you. (I. iii. 113–22)

In Henry's belief that the Percies are preventing him from ob-
taining the unquestioned obedience and respect owed to a
king, he creates new poles of rivalry, moving again into the
Adversary's strategy of destruction. He hungers for peace, but
he does not know how to achieve it. He no longer wants to feel
indebted or threatened; he no longer wants any suggestion of
taint to undermine his royalty. Too late Hotspur will discover
that he was maneuvered into the position of a rebel by the
king as well as by his own relatives.

As father, too, Henry demonstrates the limitations of mind
that baffle him as he seeks to make power do the work of understanding. A master actor who lacks the opportunities to
grow that poetry provides quickly becomes a familiar and ineffective mechanic, a dealer in old news and a failure at communication. Henry is locked and isolated in his cell of guilt
and fear as Richard never was in an actual cell. The goad of his
conscience will not permit Henry to rest until he has made
every man submit to his will, acknowledge his absolute authority, and appreciate and accept the terms of his success—
every man, and especially his son. Like another Shakespearean father, the elder Hamlet, Henry aims to flush his son
out of hiding into service to the system he creates, perpetu-

ates, and symbolizes. In the interview that he is forced to command, Henry confronts Hal with his misdoings. Yet his emphasis throughout their confrontation lies less on Hal than on himself: God has made his son his own private scourge; as Hal is, so Richard was when Henry shamed and destroyed him; Hal will not follow in his father's footsteps by limiting his public appearances and feigning humility. For forty-five lines Henry reminisces over his road to victory—haranguing, bullying, scolding, and insulting Hal until he finally presents the alternatives he has already created for the occasion: either fight for me or fight for my enemies. For reasons of his own, Hal accepts his father's linguistic analysis of the problem and vows to defeat his given enemy, Hotspur, in battle. Jubilantly Henry embraces vindication in Hal's emergence into the constricting world of politics and conflict. He has revived; his energies rise as he contemplates again the acts of war his nature produces, this time with his son at his side reflecting him.

Henry cannot heal the external split in his kingdom, nor can he keep it outside himself. This king with a guilty conscience and a thirst for absolute power rules a country where the only external possibilities for action are obedience or rebellion. Under this severe pressure, Henry's personal split has spun off a second self.[22] In the heart of England, in an Eastcheap tavern, resides the underground image of the royal court which is

22. This discussion of the relationship between Henry IV and Falstaff is based on Sigmund Freud's "The 'Uncanny,'" trans. Alix Strachey, in *On Creativity and the Unconscious* (New York: Harper & Row, 1958), 122–61. The double structure of two fathers and two sons has been studied by Ernst Kris, "Prince Hal's Conflict," *Psychoanalytic Quarterly*, XVII (1948), 487–506. Kris sees Hal rejecting the court in "silent protest" against the regicide of Richard II (p. 497), pointing out that historical sources tie the young Hal to Richard as a companion in the Irish campaign. Norman N. Holland, *The Shakespearean Imagination* (Bloomington: Indiana University Press, 1964), 177, has also noted parallels between fathers and sons, extending them to include Falstaff and Hotspur as two images of excess—Falstaff representing body, money, words, a too-slow pace, sanguine heat and travel by foot; Hotspur representing spirit, honor, deeds, a too-fast pace, choleric heat and travel by horse. The most detailed working out of the parallels between Henry IV and Falstaff is in Winny, *The Player King*, 105–31.

ruled by King Henry's double. Falstaff serves as Henry's concretizing metaphor, a physical correspondence of the sort most often found in dreams. Henry is a usurper; Falstaff is his dream equivalent, a highwayman. Henry reminisces over his former triumphs; Falstaff extends and solidifies that tendency by speaking of himself as a youth. Henry is a tyrant; Falstaff is a bully. Both are ruthless in their search for a stable personal identity in the symbolic public role of ruler. Henry faces the alternatives of civil war or holy war—in the one he protects his ill-gotten throne; in the other he expiates his sin in attaining that throne. Falstaff alternates between keeping his men in line by defeating them in practical joke-playing and word duels, and experiencing frequent, if short-lived, bouts of melancholy in which he vows to repent and lead an honest life. For neither man is the fond wish of peace and salvation more than an unrealizable and self-deluding dream. Both seek an heir. Squeezed out of the king's narrow world of politics, Falstaff—wearing the emblems of Henry's psychic nature—burgeons up as a nightmare of infinite physicality. Together they manifest two halves of the Adversary who cannot connect himself to any pattern that exists outside the self.[23]

Falstaff, however, with his greater range of syntactic possibilities and his pliant, shifting mound of flesh, plays out his limitations differently.[24] Unlike Henry, he is able to take on many roles and play many different scenes. Yet he never allows his playing to endanger his self-image. Play for Falstaff is not a medium for psychic or spiritual growth, but rather one more manifestation of his self-aggrandizing search for affirmation. In Falstaff, all growth turns to fat. From his first appearance in Hal's rooms at court , Falstaff demonstrates his form of play:

23. Wilson, *The Fortunes of Falstaff*, 17–25, discusses Falstaff as a type of Vanity, the traditional dramatic enemy of human salvation.

24. See Dorius, "A Little More Than a Little," 22–26, for an analysis of Falstaff's fatness, which represents excess, formlessness, and disorder, in contrast with the Lancastrian leanness.

> Marry, then, sweet wag, when thou art king, let not us that are
> squires of the night's body be call'd thieves of the day's beauty.
> Let us be Diana's foresters, gentlemen of the shade, minions of
> the moon. (I. ii. 23–26)

As a comic echo of the linguistic richness of Renaissance dramatic and nondramatic poetry, Falstaff's language revels in its
creative theft.[25] His language and his play activities imitate the
imitations of life found in poetry—distorted echoes of gestures, techniques, and diction separated from their governing
vision. His role-playing does not reflect his reaction to experience, nor does it provide him with the capacity to survive
amidst the threatening and the incomprehensible. Playing, for
Falstaff, is opposed to serious endeavor; it is fun, entertain-
ing—like Henry's, a means rather than an end.

Falstaff's play is always motivated by a self-seeking goal,
here no less than respectability and prestige. Closer to power,
but still concealed in the heir's apartment, Falstaff sees Hal as
his way up from darkness. His metaphors of the night—the
working hours of his profession—place him on the dark side of
the mind's experience, allowed to wander only when the sun's
eye is closed. He knows, however, that if the prince himself
rules from the night, then night becomes day and the poles of
power and slavery are reversed.

While Falstaff is working to assure his future, however, his
authority, like Henry's, is being challenged from within by
Poins, who with Hal plots to rebel by exposing Falstaff as a
coward. Hal, pliable in his quest for new roles and new situations to act out, adopts the play and his role in it, becoming a

25. Holland, *The Shakespearean Imagination*, 113, describes Falstaff's language
as a parody of contemporary theatrical styles. Waldo F. McNeir, "Structure and
Theme in the First Tavern Scene of *Henry IV, Part One*," *Essays on Shakespeare*,
ed. Gordon Ross Smith (University Park: Pennsylvania State University Press, 1965),
77, notes that Falstaff's euphuistic style and his reference to King Cambyses date
him. James L. Calderwood, "*1 Henry IV*: Art's Gilded Lie," *English Literary Renaissance*, III (1973), 135, explores fully Falstaff's blatant theatricality in an "essentially . . . realistic play"; Falstaff "keeps asserting his 'real' identity as a performer,
imposing theatricality on history."

rebel with Falstaff as he could never do with his own father, and so absorbing the other into himself. The robbery and its reversal, the robbers robbed, go according to plan. Falstaff is unhorsed, taken down from a posture of authority and made to walk the ground—an element he is no longer equipped to master.[26] He cannot acquiesce to his own deposition, however, and countermoves by tickling his nose with speargrass (II. iv. 309), bloodying his clothing, hacking his sword—trying to unite his self-image and his public image. If his audience appreciates and believes his act, that is all the reality he needs—Falstaff *is* what he pretends to be. With no lodestone of truth, he drifts in and out of roles he finds flattering and persuasive. Because his goals are restricted to the physical and the worldly, he—like the king—aims finally at popular opinion and worldly power. Accordingly his deadliest fear is public exposure; to avoid it, Falstaff uses play to deceive himself and his audience.

But when his counterplay—pretended bravery in the face of insurmountable odds—is foiled by the news that his attackers were the two rebels, Poins and Hal, Falstaff is forced to resort to his repertory of acceptable roles to shift the blame away from himself. If the role of courageous defender fails, that of loyal subject will suffice: "was it for me to kill the heir-apparent?" (II. iv. 268–69). In his anxiety to move quickly away from the trap, Falstaff characteristically suggests a play extempore to take everyone's mind off his shame, which Hal still pursues, supplying "thy running away" as the argument. Only the news from the court, demanding Hal's presence, saves Falstaff from exposure. Somewhere he holds fast to a glorious image of himself as a brave man; somewhere he believes that man is himself. His later comments on the evening's actions reveal in their ambivalent tone his attachment to that image:

26. Here Holland's association of Falstaff, in *The Shakespearean Imagination*, 177, with travel by foot seems to fail.

Bardolph, am I not fall'n away vilely since this last action? do I not bate? do I not dwindle? . . . Well, I'll repent, and that suddenly, while I am in some liking. . . . Company, villainous company, hath been the spoil of me. (III. iii. 1–10)

As his self-esteem dwindles, so too does his fort of flesh.

When the news from the court turns Hal from pursuer to pursued, the play extempore becomes a rehearsal for the up-coming scene. In it, Falstaff's relationship to play becomes clearly an imitator's genius for mimicry. He begins by appro-priately demanding the role of his double: "This chair shall be my state, this dagger my sceptre, and this cushion my crown" (II. iv. 378–79). Having accommodated himself to the role with theatrical props—the regalia of kingship having degenerated in a usurper's realm to household goods tricked up to act as royal symbols and guarded by the thief's weapon[27] —Falstaff begins to speak in King Cambyses' vein. Rather than demon-strate his capacity for regal gesture, Falstaff only succeeds in convincing Hal, if not his untutored audience, that he cannot act the role at all. Falstaff delivers himself of a theatrical re-buke to his son, his language a parody of stage royalty:

Harry, I do not only marvel where thou spendest thy time, but also how thou art accompanied; for though the camomile, the more it is trodden on, the faster it grows, yet youth, the more it is wasted, the sooner it wears. (II. iv. 398–402)

The false wisdom embodied in the mock-natural metaphors of euphuism couples with the theater rhetoric of mock kings. Be-cause his imitation is twice removed from reality, Falstaff can-not maintain the pose, breaking tenor with "thou naughty varlet"—at which point Hal, his sense of decorum offended, deposes him.

When Falstaff then turns his talents to the role of Hal, whom

---

27. Winny, *The Player King*, 106–107.

he knows well, he is no more convincing than he was as king. Falstaff's reliance on theater characterization rather than on experience indicates his inability to grow. Bounded by the huge compass of his self-interest, he cannot play any role but himself—that is, his wishful self. He is successful only when his audience is someone like the naïve Mistress Quickly, whom he can maneuver into corners. His accusation that she was responsible for the theft of a valuable ring, which is close to Henry's demand for Hotspur's prisoners in its motive[28] —to squeak out of a debt (III. iii. 65–68)—can be disproved only by Hal, who once again maintains control over Falstaff's outrageous displays of deceit.

The relationship among Henry, the Percies, and Falstaff depends on Henry's continued repressive domination of himself and his realm. From without, the Percies challenge the rule of England; from within, Falstaff challenges control of self and son. All of England lies divided in two, the inner and the outer man—the nothing in a man's soul and the role that governs his actions. Only Hal moves between the two parts, leaving Falstaff snoring behind the arras as he travels to his waking father. Hal learns how to act the Falstaffian other half of the Lancaster nature by connecting himself to the absurd bravado, slippery deceptions, and self-deceiving rationalizations of his father's comic alter ego.

The Two Harrys

Harry Percy and Harry Monmouth are each other's rivals for the love of country and of king. Of course, it is Hotspur whom Henry wishes as his son, the antipoetic, rash, active young man whose perception is framed by his attachment to war. Always willing to grasp one half of a conflict and fight it to its conclusion, Hotspur superficially resembles Henry. He is a fierce competitor, an active participant in England's play,

28. *Ibid.*, 111–12.

and a devout believer in conflict. When Henry evaluates his own son against Hotspur, he sees a seemingly time-wasting, casual, unserious, passive young man—a replica of the Richard he defeated. The rivalries mix and confuse as his son appears to be the image of his rival, and his new rival's son the image of himself. Yet the interest of the realm—the possibility of breaking through the paralyzing duality that produces tension, conflict, and war—rests not with the continuation of the Bullingbrook limits but with the revival of Richard's finest quality—the poetic perception that marks the Player-King.

In Hotspur lies the potential perpetuation of Henry's divided realm. Separating action from awareness, Hotspur can play only one role, the rigid martial hero who evaluates his world against the inflexible yardstick of a code. The indecision, self-doubt, and deliberation that drive a sensitive man to growth are not part of his obsessiveness, which overwhelms his judgment and leads him to assume a leader's role before he is capable of an adult's wisdom. He sneers at the magical, crossing Glendower's assertions of his omen-ridden birth, and reduces the patterned metaphoric vision of poetry to mechanical metrics, the "forc'd gait of a shuffling nag" (III. i. 133). Hotspur has stunted his own growth by living the narrow strictures of a single role, losing in the process his human ability to communicate with others. His ideals are not oriented to the human, nor are they shared by those closest to him.

Unlike Henry IV, and like Richard II, Hotspur's division is rooted in the blindness that makes him unable to see that he stands alone. Hotspur is an isolated man, deaf to all counsel, warning, or consequence. In his presence, his father and uncle speak to each other *about* him rather than *to* him, using the third person as if he were not there. Northumberland explains: "Imagination of some great exploit/ Drives him beyond the bounds of patience" (I. iii. 199–200). Worcester remarks: "He apprehends a world of figures here,/ But not the form of what he should attend" (I. iii. 209–10). Hotspur's world is peopled with figures of the imagination, never by the allies and enemies of his daily experience. At heart he remains a child, manipulated by others into acting out their will, isolated from the actual struggle that he is duped into believing is his own. The obsessiveness of Hotspur's search for proof of his maturity separates him from human contact—his father's and uncle's advice, his brother-in-law's pleas, his wife's bed—and precludes any accurate perception of human motive.

Always he is the supreme egotist who, as his father observes, ties his ear to no tongue but his own. Blindly assuming that he is a leader of men because he is successful in his military role, Hotspur throws himself into an enterprise that requires for its success the ability to communicate with his allies, cement their relationships to one another, and assess accurately the strengths and weaknesses of the men he leads. Noble, courageous, honorable, and faithful, Hotspur embodies all the qualities a king needs to effect justice in his community, except the sympathetic ability to understand other people through play. He has no cohesive power; he cannot understand poetry; he will not grow or learn; he believes in no strength but his own. In this narrowness and isolation, he fragments the power of his rebellion just as he would divide the kingdom were he to win—another rebel, with another divided nature, would again maintain duality in the country and perpetuate the paralysis of mode:

> Speak of Mortimer!
> 'Zounds, I will speak of him, and let my soul
> Want mercy if I do not join with him.
> Yea, on his part I'll empty all these veins,
> And shed my dear blood drop by drop in the dust,
> But I will lift the down-trod Mortimer
> As high in the air as this unthankful king,
> As this ingrate and cank'red Bullingbrook. (I. iii. 130–37)

Compulsively striking and restriking verbally at his point, inaccurately circling around and around until the sheer weight of words conveys the force of his intention to himself and his auditors, Hotspur finally falls into the either/or syntax of his opponent—either Mortimer or Bullingbrook.

In the face of that threat, victory for Hal over his rivals means more than glory and a crown. On it rests the hope of achieving the unity that his country has suffered without for two reigns. Hal's seeming idleness is actually creative dormancy; his indecision, the openness to possibility; his follies, the practice of play. Hotspur attends to his father's and his country's restricting style of action and makes it his own. On the other hand, Hal's apparent disrespect for duty and tradition is actually an ability to see outside his immediate context—the creative ability to evaluate the significance of the ceremonies he is neglecting. He guards his protective cover carefully, knowing that the polarized world of Henry IV and Falstaff is always ready to break in on him and reduce him to its scope. Both fathers would willingly narrow him to their particular boundaries in order to justify themselves and maintain their power through him. Hotspur, the other Harry, aids their attack by challenging Hal's claim to the kingdom he will inherit. Yet of them all, Hal alone has the capacity to play and, through play, to circumvent the seemingly insurmountable barriers of his world's conflict. He does not grasp role after role like Falstaff, deluding himself with sack and laughter into believing he has found eternal youth, or play one role to the obsessive border of madness as Hotspur does, or fail to attain the inner harmony of selfhood and resort to the role of the destroyer as his father does. Hal is selective in his roles, rejecting Prince of Wales, robber, ostler, shill, accomplice—yet open to the possibility of acting them all.

His opening soliloquy contains the key to the problem as Hal initially sees it:

I know you all, and will a while uphold
The unyok'd humor of your idleness,
Yet herein will I imitate the sun,
Who doth permit the base contagious clouds
To smother up his beauty from the world,
That when he please again to be himself,
Being wanted, he may be more wond'red at
By breaking through the foul and ugly mists
Of vapors that did seem to strangle him.
If all the year were playing holidays,
To sport would be as tedious as to work;
But when they seldom come, they wish'd for come,
And nothing pleaseth but rare accidents.
So when this loose behavior I throw off
And pay the debt I never promised,
By how much better than my word I am,
By so much shall I falsify men's hopes,
And like bright metal on a sullen ground,
My reformation, glitt'ring o'er my fault,
Shall show more goodly and attract more eyes
Than that which hath no foil to set it off.
I'll so offend, to make offense a skill,
Redeeming time when men think least I will. (I. ii. 195–217)

In a statement that combines the expanding consciousness contained in metaphor and the rational control of a syllogism, Hal states his plan of action. Conscious, as Hotspur never is, of the way his actions will appear in the eyes of their audience— the subjects of his community—Hal reflects the Player-King's understanding that *being* himself must be communicated to others by *acting* himself. In order to find the most effective way of enacting his strength, Hal searches through Nature's correspondences for visions that strike his eye with singular pleasure. Like his father, he discovers the principle of contrast—the sun emerging from base clouds, a holiday after work, bright metal on a sullen ground: the rare accident. He has also seen that a life of working days has sapped the energy of his father and that its polar extreme, Falstaff's life of sport, can effect the same tedium. Therefore, he resolves in this world of contrasts not to adopt either/or as his mode, but to create both/ and by becoming his own contrast, his own enemy. If he internalizes the principle of duality and makes it whole in himself, he can succeed where both kings before him failed: he can be himself. And through himself and by himself, he can communicate the spirit of oneness to his people. The biblical allusion to redeeming the time is a proper coda for his speech; Hal knows the days are evil. Although the speech is defensive, and although his vision is intuitive rather than formal—and so susceptible to temporary blindness—Hal's speech still suggests that the spontaneous pattern of his thoughts brings him from meditation to vision to language to action, like no other character before him. He falls naturally into the completeness of the Player-King's pattern.

Hiding his head in the Falstaff contagion is Hal's first step towards becoming himself. With Falstaff Hal can both release the lurking doubts and antagonism that he feels towards his own father by acting them out,[29] and also learn a new set of responses, gestures, words, again by acting. The alliance with Falstaff is for Hal a release and a seizing hold. What must be repressed in his relationship to his father the king emerges in the slanging matches he plays out with Falstaff—an elementary form of challenge that reveals the hostility beneath their camaraderie.[30] Hal will not let Falstaff's rationalizations slip by

29. Ibid., 113.
30. Huizinga, Homo Ludens, 66. M. D. Faber, "Falstaff Behind the Arras," American Imago, XXVII (1970), 206, discusses Hal's hostility as his working out of the Oedipus complex with Falstaff as his father-substitute. Faber exaggerates Hal's cruelty by viewing Falstaff with great sympathy. He exempts Falstaff from any blame for the hostility except for his constant attempts to seduce Hal away from his father. Hal's motive for being with Falstaff, therefore, is seen only as psychological release through aggression; Falstaff reacts by running away in sleep and drink, and by eventually dying in a bed in a tavern. Faber's denial of any positive motives in Hal for playing with Falstaff reduces him to a puppet and a monster.

unchallenged, nor will he countenance his thefts. On this level, Hal can right the injustices he sees in the realm. He is at once an observer and an actor, who both evaluates the actions of Falstaff and plays them out to their conclusion. He thus uses Falstaff as a trial identity while maintaining his own judgment and objectivity.

Nowhere is Hal's preoccupation with his father's guilt or his understanding of the nature of play as clearly revealed as in the spontaneous test game he stages for the drawer Francis.[31] For this limited human being, Hal creates a play situation in which he will have to attempt to be two things at once—a test that matches the one both he and his baffled country face.[32] The play, then, is not whimsical but motivated by Hal's need to

31. J. D. Shuchter, "Prince Hal and Francis: The Imitation of an Action," *Shakespeare Studies*, III (1967), 129–37, has discussed this scene in depth in terms of Hal's play abilities. He asserts that "for Hal playing is a way of knowing; dramatising a situation is a way of clarifying the various positions within the conflict or of learning what the conflict really is" (p. 133). Shuchter extends this observation to include Duke Vincentio, Hamlet, and Rosalind as other players who use play to learn to know. The Francis scene is Hal's mirroring of his own and Hotspur's conflict between a figure who represents duty (Henry IV in both cases) and figures who represent delinquency of duty (Falstaff and Worcester). Francis' duty is to serve Hal, but Poins' insistent call throws him into conflict and demands that he abandon that duty. Shuchter points to Hal's "I am now of all humors" as the scene's key line; Hal is collecting humors in preparation for becoming the state in his own person (p. 134). In contrast to Shuchter's analysis, Winny's statement, in *The Player King*, 134, that the Francis scene is an episode of "sheer inanity," a fruitless wasting of Hal's time, seems imperceptive. Winny asserts that Hal's association with low life in no way prepared him for the kingship.

McNeir, "Structure and Theme in the First Tavern Scene," 67–83, has defined the entire scene in the tavern as a miniature five-act play with a beginning, middle, end, and epilogue. Richard L. McGuire, "The Play-within-the-play in 1 *Henry IV*," *Shakespeare Quarterly*, XVIII (1967), 52, views the division of the scene rather in terms of Hal's "discovery of self through pretense, a discovery which no other character achieves," with Hal moving from thief and runagate to king. Paul A. Gottschalk, "Hal and the 'Play Extempore' in 1 *Henry IV*," *Texas Studies in Literature and Language*, XV (1974), 612–13, disagrees with McGuire's view that this scene represents the turning point for Hal, since it is followed by Hal's saving Falstaff from the Sheriff. In addition, Gottschalk terms the scene in question not a play-within-a-play, but rather two plays extempore—Hal's play, which moves towards the future, and Falstaff's play, which moves towards the unreal.

32. Holland, *The Shakespearean Imagination*, 112.

shake free of his world's premise. He too must heed two calls, free himself from the old shackles in order to grow and simultaneously keep at bay the demands of his rigid role as heir to the throne. Accordingly, the first thing he asks Francis concerns exactly that problem of bondage:

> Five year! by'r lady, a long lease for the clinking of pewter. But, Francis, darest thou be so valiant as to play the coward with thy indenture, and show it a fair pair of heels and run from it?
>
> (II. iv. 45–48)

By responding affirmatively to the joking extension and confusion of the test's premise—either serve me or answer the other call, either clink pewter for the term of your indenture or run away from your obligation—Francis reveals his inability to break loose from the mode of the game. The terms of bondage and freedom, bravery and cowardliness are indistinguishable because each relies on the other for definition.

From Francis' failure to think in any terms but those presented to him arises the next step in the series of questions that forms the circle of Hal's preoccupation: a man who is so narrow as to be either one thing or another is, in Hal's experience, a thief:

> Wilt thou rob this leathern-jerkin, crystal-button, not-pated, agate-ring, puke-stocking, caddis-garter, smooth-tongue, Spanish-pouch—
>
> (II. iv. 69–71)

The game ends here with Francis bewildered, unable to follow the tenor of Hal's metaphoric references. The term "rob" hangs loosely in the air, ready to attach itself to anyone who deserves it; and shortly thereafter, Falstaff enters the scene. Hal discovers Francis' limitations in language and act, his "Anon, sir" and his frantic to-and-fro movements, his brain's undeveloped synapses and his correspondingly limited chart of reality. Francis the Drawer, Falstaff the Highwayman, Henry the King—all are caught on the two horns of *will* and *should*, *either* and *or*. When Poins asks him the issue of the joke, Hal answers:

> I am now of all humors that have show'd themselves humors since the old days of goodman Adam to the pupil age of this present twelve a'clock at midnight. (II. iv. 92–95)

At once, Hal proclaims the good sport of the game, suggests the variety of feelings it occasioned in him, and above all expresses the results of the test for himself: the both/and of metaphor and play. After he has succeeded in using language to encompass a multiplicity of meaning, when Francis again anons him Hal rages indignantly at this and any human being's willful narrowness:

> That ever this fellow should have fewer words than a parrot, and yet the son of a woman! His industry is up stairs and down stairs, his eloquence the parcel of a reckoning. (II. iv. 98–101)

This nonplayer is ineducable.

With no transition, the image of Hal's rival—born of the scene of limitation before him—rises to turn the test back on himself:

> I am not yet of Percy's mind, the Hotspur of the north, he that kills me some six or seven dozen of Scots at a breakfast, washes his hands, and says to his wife, "Fie upon this quiet life! I want work." . . . I prithee call in Falstaff. I'll play Percy, and that damn'd brawn shall play Dame Mortimer his wife. (II. iv. 101–10)

Hal understands that he is "not yet" ready to limit himself to a compulsively competitive activity—the "work" that Hotspur always seems to want more of. He does not want to be Francis the Drawer in his role as Prince of Wales. But he knows that the only way to defeat Hotspur permanently—and all Hotspurs for the rest of his life—is to encompass his ethic; and so he calls in Falstaff to help him become his rival in play. If Hal does not do this, he will be guilty of his father's futile destruction, annihilating a man without having first absorbed the principle of his existence. The news of the robbery, momentarily forgotten in Hal's focused awareness on his problem, interrupts the intention; and they move instead into the further exploration of weakness and limit. After the jesting and the hostility, the parrying and the insults, Hal is given the opportunity to practice informed justice in play: "I do, I will" (II. iv. 481). This simple statement bridges in its parts the gap between Prince and King, between present and future, between act and volition, between understanding and intent.

But the deep insecurity of his rivalry with Hotspur, so brutally handled by Henry, flushes Hal out of hiding into the world of hostile camps on the brink of war. Taunted by his father's accusation that

> Thou . . . art like enough, through vassal fear,
> Base inclination, and the start of spleen,
> To fight against me under Percy's pay (III. ii. 124–26),

Hal vows to exchange his past for Hotspur's glory. Henry convinces Hal that the time has come for his emergence into the light, and Hal readies himself to match blood with blood and so cancel his shame.

Uneasy Victory

Hal's transformation from cipher to prince is effected offstage, just as Richard's fourth-act disappearance marked the beginnings of his renewal. For both, the transformation occurs in the words and language of those who observe them. When, to revive his confidence, Hotspur asks Vernon where the "madcap Prince of Wales" (IV. i. 95) is, Vernon answers with a description that reveals the success of Hal's exploration of possibility. The intuition of his opening soliloquy is verified in the affective power of his body, which, like a medium for light, allows the glory of the day to shine in manifest form:

> All furnish'd, all in arms;
> All plum'd like estridges, that with the wind
> Bated like eagles having lately bath'd,
> Glittering in golden coats like images,
> As full of spirit as the month of May,
> And gorgeous as the sun at midsummer;
> Wanton as youthful goats, wild as young bulls.
> I saw young Harry with his beaver on,
> His cushes on his thighs, gallantly arm'd,
> Rise from the ground like feathered Mercury,
> And vaulted with such ease into his seat
> As if an angel dropp'd down from the clouds
> To turn and wind a fiery Pegasus,
> And witch the world with noble horsemanship.
>
> (IV. i. 98–110)

The sun has emerged from the clouds to give light and guidance to its audience. Hal's appearance is the proof not only of a single metaphor, but of the metaphoric consciousness and the cohesive power of play to unite all metaphor. Hal, the Player-King, combines in his person the finest sources of natural and divine beauty. He is ostrich and eagle—the most powerful and beautiful birds in both elements, earth and air. He is simultaneously spring and summer, bearing at once the promise of youth and the fruition of adulthood. He is spiritually efflorescent and animally vital, both image and goat-bull. Bird, beast, and god—all combined in the one image of feathered Mercury—he mounts, not Hotspur's shuffling nag, but Pegasus, the flying horse of poetry, the lightning overseer of the world, the powerful grace of human imagination. The problem of achieving both/and in an either/or world—which Hal had tested on the hopeless, barely human Francis—resolves itself in his collective image astride his horse. All nature and supernature converge—regal birds, golden attire, a controlled yet orgiastic horde of warriors—in the eye of a king. Hal becomes

the synecdoche of creation, magnetic center of world correspondence, his actions the perfect communication of play.

The duality of the realm, however, flowers into war. Like
Richard, Henry has been unable to restrain the movement towards violent resolution. Confronting death, Falstaff, Henry,
and Hotspur assume their native postures before the player
Hal, who has returned vision to the eyes of England and who
sees, judges, and corrects them as they pass. When he first
meets Falstaff, on his way to battle with his army of scare-
crows, Hal's jocular manner towards his playfellow changes.
Hal calls him "sirrah," placing Falstaff securely in a position of
inferiority. At their next meeting, when Falstaff's fears form
into a plea for help on the field, Hal informs him that he owes
God a death. And on the field, when Falstaff draws sack instead of a sword, Hal's patience breaks: "What, is it a time to
jest and dally now?" (V. iii. 55). He thrusts aside the incorri-
gible, material, flaccid, overripe, unteachable imitator of
players.

King Henry pursues a parallel course of response to the fear
of defeat and death. Whereas Falstaff's gross obesity represents his form of maintaining an illusion of immortality, for
Henry that same impulse peoples the field with replicas of
himself. Both kings act out their physical, infantile desire to
survive. Hal steps into Henry's dealings with the rebels by
suggesting that a single combat between him and Hotspur
would solve the issue as well as widespread war. With that
observation, which combines both mercy and justice and corrects Henry's habitual division between them, Hal steps between Henry and his guilt and makes possible a just and
merciful offer of redress to the rebels.

Hotspur, facing the end of his actions in war, changes subtly
under the awareness of betrayal. Listing his grievances is his
attempt to arouse enough indignation to carry him into battle

with the will to victory. But the code fails him. He ranges over the reasons that, in the blindness of obsession, seemed more than sufficient motive to rebel—Henry's ill-gotten throne, the Percy disgraces, Mortimer's title—but he ends by calling the rebellion a way of ensuring safety and a dodge from the king's anticipated attack: self-defense.

With his gradual enlightenment comes the possibility of withdrawing; Hotspur reconsiders sending grievances so aggressively worded to Henry. Yet his failure to understand human psychology, his blindness to other motives than his own, and his isolation from human contact destroy him before he can pursue his awakened understanding. He sends to parley the one man whose position in a trumped-up peace would be vulnerable and unpalatable—his uncle Worcester. In counterpoint to this error, Hotspur receives from Vernon a description of his rival's demeanor on challenging him to single combat: "As if he mast'red there a double spirit / Of teaching and of learning instantly" (V. ii. 63–64). Hotspur's inability to manage two things at once—to understand and to teach—dooms his efforts to failure in a situation where failure means no less than death. Like his earlier description of Hal as spring and summer, Vernon's observation here suggests Hal's ability to teach others in play while he is still learning through it what he must master. Unlike Francis who can either serve or run away, or Henry who can be either sentimentally merciful or rigidly harsh, or Falstaff who can be either a carousing highwayman or a melancholy lush, Hal can be both a learner and a teacher, both an observer and an actor, both a moral force and a manipulator.

At once the spirit of the law and the judge, Hal returns communication to the land through his ability to act himself. The war becomes the scene in which his awareness is made manifest. Before his father, he enacts loyalty and love. Douglas supplies the scene by coming upon the kingly counterfeit[33] and maneuvering him into mortal danger. Hal sees, understands, and acts:

> King.   Thou hast redeem'd thy lost opinion,
>   And show'd thou mak'st some tender of my life
>   In this fair rescue thou hast brought to me.
> Prince. O God, they did me too much injury
>   That ever said I heark'ned for your death.
>   If it were so, I might have let alone
>   The insulting hand of Douglas over you,
>   Which would have been as speedy in your end
>   As all the poisonous potions in the world,
>   And sav'd the treacherous labor of your son.
>   (V. iv. 48–57)

Hal's response has the mathematical precision of his earlier syllogism; a proposition has been disproved. He has communicated in act what he could never render believable with words, gestures, or vows.

When he confronts Hotspur, Hal's action must include the finality of death. Their enmity, mingled on Hal's part with admiration and respect, must fulfill itself in the amalgamation of the two into one, of the two Harrys into one prince and future king.[34] The confrontation moves carefully around an orderly exchange, first of words, then blows, and finally identities. Known throughout the play by their separate names, Hal and Hotspur, they meet with great formality to acknowledge their united name.

> Hot.   If I mistake not, thou art Harry Monmouth.
> Prince. Thou speak'st as if I would deny my name.
> Hot.   My name is Harry Percy.

33. Winny, *The Player King*, 119–20, compares Falstaff's and Henry's counterfeiting in battle.

34. It is not simply that they both desire one role, as Winny states (*ibid.*, 140), but rather that the victor must be both men.

Prince.   Why then I see
              A very valiant rebel of the name.
              I am the Prince of Wales, and think not, Percy,
              To share with me in glory any more.
              Two stars keep not their motion in one sphere,
              Nor can one England brook a double reign
              Of Harry Percy and the Prince of Wales.
                                    (V. iv. 59–67)

In terms of the names they exchange, the two identities confronting each other merge and then separate. From Harry acknowledging Harry, Prince Hal moves to redefinition by correcting "Harry Monmouth" to "the Prince of Wales," thus asserting his title and right to the throne and reducing "Harry Percy" to "valiant rebel." Claiming that the time has come for him to take his own name, Hal exhibits to Hotspur's mortal surprise the superiority of his strength at his rival's own game. The one-role player bows to the all-encompassing strength of a master player. With his father, Hal proved himself a son; with Hotspur, a warrior.

In his last breath, Hotspur reveals the change that has overtaken him at the last light of his mind's consciousness:

              O, I could prophesy,
              But that the earthy and cold hand of death
              Lies on my tongue. No, Percy, thou art dust,
              And food for— (V. iv. 83–86)

The man whose life now borders on the spirit sees prophetically, unable in the shortness of his dying breath to give words to his vision of the future of England and Henry V, who must live for them both. Although Hotspur dies, his strict code of fairness and his energy of conviction live on in the Harry who courteously hides the face of the dead:

              But let my favors hide thy mangled face,
              And even in thy behalf I'll thank myself

> For doing these fair rites of tenderness.
>   (V. iv. 96–98)

Standing over the other Harry, Hal covers with his favors the ugly results of "ill-weaved ambition" and buries with Hotspur the competitive obsession that springs from the drive for solitary mastery. Both stood alone—Hotspur isolated from his community by his inability to expand himself into other minds and other postures; Hal separate by choice from the community he had to understand experientially in order to govern. In the victory of Harry Monmouth, the Prince of Wales, community survives.

As he turns away from Hotspur, Hal spies the counterfeiting Falstaff lying on the ground. The body brings to mind food harvested from a successful hunt:

> What, old acquaintance! could not all this flesh
> Keep in a little life? Poor Jack, farewell!
> I could have better spar'd a better man.
> O, I should have a heavy miss of thee
> If I were much in love with vanity!
> Death hath not strook so fat a deer to-day,
> Though many dearer, in this bloody fray.
> Embowell'd will I see thee by and by,
> Till then in blood by noble Percy lie. (V. iv. 102–10)

In contrast to the appropriately solemn, meditative eulogy to Hotspur, Hal delivers to his playmate and companion a sincere but jocular, pun-riddled speech. With Hotspur, he has buried ambition; with Falstaff, vanity. Both excesses—one of the spirit and one of the flesh—find their appropriate end in his encompassing mind, the one canceled in two paces of earth, the other divided for food to sustain life.

Falstaff, however, can die for Hal only when Hal's mind can attain its full command over his realm, when he inherits from his father and becomes the Player-King. In the meantime, Fal-

staff's life remains tied to Henry's and so to Hal's. He rises
again to usurp Hal's victory over Hotspur. Yet Hal allows him
his claim, rejecting the game that would reduce him to degrad-
ing self-assertion. Unlike Hotspur, whose quest for honor cen-
tered on self-glorification, Hal is willing to give his victory
away for a good reason. And unlike Richard, he does not believe that the usurpation has diminished him. He is delighted
to see Falstaff among the living and so allows him the favor in
return—he gives him the key to becoming a respectable and
honored man. In his magnanimity, Hal also provides Falstaff
with his last test. If he can indeed "purge and leave sack, and
live cleanly as a nobleman should do" (V. iv. 164–65), Falstaff
is capable of becoming a permanent part of the Player-King's
retinue. If he fails, he is unworthy to keep company with the
future Henry V. By elevating him to a role through which he
can focus the wisdom of play, Hal has given Falstaff the opportunity he himself seized of acting out his worthiness. The
results of the test wait for succeeding action.

The drama ends with the note of change beginning to strike,
yet the return of his former state looms imminent for Hal. Although he has defeated his rival and saved his father's life, he
cannot move naturally into the position he has assumed as
leader of the country. The realm is still not his. During battle,
Hal could rise to his position as the patterning center of play
and country; but with rebellion defeated, they again belong to
Henry. Hal's last official action is the release of Douglas, which
he effects through his brother John, again teaching his vision
and his action by having others play them out.

The widely praised structure of 1 *Henry IV*, with its alternating scenes of high and low life and its alternating language
of poetry and prose, bears a meaningful contrast to the split
structure of *Richard II*. England under Richard and Henry, as
seen in the earlier play, is compressed into the narrowness of
logical alternatives. Neither king could bring to his people the

prodigal riches of play. The contrast, therefore, becomes a parallel, a repeating structure that implies entrapment in an unbreakable, continuous mode. In *1 Henry IV*, the play mode is released from paralysis by a range and variety of styles that will be absorbed into the prince who unites them in his person. Falstaff's rich language, Hotspur's dynamic force, and Henry's clever manipulation are being encompassed by a willing poet, an energetic actor, and a knowing playwright.[35] The process of creation has germinated in the Player-King.

2 Henry IV:
The Victory of Play

The noncommunal principle which Hotspur nourished to his destruction failed when the world it fragmented reformed coherently around Prince Hal. Hotspur's failure as a leader, as Morton in *2 Henry IV* describing the process of defeat reveals, occurred because he relied on his own spirit alone to lift the dross around him to higher planes of existence:

> In few, his death, whose spirit lent a fire
> Even to the dullest peasant in his camp,
> Being bruited once, took fire and heat away
> From the best-temper'd courage in his troops,
> For from his metal was his party steeled,
> Which once in him abated, all the rest
> Turn'd on themselves, like dull and heavy lead.
> (I. i. 112–18)

The alchemical tempering of metal in the presence of the philosopher's stone cannot transform baseness permanently. Worse, even a man like Douglas loses the self-sufficiency of his courage and becomes baser than he was, as his turning to flee after Hotspur's death witnesses. As a leader, Hotspur en-

---

35. See Calderwood, "*1 Henry IV*," 137, for a discussion of Hal, who, unlike Hotspur, understands that "history is a series of roles and staged events."

ervated the will of his troops, isolating in himself the spirit of honor, bravery, and righteousness.

Hal's victory, on the other hand, rested on his maintaining the individual strength of each man and shaping it into communal form. He did not dictate Henry's just and merciful terms to the rebels, nor did he hold in his power the courage of his brothers. His play method, which will become the new mode, is a way of effecting permanent change by working from within a person, educating him by bringing him to discover the capacity within himself to handle his situation. Hal does not merely spread ephemeral glory; he transmutes baseness through the divine alchemy of play.

Rumor opens the new drama, however, perpetuating the rending duality of Henry's reign, doubling and confusing tongues' "smooth comforts false" and "true wrongs" (40), bringing in quick succession the comforting lie and the brutal truth.[36] As long as Henry IV rules, the new king must remain in the limbo of his apprenticeship. The action of 2 Henry IV is for Hal an agony of anticipation and memory, sharpened by a filial love that will not allow him to wish for his release. But his waiting functions positively as well. It forces him into a more aware introspection, which will reveal to him consciously what he had earlier understood intuitively. The metaphor that began his road to ideal kingship deepens to principle as Hal demonstrates his "double spirit / Of teaching and of learning instantly" in exercising his ability to be two things at once until he can become king and all.

The Death of the Old Mode

🕊 We see the immediate results of the king's victory on the "crafty-sick" Northumberland, who, like Richard on his return

36. John W. Blanpied, " 'Unfathered heirs and loathly births of nature': Bringing History to Crisis in 2 Henry IV," English Literary Renaissance, V (1975), 222, states that Rumor figures the dissociation of speech and act. Blanpied views the king as "both an actor in the constituted form of the play, and its interpreter, even its shaper: in other words, the surrogate playwright" (pp. 214–15).

from Ireland, is teased by Rumor's tongues from hope to despair. Because he never imagined himself in Richard's place and so never experienced in play the pain of humiliation and loss, he is doomed to live them in fact. His refusal to be a player has resulted in his abrogating the codes that maintain order against chaos. Betrayal, the prime symptom of disorder, sets its mark on his forehead: betrayal of a king, betrayal of a brother and a son. Like Henry, his partner in the game of either/or, he must face his powerlessness to change his life's repeating and increasingly personal pattern of treachery.

Northumberland's response to the news of his family's defeat is a statement of the paradoxical unity of seemingly warring poles:

> In poison there is physic, and these news,
> Having been well, that would have made me sick,
> Being sick, have (in some measure) made me well.
> (I. i. 137–39)

Poison is health-giving when it brings with it a resurrection of the will, which Northumberland lost in abandoning his cause to Hotspur. With his son dead, he moves towards the absolute antithesis of order, asserting his damned state and hurling it at the world:

> Let heaven kiss earth! now let not Nature's hand
> Keep the wild flood confin'd! let order die!
> And let this world no longer be a stage
> To feed contention in a ling'ring act;
> But let one spirit of the first-born Cain
> Reign in all bosoms, that each heart being set
> On bloody courses, the rude scene may end,
> And darkness be the burier of the dead! (I. i. 153–60)

Limited by the terms of definition that he helped Henry establish in his realm, Northumberland sees the world and its possibilities only in terms of the "rude scene" he acted in it. Macbeth-like, he curses the world he has made his prison for not allowing him to escape. He understands that the play he perpetuated cannot end except in holocaust. That play, however—Northumberland's total reality—is divorced from the larger order it seeks to destroy with its own dying hand.

With Hotspur lost, the face of rebellion assumes its proper shape in the features of the Adversary Cain, purveyor of chaos, darkness, and spite. Although rebellion forms again under a new head, this time not of courage and chivalry but of church and right, it will revive only to fulfill the fate of rebellion. Its mode is unaltered; it fights under the name of the old other, Richard. Although Northumberland will retract his ominous words under his followers' promptings, he will maintain the code of Cain by betraying again.

Northumberland's partner, Henry, drifts in his sickness closer to the sentimentality that expresses itself in his futile wish for the holy war. His chief mood is a slow, penitent melancholy that brings with it uncharacteristic amounts of meditation and metaphor—on sleep, on the past's prophecies. Yet the icier half of his nature remains hard beneath the surface. Although he seemingly balks at destroying Northumberland ("Are these things then necessities?" [III. i. 92]), Henry quickly orders what he knows is a political requirement. His last bursts of shrewdness are devoted to the preservation of those sons who will not succeed him and to the rehabilitation of the one who will. In his last hours, the alternating mode of his life establishes its mortal grip on him. Just after hearing of the rebellion's total collapse, his body fails:

> And wherefore should these good news make me sick?
> Will Fortune never come with both hands full,
> But write her fair words still in foulest terms?
> She either gives a stomach and no food—
> Such are the poor, in health; or else a feast
> And takes away the stomach—such are the rich,
> That have abundance and enjoy it not.

> I should rejoice now at this happy news,
> And now my sight fails, and my brain is giddy. (IV. iv. 102–10)

Northumberland's poison was medicine; Henry's medicine, poison. In the end both die, sharing a vision of their lives in a bloody play.

For Henry, the only hope is in the future; but that is tarnished by his feeling that Hal is a Richard, seeded with follies. He wants to believe in his son, but he does not understand the terms and implications of Warwick's prophetic defense: "The Prince but studies his companions / Like a strange tongue" (IV. iv. 68–69). Although Henry grasps at Hal's sincere explanation of the crown-snatching, he harangues him with the old-news strategies of his political career.

Henry rests his dying hope on the conviction that, with his death, the title's taint will wash off. History will prove him ultimately wrong, but his last intuition that a change is forthcoming is accurate:

> [The crown] seem'd in me
> But as an honor snatch'd with boist'rous hand,
> And I had many living to upbraid
> My gain of it by their assistances,
> Which daily grew to quarrel and to bloodshed,
> Wounding supposed peace. All these bold fears
> Thou seest with peril I have answered;
> For all my reign hath been but as a scene
> Acting that argument. And now my death
> Changes the mood. (IV. v. 190–99)

With the death, figurative and literal, of the King and the Beggar-Rebel, the "mood," or mode, of alternation indeed changes. With Henry dies the syntax of his rule, the limitation of his thought, and the medium of his power. From the ruthless, undefeatable Bullingbrook to the melancholy, hard Henry IV, the man has played a consistent role in his own play. In death, he enacts his final limitation as he discovers that Jerusalem, the place of sanctity and grace, is no more than a walled room in his own castle. Together the Percies and the king they made and tried to unmake will close their disastrous scene and leave the stage to a new play and a new playwright. Only now can the mode change, and the argument, and the king.

The Last Inheritance:
Either Falstaff or the Chief Justice

⚖ The self-deceiving equivocation of Henry's reign produces the two-sided gift he bequeaths to his son. In the one inheritance, Henry leaves the Adversary's iconoclastic rise to power. He had stripped spiritual significance from the ceremonies of kingship and rudely seized the naked crown itself, believing in power as a self-perpetuating gift he can leave to his son. In the other inheritance, he leaves the Player-King's just and orderly governance. He has held the power won and has blindly struggled to connect the island of his throne to the continent of divine kingship. On the one hand is the spirit of Falstaff, his alter ego and fellow Adversary, the actor who plays to win and to evade exposure; on the other, the Chief Justice, whose concept of law is based on the enactment of virtue. In these two, Prince Hal finds the bequest of his father. He must decide whether to alternate between them and so perpetuate the double base of the past reign, or to choose between them and become entirely an Adversary or a Player-King. In his exploration of the problem as he experiences life caught between two worlds, Hal discovers that play communicates only when it is focused through a single role. On that understanding, which forms the foundation for his continued adherence to the principle of play, Hal chooses to adopt a new father in the person of the Chief Justice.

Falstaff, since his mutilation of Hotspur, has established himself as less and less worthy of favor. Hal's magnanimous decision to allow him what he has always wanted, a position of prestige and respect, was a gift for services rendered and a test for future, more serious service. Now, with Pistol appearing as his ancient-in-arms, Falstaff's inability to change, and therefore his inability to learn, crystallizes as a damaging political and ethical failure. If the Player-King sees the world as a stage, Falstaff sees the stage as a world. The apparition of Pistol strutting out his life to the theatrical bravado of Marlowe and Peele defines Falstaff as a fellow actor, if a more versatile one. Like Henry, whose nature he concretizes, Falstaff lives an imitation of an imitation—a lie. With an audience like Mistress Quickly and Doll Tearsheet, Falstaff's theatrical words and acts of love, honor, and courage can dispel bitterness and raise tears. Before the ladies, before Shallow, he plays the distinguished, influential courtier for admiration; before the draftees, Falstaff struts for money. His motto remains as it was before his advancement: "A good wit will make use of any thing" (I. ii. 247–48). Falstaff is the living perversion of play—an accurate parallel to the seemingly humble, righteous, patriotic Bullingbrook whose coin was power.

Falstaff's failure as an actor has its origin in the fear expressed by Jonson, Prynne, and the boy-Antonio that a person will become what he acts. Rather than play a role, then, Falstaff plays at playing a role, thereby avoiding any risk.[37] The very antithesis of the one-role player, he seems infinitely elastic; but, in contrast to the Player-King, he never allows his act to touch reality at any point other than self-interest. His contempt for Shallow and his crew rests on the way they influence one another:

> It is a wonderful thing to see the semblable coherence of his men's spirits and his. They, by observing him, do bear themselves like foolish justices; he, by conversing with them, is turn'd into a jus-

37. See, too, Calderwood, "1 *Henry IV*," 131–44, especially 132–35, for a discussion of Falstaff's overt theatricality.

tice-like servingman. Their spirits are so married in conjunction with the participation of society that they flock together in consent, like so many wild geese. (V. i. 64–71)

Earlier, when he recognized Hal in the uniform of another servingman, he rebukes him with "I am a gentleman, thou art a drawer" (II. iv. 287–88). Falstaff cannot understand playing a role that is beneath his self-image because of his fear that it will become permanent. In this refusal to allow a role contact with the nothing at a man's center, Falstaff rejects the process of growth that leads to responsible participation in a community. If allowed to retain his influence over Hal, Falstaff—embodying the separation of play from learning, understanding, and communication—will merely prolong the duality of Henry IV's reign into Henry V's.

The contrast of Falstaff's nature to the Chief Justice's makes the stakes of Hal's choice clearer. In his two encounters with the Chief Justice, Falstaff plays the brash youth, the royal favorite, the sly chiseler, the unrepentant glutton—emphasizing his faults in order to demonstrate that his influence on the king-to-be exceeds judgment and law. Throughout their conversations, Falstaff refuses to communicate directly on any level with the Chief Justice, but rather adopts a studied role and acts it out. Arrogantly he flaunts his prestige and defies justice. Hal had placed himself in the hands of justice when it called him to account for a law broken, but when the Chief Justice calls Falstaff in the street to keep posted on the progress in his seeming reformation, Falstaff smugly toys with him:

> *Ch. Just.* Sir John, I sent for you before your expedition to Shrewsbury.
> *Fal.* And't please your lordship, I hear his Majesty is return'd with some discomfort from Wales.
> *Ch. Just.* I talk not of his Majesty. You would not come when I sent for you.

Fal.	And I hear, moreover, his Highness is fall'n into this same whoreson apoplexy.
Ch. Just.	Well, God mend him! I pray you let me speak with you.
Fal.	This apoplexy, as I take it, is a kind of lethargy, and't please your lordship, a kind of sleeping in the blood, a whoreson tingling.
Ch. Just.	What tell you me of it? Be it as it is.
Fal.	It hath it original from much grief, from study, and perturbation of the brain. I have read the cause of his effects in Galen, it is a kind of deafness.

(I. ii.101–17)

As he pretends deafness to the Chief Justice's page, then drops "his Majesty" and "his Highness" uncasually with metronomic regularity, Falstaff spits openly in the face of the law. His implications are clear. The king is ill and probably dying. Falstaff, an inner-circle member, is up to date on the medical reports; if the illness is as serious as it appears, his Hal will be king before long. The gross disrespect he shows in placing himself so obviously above the law is demonstrable proof that Hal cannot trust him with any authority:

> For the box of the year that the Prince gave you, he gave it like a rude prince, and you took it like a sensible lord. I have check'd him for it, and the young lion repents, [*aside*] marry, not in ashes and sackcloth, but in new silk and old sack. (I. ii. 194–98)

With the Chief Justice, Falstaff allows full vent to the destructive arrogance that will emerge in his charge: "Let us take any man's horses, the laws of England are at my commandement" (V. iii. 135–37). In public life, Falstaff is a force for disorder, lawlessness, and injustice.

Despite the blatancy of Falstaff's contempt, the Chief Justice chooses to concentrate on what he perceives to be his fundamental concern. The Gadshill robbery is past, and since then Falstaff has supposedly performed bravely on England's behalf. To the Chief Justice the act alone matters. He forgives Falstaff's tone because he believes the news from Shrewsbury, not because he fears for his position "like a sensible lord." Yet the robbery was another act committed, and the Chief Justice calls Falstaff to give him assurances that what seems to be—repentance and redemption—in fact is. The Chief Justice is the player who knows and understands what he sees, but places it firmly in the context of his office. He is thus a model for the Player-King, who must responsibly perform himself. He represents the next step for Hal, who must learn to train his new awareness on the role that will absorb him into its all-encompassing sphere. By the time the Chief Justice has encountered Falstaff twice, he has discovered and condemned what Hal himself will realize:

> Sir John, Sir John, I am well acquainted with your manner of wrenching the true cause the false way. It is not a confident brow, nor the throng of words that come with such more than impudent sauciness from you, can thrust me from a level consideration.
>
> (II. i. 109–14)

> Now the Lord lighten thee! thou art a great fool. (II. i. 194–95)

Neither Falstaff's allegations that Mistress Quickly thinks her son resembles him nor the facile twisting in and out of arguments can move the Chief Justice from what he knows.[38] In his ability to penetrate the act that convinces others, there is an overwhelming indication that he shares with Hal the key to understanding—play—and that he has gone further than Hal towards using it consciously to keep justice active.

38. Logically pursuing the discussion of Henry IV and Falstaff as parallel figures, Winny, *The Player King*, 118, sees the Chief Justice's rebuke of Falstaff as a covert rebuke of the king: "Under the rule of a usurper, justice can express itself only obliquely; but in this scene its symbolic figure contrives to speak out sharply and unequivocally against the wrongs which still go unpunished in Bolingbroke." This provides further reason for Hal's natural alliance with the Chief Justice, since he has been engaged in exposing Falstaff from their earliest moments on stage together.

Such is Hal's choice. Of the two men, he has known only the facile player Falstaff, whose nature has provided him with a needed escape from his limiting duties and whose methods have helped him become greater than he was. Through the infamously large Sir John he has learned to extend himself. But now Falstaff's own limitations become glaringly visible. As the moment for Hal to assume the serious role of king approaches, he becomes more and more aware of the kind of advisors he must have around him. Yet he still has time to observe Falstaff and the Chief Justice. The choice will remove him from the sphere of the irresponsible imitation player into that of a man whose performance of duty is an act of creative play.

Hal and the Void:
Uncertainty before Self-Awareness

With Hal, as with Richard and other Shakespearean figures, a marked absence from the drama's action signifies a private transformation. Hal's absence from Act I of *2 Henry IV* parallels his disappearance from the Act IV preparations for Shrewsbury in *1 Henry IV*. After his first disappearance, he emerged from hiding as a king heroically astride Pegasus. His second absence marks a reversal of direction. The strain and anxiety of that rapid journey to the center of England reveals itself now that leadership is no longer required of him. Hal enters the play "exceeding weary." His companion is not a Lancaster or a Percy, but Poins, whom he bitterly recognizes as a living definition of human limitation. Haunted by the Shrewsbury glory but unable to pursue it to its natural end in kingship, Hal feels the dregs of greatness—a touchy pride. His life has not totally metamorphosed into his kingly performance, and the strain in feeling it decorous to act consistently royal is almost unendurable: "Doth it not show vildly in me to desire small beer?" (II. ii. 5–6).

Yet the degradation is softened by Hal's awareness that if he cannot be king, he can bide his time by continuing to study the people around him. In Poins, Hal finds not merely a companion but the embodiment of the average subject:

> *Prince.* Shall I tell thee one thing, Poins?
> *Poins.* Yes, faith, and let it be an excellent good thing.
> *Prince.* It shall serve among wits of no higher breeding than thine. (II. ii. 32–36)

Later Hal asserts: "Never a man's thought in the world keeps the road-way better than thine" (II. ii. 58–59). Seemingly it reflects ill on Hal to be able to itemize Poins's wardrobe; but it speaks well of his ability to understand and communicate with the man whom later Hal must guide as king. Hal becomes strongly conscious once more of the problems of acting before an audience.

In *1 Henry IV*, Hal used play to test values and control deceit in others, to enlarge his consciousness in order to judge fairly their motives and actions. Now Hal refines that ability to play by practicing on Poins as the prototype of the audience he must someday convince of his kingship, teach to be just, and move to loyalty and courage:

> *Prince.* What wouldst thou think of me if I should weep?
> *Poins.* I would think thee a most princely hypocrite.
> *Prince.* It would be every man's thought, and thou art a blessed fellow to think as every man thinks.
> (II. ii. 52–57)

Although Hal finds his Everyman's thoughts vulgar and ungenerous, he must yet penetrate them if he is to create a play that involves his life. In this pursuit of the act that ideally encompasses both his own consciousness and his audience's, he continues the search of his first appearance on stage, to make what *is* also what *seems*—to be himself.

No longer here and not yet there, Hal finds a new and painful objectivity in his discovery that he is insulted behind his back, bandied about as Poins's sister's future husband, relegated to Falstaff's familiar. The separation between him and the contagion he lived among and shone through becomes apparent as he realizes with hurt that he is being used. Yet with nowhere else to go, Hal accepts Poins's suggestion that they dress as drawers, conscious of the descent and his motive for it:

> From a God to a bull? a heavy descension! it was Jove's case. From a prince to a prentice? a low transformation! that shall be mine, for in every thing the purpose must weigh with the folly.
>
> (II. ii. 173–76)

If Jove could abandon his divinity for a mortal foible, so can Hal descend from princehood for an equally mortal folly. The power and crude animality in Jove himself became the bull he chose as his manifestation; the time-serving, craft-learning servitude of the prince becomes the apprentice drawer. Even in jest, Hal knows that the correspondence is what matters. And so he moves to act out a role whose dimensions unfortunately still suit his predicament. He had asked Francis to become him; now he must become Francis.

With Falstaff, Hal tries out his old relationship, reenacting the familiar pattern of play and revelation. After Falstaff discovers the identities of the drawers, Hal pursues him as he always has, half wanting to expose him, half wanting Falstaff to pull the ace from his sleeve. But the old need to admire treachery and to expose it, the unrelenting ambivalence Hal felt towards Falstaff, which prompted him to be cruel in depriving him of self-respect and overkind in allowing him a usurped glory, no longer prevails. The terms of Hal's life have shifted, and although he probes Falstaff's excuse—"I disprais'd him before the wicked, that the wicked [*turns to the Prince*] might not fall in love with thee" (II. iv. 319–21)—it is with less than usual tenacity. Peto's news from the war and the court leads Hal instantly to repent his moment of nostalgic folly; he faces the discomfort he has felt in indulging it: "By heaven, Poins, I feel me much to blame / So idly to profane the precious time" (II. iv. 361–62). Even though he is not yet at the head of his people, Hal can no longer feel at home in the underground.

The call to court brings him to the side of his other father, who desires with a will equal to Falstaff's to make Hal into his image. Henry, in his guilty need to inhabit a world peopled with himself, fails to recognize his son as a separate being; Hal to him is only "not me." The prince's true promise, however, rests firmly on the very dissimilarity between his idea of kingship and his father's, which appears in their relationship to the central symbol of royalty—the crown. Henry IV, the usurper who wrested it from Richard's weak fingers, estimates its significance in terms of its value and power. For Henry, the crown *is* the king.

As Hal moves to his dying father's bedside, there to find the "troublesome bedfellow," the crown, he reflects an understanding of kingship that exceeds his father's literalism. The crown is a care and a duty, a symbol of majesty that will be his to guard and bequeath to his son as it was bequeathed to him. But, he explains to his father as he recounts the feelings that accompanied his seizure of the crown, it is also an enemy:

> Accusing it, I put it on my head,
> To try with it, as with an enemy
> That had before my face murdered my father,
> The quarrel of a true inheritor. (IV. v. 165–68)

Hal's need to "try with" the principle of murderous power, and so to internalize the Adversary in play, which prompted the movement of his sun behind the clouds of his vanity, appears

as he encompasses the crown's ambivalence. That crown—his
father's honor and dishonor, his prize and his failure, his ally
and inner enemy—becomes in Hal's hands the duty of a role
he must impersonally and dispassionately act. In trying with
it, he practices the inner feelings and the outer appearance
that converge in the role. He will be the first king to effect the
relationship between them without block, doubt, or distortion.
His kneeling before his father, the "exterior bending," is tutored by his "inward true and duteous spirit" (IV. v. 148, 147).
In this justification of his action, which restores hope to the
dying Henry, Hal is brought to the brink of asserting his own
play philosophy and, in asserting it, making it his conscious
motivation for further action.

In the void that extends from his just victory at Shrewsbury
to the death of his father, Hal fights the confusion of conflicting
roles. Once he has emerged from hiding into the political center of the torn country, he cannot return to the formative posturing of his test life with Falstaff. Nor can he move on to
assume permanently the position he temporarily held for England. In the hiatus between his rise from nothing to the attainment of a role, Hal discovers consciously the way to appear
and the way to persuade through appearance and action—he
has discovered how to perform. He has learned in the sobering
confusion how to become the glass that is at once transparent
and reflecting, window and mirror. He has learned to value the
person who sees, verbalizes, and enacts in himself his understanding of pattern as a work of art. He has encompassed in
himself the paradox of egoless selfhood: a person, in order to
be himself, must act the role of himself. He has rejected the
Falstaffian isolation of self from role. In Hotspur, the enemy
clearly defined himself as the atom-splitting destroyer of community—the rebel. In Falstaff, the enemy is more difficult to
perceive because he was once the friend who tutored a shal-

low intuition in the rich variety of play. Yet that principle too must be rejected as England buries the dead Henry and his mode and looks with hope to his son.

The New Mode

꿳 The two faces of choice, one embracing a seeming enemy and the other denying a seeming friend, mark the beginning of Henry V's reign. The first man the new king confronts is the Chief Justice, considered by all the court to be his enemy. In him the spirit of the law lingers from Henry IV. Yet he is a man who personally extends Henry IV's understanding of law—the necessary code to keep the king safe—to law as justice based on the sympathetic understanding of person for person.

In King Henry V's first action, he uses the play skill he perfected as an apprentice with Francis, Falstaff, and Poins to test this man's worth. He leads the Chief Justice to make a statement of belief by acting out a scene in which justice is the focus:

> How might a prince of my great hopes forget
> So great indignities you laid upon me?
> What, rate, rebuke, and roughly send to prison
> Th' immediate heir of England! Was this easy?
> May this be wash'd in Lethe and forgotten? (V. ii. 68–72)

When Hal questioned Falstaff about the indignities and insults he had heaped on him, Falstaff's response was an ambiguous dodge, the donning of another role. But here, as Hal flatly describes the outer appearance of the injury done him, he receives in response not flattery, nor chicanery, nor entertainment, but rather a direct lesson in play terms of the difference between being Prince Hal and being King Henry V:

> If the deed were ill,
> Be you contented, wearing now the garland,
> To have a son set your decrees at nought?

To pluck down justice from your aweful bench?
To trip the course of law and blunt the sword
That guards the peace and safety of your person?
Nay more, to spurn at your most royal image,
And mock your workings in a second body?
Question your royal thoughts, make the case yours:
Be now the father and propose a son. (V. ii. 83–92)

In this analysis of law and justice, based on the play extension of acting out a metaphor in which a person becomes other than what he is, King Henry recognizes the guide he has been needing to ease his way into the kingship. The scene between them is a recognition scene, where one player discovers another in the code of his language and intention. Henry V adopts the more practiced player as his father, and the Chief Justice recognizes in that action the mark of a king he can serve. That Henry's intention was not merely to expose to the Chief Justice his feelings of degradation in being arrested, but also to test his response to the accusation, becomes clear as Henry reminds him that he placed himself in the hands of the law. He quotes his father's words:

"Happy am I, that have a man so bold,
That dares do justice on my proper son;
And not less happy, having such a son
That would deliver up his greatness so
Into the hands of justice." You did commit me;
For which I do commit into your hand
Th' unstained sword that you have us'd to bear.
(V. ii. 108–14)

The proof of the Chief Justice's worth as a judge is his ability to understand a person by his acts and inculcate virtue through play. He has helped Hal reunite the word and the act—separated by both Henry IV and Richard II—by enacting law as justice.

On the firm ground of their mutual recognition, Henry can

turn to the state and begin the formal change from either/or to both/and. From the beginning of his address to the princes of the court, King Henry sets in motion the process of change. In twenty-three lines (V. ii. 122–45), the coordinating conjunction *and* appears six times, four of which emphatically begin lines of verse. (In almost double that number—forty-five lines—of one of his father's speeches [IV. v. 92–137], *and* appears only four times.) In the crucial issue of war's duality, which crippled both his father and his uncle, Henry changes strategy. He wants counsellors of wisdom equal to any other country: "That war, or peace, or both at once, may be / As things acquainted and familiar to us" (V. ii. 138–39). The new mode of play, with its emphasis on the extension of human possibilities through the reach of metaphor, on becoming more rather than less, on communication rather than power and authority, dominates the new king's court from his first royal appearance. For the first time, England is in the hands of a Player-King, a man who will not cease to grow despite the fact that he has become himself.

The rejection of Falstaff, for which King Henry has been reviled for ingratitude and a lack of imagination, occurs as it must on the heels of his recognition of his true father in the Chief Justice. When Hal says that he has placed his vain affections in the tomb with his father, he is asserting the link between Henry IV and Falstaff, a link so psychologically unbreakable that the death of one is the death of the other. Hal relegates Falstaff to the world of dreams in which they met when neither had a role to play. The object of Hal's discourse to Falstaff is to convince him that the meeting ground between them has vanished: "Presume not that I am the thing I was" (V. v. 56). Instead, Hal offers him the choice of facing the reality of his life by confronting his death, as his other half did, or of disappearing into the underground and dying symbolically. Hal had given Falstaff the opportunity of becoming a peer of the realm, the victorious knight who defeated Harry Hotspur. Now, Lancaster explains, he gives him the means to keep him from returning to highway robbery and confidence frauds. He cannot give him the awareness to tell what *seems* from what *is*: "Look you, he must seem thus to the world" (V. v. 78). Nor can he focus Falstaff's self-indulgent play on a single role in which Falstaff can lose his limiting attention to self. The choice is made with justice and compassion, but also with the necessary objectivity that must attend the role of king.[39]

Prince Hal has pursued an intuition to its end as conscious principle. With the danger of losing himself completely in the annihilation of self, he found the method of discovering and revealing the full extent of selfhood. The desire to absorb into

---

39. Ben Jonson summarizes the time's view of the ideal prince, who clearly resembles Henry V in his activities in law and religion:

[Let him] Study Piety toward the Subject: Shew care to defend him. Bee slow to punish in diverse cases; but be a sharpe, and severe Revenger of open crimes. Breake no decrees, or dissolve no orders, to slacken the strength of Lawes. Choose neither Magistrates *civill*, or *Ecclesiastick*, by *favour*, or *Price*: but with long disquisition, and report of their worth, by all Suffrages. Sell no honours, nor give them hastily; but bestow them with counsell, and for reward; If hee doe, acknowledge it, (though late) and mend it. For *Princes* are easie to be deceiv'd. And what wisdome can escape it; where so many Court-*Arts* are studied? But above all, the *Prince* is to remember, that when the great day of Account comes, which neither Magistrate, nor *Prince* can shunne, there will be requir'd of him a reckoning for those, whom hee hath trusted; as for himselfe: which hee must provide. And if *Piety* be wanting in the *Priests*, *Equity* in the *Iudges*, or the *Magistrate* be found rated at a price; what *Iustice* or Religion is to be expected? Which are the only two Attributes make *Kings* a kinne to *Gods*; and is the *Delphick* sword, both to kill Sacrifices, and to chastise offenders.

Herford and Simpson (eds.), *Ben Jonson*, VIII, 602–603. The one advantage Henry V has over Jonson's Prince is his ability to see through deception, having himself lived the roles that tutored him in its nature and expression.

Sherman H. Hawkins, "Virtue and Kingship in Shakespeare's *Henry IV*," *English Literary Renaissance*, V (1975), 313–43, provides the Renaissance background of Hal's education, defining his gained virtues as temperance and fortitude in 1 *Henry IV* and wisdom and justice in 2 *Henry IV*. Hawkins cites Xenophon's "The Education of Cyrus" and Sir Philip Sidney, who sees the aim of art as the creation of many Cyruses: "Thus Henry V, who is both king and hero, acts to a double audience, on stage and in the theater—and beyond it. By his example, both his subjects in Shakespeare's play and all who see or read it are moved to imitation: his education is also ours" (p. 343).

himself the knowledge of the Adversary experientially in the face of his father's uncontrollable need for external enemies was a movement towards healing the duality that divided the country and prevented communal, enlightened action. What began as a self-protective impulse to hide from the probing fingers of that self-sick father and king became for Hal the way to prevent the corrupting inner limitations of self. "My father is gone wild into his grave" (V. ii. 123). The need for disguise is buried in the father's death, but the results of disguise open a new world of possibility for Henry V and for England. For the first time England has a king who can bring into harmony the world of the drama and the world of the audience, a player whose portrayal of the role of king is selfless enough to convince his subjects of its validity.

Henry V:
The King Who Is Himself

Richard II understood kingship as a state of unapproachable grace in which any faults he owned as a man would dissolve in ceremony and symbol. His consequent refusal to be himself—to act the role by relinquishing the man in the king—prevented the genesis of creative act in his realm. When the usurper Bullingbrook took into his hands the will of the divided land and overthrew the king, he stifled belief in the efficacy of bare ceremony. Yet as King Henry IV, he too needed the comfort of relying on the illusion that the formal rites, which he had shattered with force, were omnipotent in themselves. The natural limitations of his mind, augmented by his guilt, confined him and England in the compulsively repeating agonistic pattern of civil war. A paralysis of mode nullified first one and then the other. Neither Richard II nor Henry IV, both bound by the limits of self, could be himself as king. Richard's ultimate escape from those limits, however—heralding the way Hal protected his unripened youth from the with-

ering touch of a corrupt authority—opened the promise of
change, growth, and fruition for all of England.

In *Henry V* that promise matures into fact. In his alienation
from the strictures of role, Prince Hal learned that either/or is
not a valid chart of the world's pattern. He learned to distrust
the power of ceremony and to rely rather on individual will to
produce response. His intuition that a person is what he acts
matured into a principle of kingship. Thus trained in play, he
becomes a king who enacts metaphors and heals division, who
creates his own realm the way an artist creates his imaginary
landscape.[40] Unlike Richard II and Henry IV, whose frustrated
wills strangled England and themselves, Henry V creates a
play world that reflects his own freedom and so bestows on his
subjects the possibility of releasing and extending their human
potential. As Player-King, he brings the cycle of human life
into a world where limit becomes extension, secrecy revelation, and distortion vision, a world where once again it is possible to exercise the will to creation over sin, indifference, and
violence. He creates the garden and gives the players in it free
will, making possible a play in which every person can make
Adam's and Eve's decision as they did—in the light of clearly
established consequences.

Yet his recreation of the garden where temptation confronted and overcame human incompleteness occurs after the

40. Edward Dowden, *Shakspere: A Critical Study of His Mind and Art* (Rev. ed.;
London: Kegan Paul, Trench, Trübner, 1892), 213, recognizes this mysterious force
in Henry: "But while Bolingbroke with his caution and his policy, his address and
his ambition, penetrated only a little way among the facts of life, his son, with a true
genius for the discovery of the noblest facts, and of all facts, came into relation with
the central and vital forces of the universe, so that, instead of constructing a strong
but careful life for himself, life breathed through him, and blossomed into a glorious
enthusiasm of existence." Rose A. Zimbardo, "The Formalism of *Henry V*," *Shakespeare Encomium*, ed. Anne Paolucci (New York: City College, 1964), 22–23, evolves
a similar view. For an excellent review of the critical arguments over whether to
read *Henry V* as heroic or satiric drama, see Moody E. Prior, *The Drama of Power:
Studies in Shakespeare's History Plays* (Evanston: Northwestern University Press,
1973), 311–41.

fall, which made perfect transparency impossible for human nature. Even art cannot consistently train the human gaze upward, away from frailty; the Player-King himself must perceive his subjects' and his own proclivity to succumb and fall away from the perfect pattern. The curse of mutability separates the imagination's will from the world it shapes to itself. While England becomes for the first time the play center for a universe that a Player-King wills into form, a last revelation awaits the man who is subsumed in King Henry V—the awareness of ultimate, unsurpassable human limit.

The Chorus and the Audience:
The Outer Circle

➴ Just as a country is an extension of a king, an audience is an extension of the drama; both are raw human material formed to the roles they are expected to play by a creating voice. 2 *Henry IV* opened with Rumor, an allegorical posture of the king, claiming the assembly and bonding the audience's imagination to a distorted play world. Rumor, dooming to futility the pursuit of the transparent act, presides over the drama of missed cues, misunderstood actions, and uncommunicated meditations. Henry V, the king and the drama, salvages the audience from Rumor's company and exposes them to the omniscient eye of the Chorus, who represents, as expositor, clarity of intent, language, and action. For the first time in the tetralogy, the circles of play extending from within the drama to the audience without, unblocked by clouded human media, move concentrically and rhythmically. A Player-King shapes the play, creating a work of art in which correspondences naturally reveal themselves in action and complete themselves in the minds and wills of the human circle that perceives it.

The Chorus, servant of communication and enemy of Rumor, appears necessarily before each act, not only to fill gaps of time and to explain actions—a dramatically avoidable service—but chiefly to maintain in his control the audience's imaginative will. He keeps the gathering consistently aware that its play faculty has the power to affect the drama before it. On his first appearance, he ingenuously begs the attention and aid of the audience to help him and a company of players bring to fruition the ideal of kingship they have long pursued:

> O for a Muse of fire, that would ascend
> The brightest heaven of invention!
> A kingdom for a stage, princes to act,
> And monarchs to behold the swelling scene!
> Then should the warlike Harry, like himself,
> Assume the port of Mars, and at his heels
> (Leash'd in, like hounds) should famine, sword, and fire
> Crouch for employment. But pardon, gentles all,
> The flat unraised spirits that have dar'd
> On this unworthy scaffold to bring forth
> So great an object. . . .
> O, pardon! since a crooked figure may
> Attest in little place a million,
> And let us, ciphers to this great accompt,
> On your imaginary forces work. (Prologue. 1–11, 15–18)

The Chorus reduces the actors to the ciphers they are, players who can never emerge as Hal did into the definition of a full role. In undercutting the illusion of drama by announcing the impotence of the actors without both a guiding and a receiving human imagination, the Chorus reveals life's and art's incompleteness, a revelation he uses to focus the otherwise variable wills of the audience on the play world. He blurs the distinction between actor and audience in order to engulf the observers in the active roles of player and playwright, lowering the critical faculty that tends to separate them and elevating the unifying imagination.

The Chorus thus enables the drama's action and the audience's response to echo the mode of Henry V's play and England's response. In contrast to the isolated group structure, the closed rooms, the secrecy and deception engendered under Henry IV and Rumor, Henry V and his Chorus manifest themselves on open terrain, in pageantry, and in public revelations. The drama's characters—Henry V's immediate audience—have conflicts that are immediately externalized because they live in a landscape designed to transform thought into word, word into act, and act into consequence. The jealous rebellions of Henry IV's reign transform to rightful war; the internal, rumor-ridden, self-devouring society recovers its health by consuming its disease in outer-directed action. Henry V is no longer the apprentice Hal; he is now the Harry the Chorus wishes could appear "like himself," fully focused in his role as king. By extending the play outward to its audience, the Chorus fulfills the expressed desire to realize the historical Henry V in fact, not by calling him back from the dead to preside again over the land, but by recreating his spirit and principle to affect the living community of spectators. He is educating his audience by having them will a Cyrus into being. In accord with Henry IV's deathbed prophecy, the mode has changed and with it the play scene of England and the drama that contains it.[41]

The Player-King and the Country: The Inner Circle

⚔ Prince Hal's dangerous but successfully completed struggle as a man with his nothingness produces the change in

41. The Chorus does not point to a waning belief in the power of illusion, to a "new and not altogether cheerful note" (Righter, *Shakespeare and the Idea of the Play*, 174). Nor is the Chorus "an admission of structural weakness in the play" that prevents the spectators from becoming personally involved (Winny, *The Player King*, 168–69). The Chorus' place within the drama depends not on Shakespeare's general attitude towards the stage at this point in his career and not on his attitude towards this particular drama, but on a desire to will this king into being. Mark Van Doren, too, sees the prologues as a sign of Shakespeare's waning faith in the drama, and so believes the play itself defective. His argument appears in *Shakespeare* (New York: Holt, 1939), 171–72.

the form and language of Henry V's drama. The first movement of his reign proceeds according to the pattern of enacted
justice that he had finished forming when he adopted the
Chief Justice as father. To create his realm as a ground on
which human potential can be realized in act, he first creates
the center of his pattern by staging himself as a living, selfless
nexus of correspondences. The first part of his play's action,
from the drama's opening to the eve of Agincourt, succeeds in
manifesting the plan. Not until he faces the possibility of an
unjust and ignominious death for himself and the men he
leads does self-doubt reveal to Hal his own limitations. Until
then he realizes himself as king, using his training in play to
fulfill the private and public needs of his role:

> Hear him but reason in divinity,
> And all-admiring, with an inward wish
> You would desire the King were made a prelate;
> Hear him debate of commonwealth affairs,
> You would say it hath been all in all his study;
> List his discourse of war, and you shall hear
> A fearful battle rend'red you in music;
> Turn him to any cause of policy,
> The Gordian knot of it he will unloose,
> Familiar as his garter; that, when he speaks,
> The air, a charter'd libertine, is still,
> And the mute wonder lurketh in men's ears
> To steal his sweet and honeyed sentences. (I. i. 38–50)

Play allows him to move inward toward the nothingness at the
human center, to drop his given role and encompass another—
divine, politician, general, judge—and to act out the new role
with the art of Orpheus, mesmerizing his audience with his
pleasing performance.[42] Henry V keeps the movement from the
inner man to the acted man unimpeded. He can comprehend,
interpret, and speak to any person in his kingdom; he can focus
on himself the will and imagination of his people; he can cre-

ate a play world where virtue and vice reveal themselves even to themselves.

The reign of Henry V is consequently a series of revelations and judgments, both in word and in deed. In their assertive candor, the language and images of his realm overthrow Henry IV's mode of withdrawal and duplicity, and all of England understands and responds to the change. In explanation of Prince Hal's transformation, Ely finds the appropriate correspondence in the natural realm:

> The strawberry grows underneath the nettle,
> And wholesome berries thrive and ripen best
> Neighbor'd by fruit of baser quality;
> And so the Prince obscur'd his contemplation
> Under the veil of wildness, which (no doubt)
> Grew like the summer grass, fastest by night,
> Unseen, yet crescive in his faculty. (I. i. 60–66)

The image of growth protected from the searing influence of the sun suits the natural process of discovery in which Hal had been engaged. His "crescive" faculty, while it was vulnerable to the pinch and thrust of a hostile element, remained in hiding, but now with maturity it emerges from its cover.

The king himself has initiated this movement towards openness, and in all his actions and statements he advances it further. His right to move on France, which forms the basis of the drama's action, is "unhidden" (I. i. 86), in contrast to the sinuous path Henry IV traveled to the English throne. When the French ambassador suggests that he relay the Dolphin's mes-

---

42. Winny, *The Player King*, 174, in making Henry V a figure of folklore, fails to note any connection between his apprenticeship as Hal and his arrival as King Henry V. Commenting on the Archbishop's speech, he states: "But Shakespeare is not asking his audience to suppose that the Hal of Eastcheap has been transformed into this paragon of learning and discretion" (p. 175).

sage to this new king in private, Henry demands that they speak "with frank and uncurbed plainness" (I. ii. 244), thus tutoring even the French in the new play atmosphere of openness and candor. He undercuts the effect of the Dolphin's snide insult by using the gift of tennis balls to expose further to his people the motives for his seeming idleness:

> And we understand him well,
> How he comes o'er us with our wilder days,
> Not measuring what use we made of them.
> We never valu'd this poor seat of England,
> And therefore, living hence, did give ourself
> To barbarous license; as 'tis ever common
> That men are merriest when they are from home.
> But tell the Dolphin I will keep my state,
> Be like a king, and show my sail of greatness
> When I do rouse me in my throne of France.
> For that I have laid by my majesty,
> And plodded like a man for working-days. (I. ii. 266–77)

Henry confesses openly that he was not himself but an alien to England and his birthright when he was guilty of the follies charged to him. It is a way of explaining his tutelage as Adversary. But he also asserts his awareness that his alienation was fertile; he knows he is more kingly for having "plodded." In war, Henry will demonstrate that what seems mere jest is serious, that play is not simply the Dolphin's jeers but also the life-and-death struggle that will mock men out of their lives. In attacking France, Henry takes on himself the burden of enacting before the French the efficacy of play for a king.

In this way, language in the realm of a Player-King does not rest unfulfilled in act. Sanctified with the absolute ceremonies of kingship, which he fuses with play, Henry V systematically saves what is capable of redemption, extirpates what is beyond it. In all cases, he allows the individual potential for salvation

and damnation to release itself from within. Falstaff dies of a
fever, melting in the fire associated with Henry's purgatorial
influence from the first line of the play. And, as Mistress
Quickly assures Bardolph, Falstaff lies in Arthur's bosom, but
only because Henry denied him the temptation of power. The
refrain of "Look to thy end," which haunted Falstaff throughout 2 *Henry IV*, comes to its fruition in his touching final hours:
"'A made a finer end, and went away and it had been any chris-
tom child" (II. iii. 10–12). When the bishops lay before Henry
the grounds for his claim to the French throne, plot though it
is to keep their lands and revenues from legal confiscation, he
extracts from them the facts of his right, forcing them to speak
through the mask of the role he carefully prepares:

> My learned lord, we pray you to proceed,
> And justly and religiously unfold
> Why the law Salique, that they have in France,
> Or should, or should not, bar us in our claim. (I. ii. 9–12)

Henry describes for the prelates their status in the realm and
the consequences of their words, which, in the natural way,
flow directly into action. With the skill he had perfected with
Falstaff, Henry cuts through the tangled web Canterbury
weaves with a simple question: "May I with right and conscience make this claim?" (I. ii. 96). Canterbury, forced by
Henry to accept his responsibility for the acts his words will
engender, answers: "The sin upon my head, dread sovereign!"
(I. ii. 97). Henry knows the bishops' base motives for wanting
him to engage France in war, but he takes up the sword for his
own reasons, just as he did after hearing his father's harangue
about duty.

With his peers, too, Henry reveals both understanding and
justice. "By interception which they dream not of" (II. ii. 7),
Henry has discovered the treachery of the trusted Scroop,
Cambridge, and Grey. The means of his knowledge is left mys-

terious, suggesting that Henry somehow sees through sur-
faces. Under Henry IV, the traitors York, Mowbray, and
Hastings were prejudged, deceitfully apprehended, and speed-
ily executed. In contrast, Henry V exposes treason by carefully
staging a scene in which the traitors themselves can enact
their treachery, pass their own judgment, and come to their
own realization of sin and its consequence. The king establishes his play's *donnée*:

> Uncle of Exeter,
> Enlarge the man committed yesterday,
> That rail'd against our person. We consider
> It was excess of wine that set him on,
> And on his more advice we pardon him. (II. ii. 39–43)

In full complement, Scroop, Cambridge, and Grey protest the
act of mercy, instead demanding rigid justice. Their judgment
of the situation is the Adversary's, based on disconnecting person from community, act from corresponding act. But Henry V
forces the pattern of correspondence they blindly reject:

> The mercy that was quick in us but late,
> By your own counsel is suppress'd and kill'd.
> You must not dare, for shame, to talk of mercy,
> For your own reasons turn into your bosoms,
> As dogs upon their masters, worrying you. (II. ii. 79–83)

In publicly staging the deception of these seemingly dutiful,
grave, learned, noble, religious men, Henry exposes the Adversary's nature, which projects its hypocrisy onto the world
around it. In play, he has simultaneously judged and taught
justice not only to himself and to his court but to the traitors as
well, who, faced with the nakedness of their crime, plead for
forgiveness but not for the mercy they extinguished. Even in
the men who would have murdered him, Henry instills the
grace of redemption. The traitors must die, not because Henry
seeks personal revenge but because they would have sold

their land, their king, their nobles, and their commons into slavery without ever realizing, until Henry points it out, that in doing so they sold themselves.

The executions of the commoners Nym and Bardolph in France parallel those of Scroop, Grey, and Cambridge. What nobles can effect in villainy is matched on a smaller scale by the pettier but no less vicious sins of the commons. Again the crime manifests the Adversary's denial of his likeness to others, and again Henry will not confuse mercy with justice as he deals with those who have broken an openly declared law. He does not reject human compassion when he approves the execution of Nym, the taker, and his own former companion Bardolph, but rather embraces the sense of justice that forced him in another time to place himself in the hands of the Chief Justice.

Before Harfleur, too, Henry proceeds according to the ethic of play. He has parleyed before and been unsuccessful in convincing the town to yield to his forces. Rather than use vain words again, Henry delivers a vivid account of the fate of a town taken in war. With words, he creates the picture of what will become fact if Harfleur remains stubborn: "for as I am a soldier, / A name that in my thoughts becomes me best" (III. iii. 5–6), Henry begins, establishing the role he is playing. Virgins raped, infants piked, old men brained—all these are the results when men's better natures are loosed to the "licentious wickedness" (III. iii. 22) of war. Henry, so much in control of his army, tells Harfleur that, once begun, the siege and its brutalities cannot be stopped, even by him. In portraying verbally the devastations of war, Henry has accomplished two objectives: first, he fixes the scene to come in the minds of the representatives of Harfleur, and, second, by doing so, he fixes responsibility for the potential carnage on those who will suffer by it:[43]

43. Traversi, *Shakespeare from "Richard II" to "Henry V,"* 167–98, especially 182–83, views Henry as excluding humanity from his public role. Yet the results of

What is't to me, when you yourselves are cause,
If your pure maidens fall into the hand
Of hot and forcing violation? (III. iii. 19–21)

What say you? Will you yield, and this avoid?
Or guilty in defense, be thus destroy'd? (III. iii. 42–43)

Again he has given free will to those he encounters, just as he
had with the Archbishop of Canterbury, the three traitors, and,
later, the two thieves. If they go to death or damnation, the
burden rests on them and them alone. They are all characters
in Henry's play, where every person is held responsible for the
consequences of his decisions. Harfleur's governor, like the
traitors, recognizes his town's doom in the scene Henry's words
create:

Our expectation hath this day an end.
The Dolphin, whom of succors we entreated,
Returns us that his powers are yet not ready
To raise so great a siege. Therefore, great King,
We yield our town and lives to thy soft mercy. (III. iii. 44–48)

Through their power to call up the image of the future—the
power of conjuring up the patterns that life makes—Henry's
words save rather than destroy.

Throughout his reign, Henry falls time and again into the
figures of play to explain his actions and communicate an atmosphere or desire. He adopts the tennis game as the original
metaphor for his war, uniting his people under the communal
spirit of a team engaged in competition. Once the English are
in France, "the game's afoot!" (III. i. 32), and Henry instructs
his troops to act the role of warrior, not with "modest stillness
and humility" (III. i. 4), which suits the man in peace, but with
the "hard-favor'd rage" (III. i. 8) of the tiger. His reason for
passing the law that prohibits the English from pillage and

---

his speech are salutary for Harfleur. He has forced the city to see its fate, and that
frees it from inhuman strictures, such as burning, in the hope that the Dolphin will
defend it.

insult is based on the same metaphor: "for when lenity and cruelty play for a kingdom, the gentler gamester is the soonest winner" (III. vi. 112–13). The atmosphere of play never belies the seriousness of Henry's engagement, which he sees clearly in the images of death and destruction occasioned by any war. Rather he knows and brings all England and eventually all France to know that no contradiction exists between play and earnest, just as no contradiction exists between self-interest, rightly understood, and common interest.

The Edenic cast of Henry's England—its play world unified by a language of action that brings crime to punishment and virtue to revelation—is defined by the specter of temptation in the French Adversary. The French are Henry's enemies not only because he claims the French throne but also because they embody his antithetical qualities: arrogance, self-seeking, and showiness. The French code is perhaps best expressed by the Dolphin as he bullies even his father into believing him brave and courageous: "Self-love, my liege, is not so vile a sin / As self-neglecting" (II. iv. 74–75). The French rely on the appearance of things, a natural consequence of their over-blown self-esteem. Their narrowness realizes itself in the smug Montjoy, the man chosen to represent the French, who limits his humanity to his function:

> *Mont.*   You know me by my habit.
> *K. Hen.*   Well, then, I know thee. What shall I know of thee?
> (III. vi. 114–15)

The French represent the amalgamation of two dark areas in Henry's life, Hotspur and Falstaff: they are isolated egotists, each of whom believes himself the heart of the French army, and they are cowardly buffoons who cannot connect their self-images to the reality they are supposedly based on. The danger of the French, then, is in their resurrection of old, defeated impulses. Henry finds himself suddenly and uncharacteristically boasting to Montjoy that one Englishman is worth three Frenchmen:

> Yet forgive me, God,
> That I do brag thus! This your air of France
> Hath blown that vice in me. I must repent.
> (III. vi. 150–52)

The French pride in their purity of blood, which the Dolphin assumes will defeat the "emptying of our fathers' luxury" on "wild and savage stock" (III. v. 6–7); their petty, divisive squabblings; their reliance on surface show—"Do but behold yond poor and starved band, / And your fair show shall suck away their souls" (IV. ii. 16–17); their undetermined leadership: all these characteristics establish them as the company of an Adversary.

Yet Henry's momentary lapse into the Adversary's mode, which as Prince Hal he had acted out, brings with it his rediscovery of the balance struck at Shrewsbury. Henry asks Montjoy to deliver this message to his master: "We would not seek a battle as we are, / Nor, as we are, we say we will not shun it" (III. vi. 164–65). With that denial of Hotspur's foolish bravery and Falstaff's shrewd cowardice, Henry reasserts himself as Player-King. And as Player-King, he will create the patterns that reveal even to the Adversary the shallowness of bare show, here to the French who, judging by appearance, choose to abandon Harfleur and, again judging by appearance, choose to fight at Agincourt. Henry faces the newly resurrected specter of the ego-bound player, and his choice is again to assimilate him or be destroyed by him. Richard II could not summon for himself one angel to help repel the invader, but Henry can draw to himself the power of divine will, which he can both read and reveal in action.

The basic pattern of Hal's preparation for kingship was complete by the opening of *Henry V*: he had discovered how to read human nature and motives; how to stage himself to elicit the response that echoes the intent; how to teach human nature to judge itself in an act of creative play. Underlying all Henry's individual discoveries was play—his technique for probing motives, testing doubts, and inducing realizations. Yet in the ceremonial robes of King of England, Henry V can no longer take part in his own process of growth. His status as king renders him transparent and selfless, a perfect medium of communication but no longer an individual man seeking individual fulfillment. Henry has joined himself to ceremony in order to complete the pattern of play. The totally external character of the life that results, however, precludes the opportunity of further conflict and further exploration; and even in Eden human frailty found its manifestation.

"Your Majesty came not like yourself"

⚜ No artist can create without periods of gestation to enrich the connections and significance of the art he produces, and the Player-King himself finds it demanding to subsist on the period of preparation alone for his relationship to play. When a dilemma he has not foreseen arises or when an experience he cannot encompass from within his role occurs, doubt resurrects the self's demands and clouds the transparency of his role. The eve of the battle of Agincourt presents such an occasion for Henry. In the sudden appearance of what seems certain disaster for himself and his troops, the circles of ceremony dissolve back to the point from which they emanate and the created pattern, now found incomplete, shatters. The Chorus assures us that Henry's kingly face never shows his anxiety, just as the demeanor of the madcap Prince of Wales never betrayed the fears engendered by his father's guilt, fears that now assault him in the dawn. From the king still flows "a largess universal, like the sun" (Chorus. IV. 43). Yet the resurrected need to disguise himself and walk unknown in the night to debate with his bosom betrays the hard necessity of coming to terms with an as yet unencompassable problem—the degree of a king's guilt in bringing soldiers to fight a war they could die losing.

Henry eases himself into the night to center the growing fear and resentment he senses among his men on himself as on a target, acknowledging what cannot be changed in the present circumstance and guiding it into safe channels. Under the cloak of the loyal and wise Sir Thomas Erpingham, he first encounters Pistol, whom he draws out on the subject of the king. Even though Pistol praises him profusely, thus stilling one painful doubt, Henry still retains his judgment sufficiently to own Fluellen as friend, kinsman, and fellow Welshman. The first challenge to be answered after the battle of Agincourt is delivered.

With the common soldiers Bates, Court, and Williams, Henry probes more deeply into the problem that sent him into the night. The burden of greatness, already exposed to him in hearing himself bandied by Pistol as "the lovely bully" (IV. i. 48), he gratefully releases as he plays out the fears he could not expose in his kingly role:

> I think the King is but a man, as I am. . . . His ceremonies laid by, in his nakedness he appears but a man; and though his affections are higher mounted than ours, yet when they stoop, they stoop with the like wing. Therefore, when he sees reason of fears, as we do, his fears, out of doubt, be of the same relish as ours are.
>
> (IV. i. 101–109)

From then on, he uses his companions in the night to hone his understanding and reveal to himself the nature of his feelings in that time. To Bates' assumption that the king would "wish himself in Thames up to the neck" (IV. i. 114–15), Henry replies with assurances that he would neither wish himself in England, nor, he retorts to a further expression of fear, would he believe that any of his men would really wish him in France alone, his cause being just. At that point, the issue is brought up squarely first by Bates, who expresses the common man's bitter and potentially vindictive sense of being manipulated by causes he cannot possibly judge, and then by Williams, who uses the only sense of justice he can muster, that if the king's cause is unjust, he will pay for all the wounds and deaths it brought about.

The attitudes and fates of his soldiers are Henry's prime interests, and now, prompted by the scene he staged for his instruction and that of the men he visits, he reasserts his one ruling belief—that every man is responsible for his own acts, that war with its fire is a means beyond human control of purging a society of its unredeemable elements:

> Every subject's duty is the King's, but every subject's soul is his own. Therefore should every soldier in the wars do as every sick man in his bed, wash every mote out of his conscience; and dying so, death is to him advantage; or not dying, the time was blessedly lost wherein such preparation was gain'd; and in him that escapes, it were not sin to think that making God so free an offer, He let him outlive that day to see His greatness and to teach others how they should prepare. (IV. i. 176–85)

The pattern the king creates echoes the biblical pattern in Genesis as circle echoes circle. For Henry, the individual integrity of a person's conscience, in which he judges himself as he will be judged, touches both divine and human communities. The prepared, educated soul functions on earth as a teacher. The sincerity and logic of Henry's reasoning prompts a chorus of agreement from the soldiers who are willing to accept responsibility for their own lives and deaths. Henry has again manifested his gift for simultaneously teaching and learning through play.[44]

44. His ability to share his purview with the soldiers denies Winny's assertion, in *The Player King*, 193, that in this scene "the common touch acquired by Hal about Eastcheap seems to desert him."

But the distrust between the common man and the nobility, which is greater from below, reasserts itself as Williams cynically rejects Henry's word that he will not be ransomed and mocks his companion for saying that he will not trust the king ever after if he breaks his word:

> You pay him then. That's a perilous shot out of an elder-gun, that a poor and a private displeasure can do against a monarch! You may as well go about to turn the sun to ice with fanning in his face with a peacock's feather. (IV. i. 197–201)

At this point, Henry's knowledge of his long and arduous journey to awareness and his intense sense of his own human infirmities rouse him to anger, and he exchanges gauges with Williams. In effect, he will prove by answering the challenge that his act will be as good as his word.

The self-deception, however, is there. In the heat and anxiety of a trying time, Henry doffed his ceremonial robes and allowed himself the confession, the emotional release, and the anger of a common man. He has rebelled against the role that denies him the flexibility of his player's nature. No one, not even the ideal player, can emerge from exploration as a cipher into a defined role and never regret the limits placed on his existence. Certainly Hal, who plodded like a common man and felt the crescive faculty within him grow and mature until he was exposed by his father's death, cannot deny himself the release of being again free of role when, on the brink of certain-seeming destruction, he faces death.

And so, addressing himself to the night, he rails on the culprit ceremony, the soul of the hierarchical structure that denies him earned homage, sleep, happiness, and gives him personally nothing in return, no rents or comings-in, no cures for the fever. His complaint is spoken in the voice of his fathers, Henry and Falstaff. But the satisfaction of achieving personal gratification is denied a king; and in this night that seems the last, Henry wishes again to be the protected instead of the

protector, the led instead of the leader, the beggar instead of
the king:

> The slave, a member of the country's peace,
> Enjoys it; but in gross brain little wots
> What watch the King keeps to maintain the peace,
> Whose hours the peasant best advantages. (IV. i. 281–84)

The former Hal, an intuitively accurate player, knows that the
only release from his doubts and his desires is in acting them
out of himself; in his journey through the night, he gives vent
to the unkingly but human aspects of his nature. As he ends
the expression of his secret wish, Sir Thomas Erpingham comes
to prompt the king to return as himself. The desire to be Hal
again fades under the responsibility of being King Henry V in
a time and a place that he as king created. With the solemn
reminder that his nobles seek him in their need, Henry reasserts his kingship by speaking, not to the night, but to God, the
only being who can understand his troubling feeling of isolation. He speaks in prayer for his soldiers and his land, asking
that the father's sin, whose punishment will come, not be visited upon them that day at Agincourt.

By dawn and battle, the French and the English have reas-
serted their polarities, the one relying on braggadocio and
show, the other on hearts that "are in the trim" (IV. iii. 115),
the French moving into battle with internal divisions and com-
petitions, the English as "we band of brothers" (IV. iii. 60).
Within the day's compass the French, like Northumberland,
manifest their natures by defying order—the Constable acknowledging disorder as the source of their defeat, Bourbon
retaliating with "The devil take order now!" (IV. v. 22)—as
they spitefully turn their strength on the defenseless boys and
luggage, while the English, Suffolk and York, affirm the bond
of love even in death. Agincourt marks the inevitable absorption of the Adversary's destructive, shallow egotism into the
Player-King's patterning will.

Recovery of the Concentric Pattern

≥≤ The English victory at Agincourt, against all rational expectation, releases Henry from the anxieties of his night's debate. In his impassioned plea to God to forget his father's sins
until another time, Henry discovered a comfort in his isolation,
a companion in his solitude. His victory demonstrated to him
that he was not and is not alone on the pinnacle of ceremony.
Again in the agony that drives a person to release himself from
the limits of his role, Henry has made a discovery of great magnitude. Through his frustrated denial of ceremony, he has
found that the role ceremony bestowed on him was in fact no
greater than the role of a common man. The common man
sleeps in his reliance on the king, but the king can find the
quietude of sleep if he learns to rely on God, for whom he
reigns if he is a just player, and in whose name and no other
he is victorious or defeated. War, Henry finds, is what he had
explained to the soldiers on the eve of battle—God's manifestation and tool of justice:

> Come, go we in procession to the village;
> And be it death proclaimed through our host
> To boast of this, or take that praise from God
> Which is his only. (IV. viii. 113–16)

Yet the conflicts he had focused on himself in the night remain to be worked out. With the French defeated, Henry finds
he must come to a decision about his personal quarrel with
Williams. In the light of day, with ceremony again elevating
him above his common humanity, he becomes aware that he
cannot fulfill the rules of the challenge because he would put
Williams in the mortally dangerous position of striking a king.
Yet in order to keep his word and so act out his verbal commit-
ment, he must find a way of answering the challenge. His answer resides in the Welshman Fluellen, whom he has owned
as countryman and relative and whose fidelity to rules parallels Henry's devotion to law.

While answering the challenge through Fluellen and assuring Williams' safety, Henry sees too the possibility of using the play as a test of his night's performance. Once he has made sure, by sending Warwick and Gloucester after Fluellen, that no harmful effects can occur, he follows, coming upon the combatants after the blows that fulfill the challenge have been struck. He stands before them as both judge and participant, the king and the soldier of the night before, just as he stood before the Chief Justice as both his king and his prisoner. Again Henry reacts by testing the worth of his supposed antagonist through playing the injured king: "'Twas I indeed thou promisedst to strike, / And thou hast given me most bitter terms" (IV. viii. 41–42). But Williams, with simplicity and candor, separates, as the Chief Justice did, what the king has united—the two different roles played. Williams would not have insulted the king had he known he was speaking to the king. Falstaff, after Gadshill, at once denied the efficacy of Hal's disguise and covered his own cowardice by saying that he knew the robber was Hal all along. Falstaff was a coward on instinct: "the lion will not touch the true prince" (II. iv. 271–72). Henry V, like Richard II, has discovered otherwise: ceremony alone will not make a lion stop short of feasting on royalty. Williams affirms both Henry's ability to act and his understanding that only the enactment of kingship makes a king:

> Your Majesty came not like yourself. You appear'd to me but as a common man; witness the night, your garments, your lowliness; and what your Highness suffer'd under that shape, I beseech you take it for your own fault and not mine; for had you been as I took you for, I made no offense; therefore I beseech your Highness pardon me. (IV. viii. 50–56)

Williams has placed before Henry the grounds of his own kingship—individual responsibility—and returned the judgment back to him in play, just as the Chief Justice did in asking

Henry to put himself in his father's place. In doing so, Williams demonstrates his understanding of the lesson Henry was teaching that night to himself as well as to the soldiers. The king is a man like any other, who can be trusted to keep his word and called to account if he does not. For his simple apprehension of Henry's humanity, for his clear vision in seeing the man apart from the role, and for the honest reminder of Henry's own weakness, Williams is rewarded with crowns filling the challenge glove—the symbols of kingship in the glove of a common man.

To complete the illumination of what occurred that night, Fluellen unmasks the pretender, Pistol. Unlike Henry, Pistol takes on a role he is unwilling to stand behind. This follower of Falstaff plays the theatrical role of the swaggering soldier to perfection, but without turning those qualities into military channels. In the course of Henry V's exposure of all secrecy and deception, Pistol is placed in a real war where he exposes himself for what he is—a coward and a bully. Fluellen forces the leek down Pistol's jeering throat just as Henry mocked the Dolphin's tennis balls into cannon balls. Gower forces the lesson home on Pistol:

> Go, go, you are a counterfeit cowardly knave. Will you mock at an ancient tradition, begun upon an honorable respect, and worn as a memorable trophy of predeceas'd valor, and dare not avouch in your deeds any of your words? (V. i. 69–73)

In the corresponding echo of Henry's exemplary teaching, the strength of tradition and ceremony is upheld and the man whose words and gestures fall short of action exposed. Pistol is unredeemable in himself, but he can no longer live undetected in Henry's open realm.

Having consolidated his own men and country into a united people again, Henry officially ends his dramatic reign by drawing the defeated French into his magnetic field. While his

trusted relations dicker with the French royalty over the formal demands of the military victors, Henry engages in the pursuit of true unity—love and marriage. Released from his feeling
that ceremony restricts and burdens him, Henry chooses to
speak "plain soldier" to "Kate" (V. ii. 149) and to ingratiate
himself not by imitating the praises of sonneteers and so wooing
her with deception, but by telling her who and what he is, a
king and a man. He teases her out of her coyness, which he
perceives is staged, and manages the kiss she would deny on
the basis of the customs they should govern. He will repeat in
public the kiss that united them in private. Henry knows that
love is not based on the pale adorations of the sonnet and is
not above a bawdy response to Burgundy's joking reference to
maids who are like flies at Bartholomewtide. The play principle of metaphoric extension, encompassment, and creativity
finds its proper external vehicle in his union to Katherine of
France.

Henry V completes the long struggle of a playwright and a
people to find the ideal king. After a series of failures, each of
which teaches more about the nature of success, Henry V,
through his process as the strawberry growing beneath the
nettle, emerges to unite into a pattern that imitates the universal pattern the circle of his realm and the circle of spectators
who observe it. The Chorus ends the play with a reminder of
the incompleteness of dramatic illusion on the one hand and
the incompleteness of human life on the other:

> Thus far, with rough and all-unable pen,
> Our bending author hath pursu'd the story,
> In little room confining mighty men,
> Mangling by starts the full course of their glory.
> Small time, but in that small most greatly lived
> This star of England. Fortune made his sword;
> By which the world's best garden he achieved,
> And of it left his son imperial lord. (Epilogue. 1–8)

The frustration of the Player-King's art form—his community—
and the art form of the playwright who recreated him—the
drama—is the mutability to which they and all life are subject.
Only if the audience of the drama's creative act can "piece
out" the imperfections with its own collective imagination—
the faculty that seeks perfection—can the mutability of life for
a brief time stop exerting its influence. Art fails and life fails.
The Player-King—star, son of Fortune, achiever of the world's
best garden, who unites in himself the firmament with the
earth—is doomed also to death and to having his accomplish-
ments, based not on the magic of kingship but on his human
ability to learn and teach through play, wither in the hands of
his son. "Nor I, nor any man that but man is, / With nothing
shall be pleas'd, till he be eas'd / With being nothing" (V. v.
39–41). Given the limited possibilities for human redemption,
the Player-King stages the scene to reveal the way to attain it.
Yet the Player-King is also a human being, not a god, who can
be dissatisfied with his lot, who can doubt himself again when
difficulties arise, who is susceptible of yielding to old vices.
The miracle of the Player-King is that he is fallible, yet also
the king who is himself.

CHAPTER III

Love Play in the Early Comedies

⚓ In Shakespeare's early comedies, love, the drive towards human perpetuation and harmony, lures the drama's characters into the educating world of play. As a metamorphosing force, creating selflessness from egotism, love is itself a play form. It opens the vision of the lover to the good, the beautiful, the ideal; it causes him to abandon his definition of self in the face of another image, his love, whose self becomes his own. The comedies insistently ask, "Who is myself?"[1] In *The Comedy of Errors*, individual identity is threatened by the existence of a double; in *The Two Gentlemen of Verona*, the changing of clothing and mind leads to frequent questionings about shadows and selfhood; in *A Midsummer Night's Dream*, the metamorphoses of love produce the confidence that grows out of enlightened self-doubt. Confronting exile from Silvia in *The Two Gentlemen of Verona*, Valentine remarks: "To die is to be banish'd from myself, / And Silvia is myself: banish'd from her / Is self from self, a deadly banishment" (III. i. 171–73).

The process leading to love takes various play forms—the wit match, the disguise, the eavesdropping—that gradually entice the character to abandon himself as an isolated entity. The wit exchanges begin the encounter, expressing an initial attraction and testing its object. But as long as they embroil two potential lovers—Petruchio and Kate, Berowne and Rosalind, Beatrice and Benedick—love cannot take hold. In the

1. Northrop Frye has noted that the focus of the comedies is the process of achieving selfhood in "The Argument of Comedy," *English Institute Essays, 1948* (1949), 58–73.

verbal confrontation, each clings to his or her own self-image, seeking triumph rather than submitting to a mutual self. Only the character's experience of playing breaks that isolation. Kate dwindles to a wife when Petruchio mirrors back to her in play her own ungenerous impatience, making her see from without the ugliness of her self-bound love. Because the lovers of *Love's Labor's Lost* use masques and dances as competitive sex plays, the intruder Death is needed to shatter their self-gratifying isolation, forcing the lesson that the restricting ego is destroyed with the body it loves. In *Much Ado about Nothing*, only when the defensive barrier of self-love is penetrated by the plays staged to convince Benedick and Beatrice that each worships the other does their love flower.

Within the couples, the women prove apter in love's ways. They readily adopt the defacing disguise, all from Julia to Jessica feeling it humiliating to abandon the costume of their sex yet willing to gamble away its safe definition. The women also discover sooner the contention between love's quest for perfection and the cold facts of a fallen world, and instinctively they play to bridge the gap. The ladies of *Love's Labor's Lost* withdraw from their competition to enforce a year's practice in using play to come to terms with mortality; Beatrice insists on Benedick's challenging his friend and soul mate as her due since they have become each other's self; Rosalind-Ganymed tests Orlando's poetical stamina by forcing him to imagine and love her in a different sex form; Viola-Cesario shatters the empty imitations of love and death in Orsino and Olivia. With the exception of Kate and Titania, who are metamorphosed by their lovers, it is the heroines who form their dramas from within because they possess a greater detachment from self and situation than the heroes and a consequent willingness to abnegate both in quest of a greater good.

Of all the heroines, Portia attains most fully the power of the Player-King in her ability to control not only the single character of her lover but the entire play world of her drama.[2] Because she cannot assert herself by choosing a husband, Portia must live in a state of receptive passivity. Her father's will creates her experience of love as a mixture of detachment and passion: she must remain open to the possibility of defining herself in terms of any suitor who submits to the test; she must master her urge to choose the image for her own life. Despite an initial resistance to her situation, Portia gradually discovers that the play her father has placed between her and her future has the wisdom of exposing publicly her suitors' weaknesses and of confirming her own choice of Bassanio. Through that discovery, Portia becomes the conscious educator of her play's relative, incomplete worlds—a Player-Queen.

The Merchant of Venice:
"Who chooseth me must give and hazard all he hath"

Both and Neither

Antonio, a merchant of Venice, in the drama's opening speech proclaims his vexing and puzzling melancholy:

> In sooth, I know not why I am so sad;
> It wearies me, you say it wearies you;
> But how I caught it, found it, or came by it,
> What stuff 'tis made of, whereof it is born,
> I am to learn;
> And such a want-wit sadness makes of me,
> That I have much ado to know myself. (I. i. 1–7)

His words provide the key terms of his experience in the drama—sadness, self-surrender, and impending revelation. In the quest for selfhood, Antonio describes the opening stage of the Player-King's education: an apparent dullness to his im-

---

2. Kirby Farrell's discussion of Portia and *The Merchant of Venice*, in *Shakespeare's Creation*, 140–62, also uses this concept. He sees her "as an actor-dramatist among simple actors" (p. 161).

mediately defining identity which, though personally and socially burdensome, will open for him the possibility of growth. It is the same dangerous dissatisfaction that leads to Hal's abandonment of role, Vincentio's disguise, Hamlet's antic fit.

In a series of responses that will take form in the drama as the three caskets, Salerio, Solanio, and Gratiano suggest the logical causes for Antonio's depression: his wealth adrift at the mercy of the sea (I. i. 8–14); his heart at the mercy of love (I. i. 46); his self-image at the mercy of public opinion (I. i. 86–102). Although Antonio's position suggests that any of these reasons could be accurate, he denies them all. After all, he seems master of the world's tangible gifts—his ships secure, his fellow merchants respectful. Love he dismisses with a "Fie, fie!" (I. i. 46). His dissatisfaction, incomprehensible in the given terms, transcends the boundaries of worldly logic. It is as if all the world's ills rested on him. Using the single metaphor that best describes his state of mind, Antonio explains it as a role:

> I hold the world but as the world, Gratiano,
> A stage, where every man must play a part,
> And mine a sad one. (I. i. 77–79)

Denying responsibility for having sought his unhappiness, Antonio finds in the metaphor an explanation for the inexplicable.

Bassanio, on his entrance into the play, is as irrationally carefree as Antonio is melancholy. His first words—"Good signiors both, when shall we laugh?" (I. i. 66)—establish him as Antonio's complement, an insouciant young man whose faith in good times to come allows him to brush aside life's unpleasantness. Although he is a gambler, Bassanio generates a will to succeed so powerful that it absorbs even failure:

> In my school-days, when I had lost one shaft,
> I shot his fellow of the self-same flight
> The self-same way with more advised watch
> To find the other forth, and by adventuring both

> I oft found both. I urge this childhood proof,
> Because what follows is pure innocence.
> I owe you much, and like a willful youth,
> That which I owe is lost, but if you please
> To shoot another arrow that self way
> Which you did shoot the first, I do not doubt,
> As I will watch the aim, or to find both
> Or bring your latter hazard back again,
> And thankfully rest debtor for the first. (I. i. 140–52)

Impatient to woo Portia and to repay his debt to Antonio, Bassanio urges his "childhood proof," asserting the principle that will appear later as the legend on the lead casket—to gain, one must give and hazard. Indeed, were the world still in its childhood, were there no need to educate human nature, Bassanio would be its Player-King. He gives himself easily and gracefully to roles that suit his fellow characters' desires—boon companion to Salerio and Solanio, charming prodigal to Antonio, indulgent friend to Gratiano, employer and savior to Launcelot. But such "pure innocence" will not expose or contain evil, and Bassanio's easy changes of identity seem almost meretricious in the postlapsarian world.

Portia, Venice's dream of fabulous wealth, mirrors the pervasive Venetian feelings of melancholy and impatience as she confesses, "By my troth, Nerissa, my little body is a-weary of this great world" (I. ii. 1–2). When, in response to her complaint, Nerissa preaches the doctrine of moderation, Portia responds with an awareness of the contradictory and partial truths of human life:

> If to do were as easy as to know what were good to do, chapels had been churches, and poor men's cottages princes' palaces. It is a good divine that follows his own instructions; I can easier teach twenty what were good to be done, than to be one of the twenty to follow mine own teaching. (I. ii. 12–17)

Portia understands that teaching requires something other than wise and empty words, that the very divine who espouses doctrine frequently leaves it unacted. She is aware of the postlapsarian division of word from deed.

She even provides the example of her own verbal wisdom by ignoring it. Held as she is in the closure of her father's behest, she cannot act until a suitor releases her from her casket; but if it were not for that stricture, Portia would commit herself as freely and as impetuously to action as Bassanio:

> The brain may devise laws for the blood, but a hot temper leaps o'er a cold decree—such a hare is madness the youth, to skip o'er the meshes of good counsel the cripple. But this reasoning is not in the fashion to choose me a husband. O me, the word choose! I may neither choose who I would, nor refuse who I dislike; so is the will of a living daughter curb'd by the will of a dead father. Is it not hard, Nerissa, that I cannot choose one, nor refuse none?
>
> (I. ii. 18–26)

Portia's syntax pits opposites against each other, setting "madness" against "good counsel," "the youth" against "the cripple," will against will; and that syntax clearly exposes her own canceled state. She does not yet affirm her father's wisdom, which his will forces out of the realm of words into action, nor can she understand it until she discovers the concert of choice and obligation in Bassanio's victory. She has yet to draw a conclusion from her own rejection of those suitors whom her father also rejects—the motley group of types who come to win but not to hazard, to get but not to give. But her syntax, which now expresses the neither/nor consciousness of the cipher, holds the promise of the Player-King's both/and.

At the play's beginning, Antonio and Bassanio are incomplete as separate individuals, disabled rather than strengthened by their alliance. Bassanio's ability to give and hazard rests on Antonio's solid position in the world, and Antonio, as

Solanio observes, only loves the world for Bassanio (II. viii. 50). If either man is to grow, the terms of the friendship must change. Bassanio must be allowed to control the world's substance and so to understand its exact limits, Antonio to respond to human bonds without the cushion of wealth. Initially, their tie is based on mutual need, and it is precisely that restraint that will bring each to act out and break through his personal limitations. Because of Bassanio, Antonio will risk annihilation and learn a new part on his life's stage, and because of Antonio, Bassanio will cease being all things to all people—an eternally ingratiating young actor—and focus himself through a single role. First, however, they must be drawn into the play world where such learning can take place, and since neither is a Player-King, both must be directed by one.

With and without an identity, young yet enclosed in a casket as if dead, Portia combines Venice's opposites. Her impetuosity is modulated by constraint, her passivity lightened by energy and will. She is both Antonio and Bassanio and neither of them. As a cipher, she simultaneously lives outside and at the center of the play's communities. She faces a future that could mean permanent bondage, but the risk brings with it a commensurate reward—the possibility of playing all human experience. Her father's message to her and to her husband— "Who chooseth me must give and hazard all he hath"—is the key to her freedom. It is the pure wisdom of play.

The Choices

≈ Indeed, the function of play is to educate by substituting experience for abstraction, turning words into acts and, in the process, imprinting them indelibly on the human consciousness. A problem is capable of solution in the mind and in the body: in the mind the solution affects the one; in the body it manifests itself to the many. True education, then, must involve both.[3] Portia's father's wisdom in giving his daughter away according to the result of his three-caskets test lies in forcing her suitors to release the unconscious tendencies of their minds into act. The gold, silver, and lead caskets, hidden behind a curtain and exposed at the critical moment of choice, are the only props for the play in which the suitor must recognize and wed himself. In establishing the test as a play, Portia's father extends his wisdom beyond his daughter: metaphor when forced into act affects the entire world surrounding it— in this case the world of the drama. And in Portia's ability to learn the aim of the test that she at first considers an unnecessary limitation on herself rests the possibility of redeeming the drama's world. She must play out the possibility of marriage to each of her suitors, yet remain detached from them all until the mirror of their choice is exposed from within the casket. In acting out many identities, she learns how to play; in observing the full nature of her father's play test, she learns how to teach others through play. As the Princes of Morocco and Aragon reach out for the touch of what they treasure, Portia learns the principle of play justice and how to manipulate it towards a worthy end.

The first suitor to venture the terms of the will and act in the play-within-the-play is the Prince of Morocco, a Moor and, from his plea for judgment based on inner worth rather than appearance, as great an object of prejudice as Shylock. Portia, in the terms of her father's play, entertains him as a prospective husband:

> In terms of choice I am not soly led
> By nice direction of a maiden's eyes;

3. Albert Wertheim, "The Treatment of Shylock and Thematic Integrity in *The Merchant of Venice*," *Shakespeare Studies*, VI (1970), 75–87, treats the play as educative from beginning to end, with money and spirit its thematic lesson. Farrell, *Shakespeare's Creation*, 152, states it is "about the creation of identity: about 'making it' or 'finding oneself.'"

> Besides, the lott'ry of my destiny
> Bars me the right of voluntary choosing.
> But if my father had not scanted me,
> And hedg'd me by his wit to yield myself
> His wife who wins me by that means I told you,
> Yourself, renowned Prince, then stood as fair
> As any comer I have look'd on yet
> For my affection. (II. i. 13–22)

The petulance of Portia's attitude towards the required terms of her wooing, coupled with her choice of the word *lott'ry* to describe the process, demonstrates how far removed she is at this point from understanding her father's import. Morocco echoes her concept of the play by complaining that "blind fortune" (II. i. 36) might bar his winning and bestow her on a fool or beggar.

The results of the play, however, begin to remove that fear. Even though Morocco has pleaded for a judgment of the mind and not the eyes, he himself chooses according to appearance. The gold casket bears an inscription reading: "Who chooseth me shall gain what many men desire." He reasons that Portia is intended thereby, not being self-aware enough to consider whether he and others desire her for her visible fortune, represented by the gold casket, or for her less tangible assets. Following his association of Portia with gold, he believes that her picture must lie in the gold casket. But what his conscious faculties do not recognize, his language begins to reveal as he approaches the act of choosing—Portia's beauty for him lies more in her coffers than in her person:

> never so rich a gem
> Was set in worse than gold. They have in England
> A coin that bears the figure of an angel
> Stamp'd in gold, but that's insculp'd upon;
> But here an angel in a golden bed
> Lies all within. (II. vii. 54–59)

Dazzled by the appearance of the commodity he seeks, Morocco opens the casket to find his appropriate reward: a skull. The human lust for possessions, the costly tokens hung on mortality, vanishes with the flesh.

Morocco plays his role and is caught in the grip of his own life choice, exposed by the act of opening the apparently valuable box and finding himself within:

> "All that glisters is not gold,
> Often have you heard that told;
> Many a man his life hath sold
> But my outside to behold.
> Gilded tombs do worms infold.
> Had you been as wise as bold,
> Young in limbs, in judgment old,
> Your answer had not been enscroll'd.
> Fare you well, your suit is cold." (II. vii. 65–73)

Playing forces self-realization. The cliché—all that glitters is not gold—is unable to arouse Morocco's mind and body to the denial of the material—flesh and wealth—but its meaning is revived when he acts out his adoration of the ephemeral idol and confronts the consequence. And, to answer both Morocco's and Portia's belief that luck alone could prompt a man to the right choice, the scroll instructs the chooser that his judgment, not his fortune, failed him. The conditions of the will, that the unsuccessful suitor must leave immediately and never marry, bring Morocco's self-realization to its natural conclusion. The gold casket is the choice of death over life, money over love, and so the will prevents such a man from ever seeking to engage that self in marriage. With relief, Portia sinks back to her dormant state, willingly relinquishing her play role as Morocco's wife and with it the principle he embodies.

The second play-within-the-play opens on the Prince of Aragon facing the stage that bears the caskets. With a tactless gesture of contempt, he immediately rejects the lead casket: "You [the lead casket and the real Portia] shall look fairer ere I give or hazard" (II. ix. 22). He has accepted Portia's own statement that he has come "to hazard for my worthless self" (II. ix. 18), her play enactment of the woman who would be a wife to Aragon. From the beginning, he exhibits the inflated self-esteem that will lead him to accept his own merit and reach for the silver that hides within it the ugly portrait of human pride. He considers the gold casket, but rejects it because the many who desire it and its real image within are merely "the fool multitude that choose by show" (II. ix. 26)—a just objection were it not for his own underlying, personal reason for spurning it:

> I will not choose what many men desire,
> Because I will not jump with common spirits,
> And rank me with the barbarous multitudes. (II. ix. 31–33)

And so he reaches for the silver casket, whose inscription reads: "Who chooseth me shall get as much as he deserves." Like Morocco, his rationalization for choosing what attracts him most has the appearance of worthiness: those who truly merit respect would be elevated to honor; those who have merely derived their honors from ancestors without deserving them would be plucked down from positions of respect. Yet the sense of justice based on public opinion is as mortal as the voices who pronounce it. As he reaches to open the silver casket, he adds: "I will assume desert" (II. ix. 51). For all his words' wisdom, Aragon is blind to his own true merit, narrowly circumscribed by his unnaturally high, though typically human, opinion of himself.

The mirror of Aragon's proud image is the portrait of an idiot:

> "The fire seven times tried this:
> Seven times tried that judgment is,

That did never choose amiss.
Some there be that shadows kiss,
Such have but a shadow's bliss.
There be fools alive, iwis,
Silver'd o'er, and so was this.
Take what wife you will to bed,
I will ever be your head.
So be gone, you are sped." (II. ix. 63–72)

The fool is but a human shadow, as is the man who considers public opinion and self-estimation greater than real worth. No matter how honorable his reasons sound, it is glory he seeks, the sounds of acclaim from other people. Again a shallow sense of value, forced to act by the play, comes to public recognition. Aragon leaves according to the terms of the test, but in leaving he acknowledges the justice of his prize: "With one fool's head I came to woo, / But I go away with two" (II. ix. 75–76). The play's success resolves Portia, too, who affirms its justice: "O, these deliberate fools, when they do choose, / They have the wisdom by their wit to lose" (II. ix. 80–81).[4] The curtain is drawn on the second play and the second failure. Meanwhile, however, a third suitor has arrived bearing the gold of rich gifts, the silver acclaim of those who observe him, and the lead simplicity of love.

Bassanio's entrance into Belmont produces in Portia the worst conflict she has yet faced. Instead of engaging her will negatively by pitting it against the suitors and desiring their failure, she finds herself wanting passionately for Bassanio to succeed. Eager to play the role of his wife permanently, yet fearful that he will choose wrongly and remove with him the self she wants to become, she suggests that he remain a while before trying himself in play. Bassanio, however, insists on hazarding

---

4. Traversi, *An Approach to Shakespeare*, I, 195, notes that both Morocco and Aragon have chosen self over love and are mocked by the consequences of that choice.

immediately. By nature open and by principle daring, he demonstrates his characteristic impatience. While that quality will echo negatively later in the play, it now cheers Portia into hopeful resignation: "Away then! I am lock'd in one of them; / If you do love me, you will find me out" (III. ii. 40–41). Her final assent to her father's will demonstrates that she has become aware that wisdom and love, and never greed or pride, will free her.

Yet she begins the play with music, a concert of harmonious sounds and words that reveals the lesson of Belmont to the man who will listen:

> Tell me where is fancy bred,
> Or in the heart or in the head?
> How begot, how nourished?
> Reply, reply.
> It is engend'red in the eyes,
> With gazing fed, and fancy dies
> In the cradle where it lies.
> Let us all ring fancy's knell.
> I'll begin it. Ding, dong, bell. (III. ii. 63–71)

Perhaps in response to the song's hint, Bassanio comments: "So may the outward shows be least themselves" (III. ii. 73). The definition of self does not spring from a person's own physical reflection or from the reflection one finds in the glance of others. With the kind of wisdom he has before demonstrated to Antonio, Bassanio discourses on the deception of appearances, on the ease with which a coward or a sinful man can adopt the show of bravery or virtue. A promise made by the face that a person adopts to show others what he would like to be deceives as much as the wish to be held in respect. Thus are gold—"hard food for Midas" (III. ii. 102)—and silver—"pale and common drudge / 'Tween man and man" (III. ii. 103–104)—linked and damned. Nor does Bassanio belie his verbal wisdom when it is time to act. Having rejected the two base reasons for wooing Portia, disguised in the apparently valuable containers, Bassanio reaches for the lead, embracing the threatened risk in accord with his principle that an arrow lost is found only by venturing another arrow. For love, one hazards and gives all.

Portia, liberated by the outcome, banishes her doubts, her despair, her fear, her jealousy and becomes the woman she wants to be as Bassanio finds her portrait encased in the lead casket. In Bassanio's love, she finds escape from the deathlike stasis of her unresolved self. In her portrait, he finds her image; yet the portrait, as perfect as it paints her, he dismisses as mere shadow. Word and act, picture and self: the play has brought together what the human fall from grace separated. It is Portia's self that Bassanio seeks, and in her himself. For that reason, he will not take her as a prize "until confirm'd, sign'd, ratified by you [Portia]" (III. ii. 148). Portia, who has been held from becoming herself by the terms of this very play, now on reaching the end has achieved an identity that is not individual but the mutual image of a lover. She too gives all:

> You see me, Lord Bassanio, where I stand,
> Such as I am. Though for myself alone
> I would not be ambitious in my wish
> To wish myself much better, yet for you,
> I would be trebled twenty times myself,
> A thousand times more fair, ten thousand times more rich,
> That only to stand high in your account,
> I might in virtues, beauties, livings, friends,
> Exceed account. But the full sum of me
> Is sum of something; which, to term in gross,
> Is an unlesson'd girl, unschool'd, unpractic'd,
> Happy in this, she is not yet so old
> But she may learn; happier than this,
> She is not bred so dull but she can learn;
> Happiest of all, is that her gentle spirit
> Commits itself to yours to be directed,

As from her lord, her governor, her king.
Myself, and what is mine, to you and yours
Is now converted. But now I was the lord
Of this fair mansion, master of my servants,
Queen o'er myself; and even now, but now,
This house, these servants, and this same myself
Are yours—my lord's!—I give them with this ring,
Which when you part from, lose, or give away,
Let it presage the ruin of your love,
And be my vantage to exclaim on you. (III. ii. 149–74)

With the perfect circle of the ring, Portia gives to Bassanio her self and all her possessions. The ecstasy that she had experienced when Bassanio chose rightly he describes at this moment in the metaphor of a beloved prince appearing in a crowd: "every something, being blent together, / Turns to a wild of nothing, save of joy / Express'd and not express'd" (III. ii. 181–83). For one rich moment, perfect harmony falls on Belmont, the ineffable sense of perfection achieved, the spiritual and physical ecstasy of ideal lovers matched.

So fully Edenic is this moment that it contains the human history of paradise, its loss and its restoration. Portia's injunction against Bassanio's parting with the ring establishes the premise for her last play, the one in which she will bring her marriage into the world of relative truth. As a reminder of that world's dangers and needs, the news from Venice intrudes on Belmont; the city is moving towards the tragedy only Portia can avert. Brought to life from within her lead casket, she now possesses her full inheritance. She has been audience to and actress in her father's play, learning from it the principle of attaining selfhood and the means for exposing and educating human nature. Her will and his will are now one. She is an untried Player-Queen, and before her are two situations that require her attention. She must playwrite Bassanio's confrontation with the world's harsher realities—conflict, betrayal, death—but before she can attend to that immediate need, she must rescue Antonio and Venice from the obsessive hatred of the play's Adversary, Shylock. Like Prospero, she will discover in the process that teachers always learn from their students.

The Adversary:
"Fast Bind, Fast Find"

⚓ While Antonio waits vulnerably, Shylock moves against him. His motive is hatred, his goal revenge. The two merchants confront each other over the heads of their fellows on the Rialto, two men separated from human society and motivated by opposing philosophies. Antonio remains uninvolved and unmoved in the midst of well-meaning friends; Shylock stands outside the Christian circle. For Venice to be saved from Shylock—that is, from its own prison of wealth and prestige—Antonio must be freed from his melancholy.

Shylock represents all that is extreme in a mercantile society. He has allowed his lust for possession and the opinion of the surrounding Christian world to define him. Like all Adversaries, Shylock is not merely isolated but also trapped within that isolation by his insistence that the world conform to him. Unimaginative, he cannot conceive of human growth in spiritual terms. Instead he grows money, invoking Jacob's husbandry with his sheep as if flesh and metal were the same. Gold grows more gold, silver more silver, just as Falstaff's flesh grows more flesh—the pattern is the repetition compulsion of the materialist. Gradually the identification of the self with material acquisition and of flesh with metal leads to a subtle cannibalism that expresses itself in Shylock's bargain with Antonio: for my gold I demand your flesh. The bargain itself becomes the image of this society's tendency—Shylock's face within Venice's gold and silver caskets. The principle is quantitative rather than qualitative.

Shylock's nature as an Adversary is marked dually by his

unwillingness to play towards selfhood and by his consequent linguistic pattern of repetition.[5] The nonmaterial growth of play, with its inherent danger of self-annihilation and its reward the totality of the human self, contradicts the Adversary's fixed perspective on his own limited, inflexible being and his venomous hatred of any who encroach on it, indeed his hatred of all he does not see as himself. The mode for his play is flat deception rather than imitative growth. For Shylock, the crucial play act necessitates his convincing Antonio that he is well disposed towards him when they strike their bargain. Thus his only play is the acting out of a lie. His other characteristic actions demonstrate the Adversary's dialectical opposition to the principle of play, which is to give and hazard all. Instead of being open to possibility, he takes every opportunity to lock himself and all that is his away from the world. He treats both his daughter Jessica and his servant Launcelot as extensions of himself, assuming that his own values and habits suit them, and blindly ignores Jessica's conflict and Launcelot's discontent. So thoroughly bound by self that his daughter's love for Lorenzo goes unnoticed, Shylock cannot recognize in her any difference from himself. Solanio's remark about Jessica's elopement—"And Shylock for his own part knew the bird was fledge" (III. i. 28–29)—is callous but accurate. Jessica is part of nature and responsive to its laws. She is neither Shylock nor his property, although he treats her alternately as both: "My own flesh and blood to rebel!" (III. i. 34); "my ducats, and my daughter!" (II. viii. 17).

He turns his contempt on the surrounding Christian society,

---

5. Shylock's linguistic patterns have been studied by C. L. Barber, *Shakespeare's Festive Comedy* (Princeton: Princeton University Press, 1959), 172, who notes that his speech echoes his miserliness and his isolation; by John Palmer, *Political and Comic Characters of Shakespeare* (London: Macmillan, 1961), 68–70, who discusses at length Shylock's syntax as compulsively repetitive, stubborn, obsessive, and literal. Farrell, *Shakespeare's Creation*, 154, has commented on the cannibalistic turn of Shylock's language.

particularly on its play forms, which he views as prodigal and tinged with immorality:

> What, are there masques? Hear you me, Jessica:
> Lock up my doors, and when you hear the drum
> And the vile squealing of the wry-neck'd fife,
> Clamber not you up to the casements then,
> Nor thrust your head into the public street
> To gaze on Christian fools with varnish'd faces;
> But stop my house's ears, I mean my casements;
> Let not the sound of shallow fopp'ry enter
> My sober house. (II. v. 28–36)

The house that contains Shylock and his possessions, both human and material, is another extension of himself. The house's ears and Jessica's ears are Shylock's ears, all polluted by the free, loud exhibition of the masque. Shylock particularly hates the music. Only the urge to feed off the prodigal—his cannibalistic impulse—prompts him to leave his house on a night of reveling. The antiplay principle is his proverb: "Fast bind, fast find— / A proverb never stale in thrifty mind" (II. v. 54–55). The proverb, however, plays him false, for the danger cannot lie outside the house if it does not begin within it. What is bound either escapes or dies.

The limitation of Shylock's humanity and self-image to owned things is reflected in the habit of speech that he shares with other Adversaries: a rigid, compulsively repetitive pattern. Even before his crisis begins with Jessica's escape from his circle with an appropriated dowry of gold and jewels, Shylock's incurable prison of self manifests itself in a linguistic stinginess:

> *Shy.* Three thousand ducats, well.
> *Bass.* Ay, sir, for three months.
> *Shy.* For three months, well.
> *Bass.* For the which, as I told you, Antonio shall be bound.
> *Shy.* Antonio shall become bound, well. (I. iii. 1–6)

Shylock takes Bassanio's words into his mouth, but without allowing them to penetrate his consciousness. The concept of Antonio's being bound pleases him; it puts Antonio in a vulnerable position where Shylock can devour him and increase himself by the weight of his antagonist. Bassanio's words enter his mouth with the taste of gratification, but Shylock withholds himself from taking them as Bassanio means them by repeating his note of ironic noncommitment: "well." His true response is indicated later when Antonio enters the scene and Shylock greets him with a characteristically cannibalistic expression: "Your worship was the last man in our mouths" (I. iii. 60). The Player-King assimilates the enemy; the Adversary devours him.

When the thoughts he wishes to express grow more complex, Shylock expands them according to syntactic repetition, the parallelism of simple sentences with only diction differing from element to element:

> Ho, no, no, no, no! my meaning in saying he is a good man is to have you understand me that he is sufficient. Yet his means are in supposition: he hath an argosy bound to Tripolis, another to the Indies; I understand moreover upon the Rialto, he hath a third at Mexico, a fourth for England, and other ventures he hath, squand'red abroad. But ships are but boards, sailors but men; there be land-rats and water-rats, water-thieves and land-thieves, I mean pirates, and then there is the peril of waters, winds, and rocks. The man is notwithstanding sufficient. Three thousand ducats: I think I may take his bond. (I. iii. 15–27)

The language, indicative of obsession before the calamity awaiting Shylock's imprisoned spirit, becomes uncontrollable after he discovers that Jessica has run off with one of the prodigals and, by Tubal's reports, become one herself. First his servant, then his daughter and his wealth slip from his house to the Christians. The inability of his nature to cope with change prompts him to greater hatred and the further narrowing of his scope to the one aim of vengeance. From his first reaction to the discovery, it is an easy step to the inflexible pursuit of the only gratification he has left:

> "My daughter! O my ducats! O my daughter!
> Fled with a Christian! O my Christian ducats!
> Justice! the law! my ducats, and my daughter!
> A sealed bag, two sealed bags of ducats,
> Of double ducats, stol'n from me by my daughter!
> And jewels, two stones, two rich and precious stones,
> Stol'n by my daughter! Justice! find the girl!
> She hath the stones upon her, and the ducats." (II. viii. 15–22)

> Let him look to his bond. He was wont to call
> me usurer, let him look to his bond. He was
> wont to lend money for a Christian cur'sy,
> let him look to his bond. (III. i. 47–50)

Only in degree does Shylock's linguistic pattern change from the beginning to the end of the drama. Consistently his language emerges barren of harmony, a monotone of envy and hate. Lorenzo will later comment on the man who has no music in him, the treacherous, violent destroyer, a man who cannot create metaphors or play them out. Shylock holds rigidly to his own pattern of life, which encases him in the tomb of repetition as he, Midas-like, stamps himself again and again on everything he touches.

The Player-Queen in Venice

ᕭ The first principle of Portia's father's play is disguise, the concealment of what *is* within what *seems*. The disguise functions as a test in which a person is given the chance to become in act what he is in word; the result is personal and public revelation. As the news of Antonio's misfortunes disrupts Belmont's marriage harmony, the only hope of saving Antonio and Bassanio with him is for Portia to bring the play of Belmont to Venice where Shylock has claimed the empty throne of the Player-King and staged his own play of vengeance and self-justification.

Bassanio has left the beggary of his initial state when he rated himself as worse than nothing (III. ii. 260) and risen to the fullness of wealth, prestige, and love with Portia. Antonio, on the other hand, has lost all his worldly goods, is a prisoner of the law, and stands in immediate danger of his life. The only lure he now has to call a friend to his side is love: " 'if your love do not persuade you to come, let not my letter' " (III. ii. 321–22). The two incomplete Player-Kings of Venice have switched roles; moreover, they have been brought into a new relationship by Bassanio's union with Portia. Since Portia and Bassanio are one, and Bassanio and Antonio are one, then Portia, Bassanio, and Antonio should also be one. So Portia assumes: "Antonio, / Being the bosom lover of my lord, / Must needs be like my lord" (III. iv. 16–18). In fact, however, the friends are not alike, and the triangle's possibility of becoming a working unit rests on Bassanio's and Antonio's becoming complete as individuals.

Before that is possible, however, they must experience the either/or of their complementary natures. Antonio's melancholy moves from complaint to the acceptance of death:

> I am a tainted wether of the flock,
> Meetest for death; the weakest kind of fruit
> Drops earliest to the ground, and so let me. (IV. i. 114–16)

Bassanio recklessly hazards all he has to save his friend, this time volunteering "life itself, my wife, and all the world" (IV. i. 284) as sacrifice, no doubt believing he will be able to regain them. The flaws in both men, indicated from their first appearances in the play, reveal themselves, if not to all of Venice, certainly to Portia and Shylock. The outsiders, both attempting to control the play before them and reveal Venice to itself, function as observers and critics of Venice's performers.[6] Portia,

---

6. Farrell, *Shakespeare's Creation*, 156–57, sees Shylock as parodying the Christians, like Lucifer parodying God, and Portia as achieving her victory by parodying Shylock.

hearing Bassanio offer to give all, says: "Your wife would give you little thanks for that / If she were by to hear you make the offer" (IV. i. 288–89). Shylock rejects the court's plea to show Antonio mercy by using the Venetians' own acts—insulting Jews, mistreating slaves—in defense of his cruelty, and comments on Bassanio's offer with the aside, "These be the Christian husbands" (IV. i. 295). Portia's education in human fallibility is continuing.

Upon her entrance into Venice, Portia brings with her the fruitful both/and of self-surrender and self-enactment. While she is learning even further, she is performing the principles of her own education:

> "I beseech you let his lack of years be no impediment to let him lack a reverend estimation, for I never knew so young a body with so old a head. I leave him to your gracious acceptance, whose trial shall better publish his commendation." (IV. i. 161–66)

The letter suggests the mystery of opposites united in one being. The advocate for Antonio is a seeming youth whose head is older than his body—Portia is now both herself and her father. The acknowledgment of public opinion, sought after by the Prince of Aragon, will be bestowed on the lawyer not by the words of Bellario but by trial. Old and young, unknown and reputed, male and female, Portia in her disguise is the complete player.

She begins her part by asserting the legality of Shylock's case, thus avoiding the breach of justice tempting all Venice and later expressed by Bassanio, who asks the court to throw the case out. Instead, she creates a bond between herself and Shylock, offering him affirmation and sympathy and asking him to bestow an act of mercy in turn. In the situation she has staged for him, Shylock can respond to the plea as if he had not steadily refused it, as if it were a fresh possibility. She gives him the chance to play to her, a new and receptive audience, by putting himself in the position of one who seeks mercy:

> [Mercy] becomes
> The throned monarch better than his crown.
> His sceptre shows the force of temporal power,
> The attribute to awe and majesty,
> Wherein doth sit the dread and fear of kings;
> But mercy is above this sceptred sway,
> It is enthroned in the hearts of kings,
> It is an attribute to God himself;
> And earthly power doth then show likest God's
> When mercy seasons justice. Therefore, Jew,
> Though justice be thy plea, consider this,
> That in the course of justice, none of us
> Should see salvation. We do pray for mercy,
> And that same prayer doth teach us all to render
> The deeds of mercy. (IV. i. 188–202)

Portia carefully establishes the difference between the mutable laws of the human community, which can touch only the physical person, and the eternal laws of the spiritual community, which affect the permanent life of the soul. For the Venetians, she paints the two aspects of their city. For Shylock, she describes a world where what a person wills for himself is connected to what he wills for others, where the role a person chooses to play is not merely a deception but part of his life and of all life. Like Henry V with the traitors, she demands that Shylock acknowledge the natural connection between the human and the divine, a connection that play reveals and enacts, as she substitutes the bond of love for the bond of flesh.[7]

Shylock's only response, however, is to reassert his separation of the temporal from the eternal, of law from justice, of self from other: "My deeds upon my head! I crave the law, / The penalty and forfeit of my bond" (IV. i. 206–207). "Fast bind, fast find" remains Shylock's principle and strategy, and

7. John P. Sisk, "Bondage and Release in *The Merchant of Venice,*" *Shakespeare Quarterly,* XX (1969), 217–23, has a full discussion of the bond's meaning and use as the unification of the casket and ring stories.

he still believes that it will give him control. He insists upon maintaining his isolation in spite of Portia's affirming his bond's legality and offering him money. All Shylock's other motives— the accumulation of wealth, the tricking and shaming of the Christian community—have vanished. His hatred, the mark of the Adversary, has finally shrunk him to one fixed, immovable point—the pound of Antonio's flesh.

When all words fail, Portia moves towards the enactment of justice. She brings Shylock breathtakingly close to fulfilling his single obsession; she draws to the surface the feelings beneath his desire to cut out Antonio's heart. At any point along the way, Shylock might satisfy himself and drop the knife. When he presses forward, Portia turns the desire back on itself. His purpose for Antonio becomes the court's purpose for him: the forfeited pound of flesh does not include a drop of blood. Shylock senses the reversal and moves quickly to take the money. But what was offered before when he was asked to show mercy of his own free will no longer suits his present situation. The pattern Henry V establishes with the traitors is present here: he who will give no mercy will receive none. Bassanio, always precipitate, extends the money, but Portia withdraws it:

> *Shy.* Give me my principal, and let me go.
> *Bass.* I have it ready for thee, here it is.
> *Por.* He hath refus'd it in the open court;
> He shall have merely justice and his bond.
> (IV. i. 336–39)

To fulfill the parallel situation, Portia cites the law that states that any Venetian who conspires against a fellow citizen's life is at the mercy of the court, half his goods to go to the state, the other half to the man he would have murdered. Shylock is as totally at the mercy of Venice as Antonio was at his. Suddenly nothing is bound fast—not Shylock's bond nor his wealth nor even himself. Portia has forced him to play the role of Antonio.

She now leaves to Venice and Antonio, who are suddenly in Shylock's place, the opportunity to bestow free and unconstrained mercy on him. As a Jew and a would-be assassin, Shylock arouses the hatred that breeds blind injustice—the very hatred he had felt towards Antonio only moments before. Venice, however, takes the lesson of Portia's play: the Duke pardons Shylock's life and reduces the penalty of half of his estate to a fine. When it is Antonio's turn to enact the mercy he had sought, he does not simply return the gold to Shylock, which would leave uncorrected the unnatural equation of ewes with gold, nor does he accept the gold unconditionally as his due. Instead he subordinates the gold to love, establishing its proper place in human life by finding a natural use for it: the half that falls to him he will use and bequeath to Lorenzo; the other half that is left to Shylock is to go after his death to Jessica. Thus the children of Venice can return, their love, like Bassanio's, bringing with it wealth and prestige.

Antonio's other condition, that Shylock convert to Christianity, is the formal assertion of the play's doctrine. Once he has played, compelled to act not only as attacker but also as victim, Shylock cannot return to his initial state. He has been forced outside himself for the first time, reduced to the state of nothing from which all redemption springs, and then restored to partial wealth. Like Morocco, he had asked for what he was not willing to give; and like Aragon, he had assumed personal desert. He leaves the courtroom exposed and taught. Portia has put him through the ritual of self-abnegation and surrender that precedes all enlightenment, and his response is at once bitter and affirmative: "I am content" (IV. i. 394).

Portia's play has brought the world of Belmont to Venice. Through play she inculcated experientially the principle of love in the city that had for too long acted out only its baser impulses. Antonio, although considered good by his fellows, was not proven so until he performed the act that restored him to life—the exchange of mercy for cruelty, of love and life for money and hatred. In that act, staged by Portia, Antonio frees himself from his prison. The withdrawn, passive man who had much ado to know himself when the world gave him greatest cause to think he did commands the conversion of Shylock and announces his debt to Balthasar-Portia. Now that he is living on borrowed wealth, owning nothing but himself, Antonio is free.

The Player-Queen in Belmont

⚔ Antonio, weighed down by human evil and pain, is reborn through Portia's play. In him the feelings of sadness and burden are now mixed with joy. For Bassanio, however, Portia must stage the fall he has been steadily approaching since the play's beginning. In the courtroom, he exposed his weakness: when the world's wealth could not buy his friend's life, he offered himself (IV. i. 112–13); he advocated injustice by asking the Duke to "wrest once the law to your authority" (IV. i. 215); and finally, desperate, he volunteered to sacrifice self, wife, and all. He would shoot all his arrows, leaving none to help find those he lost.

Rather than have him forget those failures of nerve and understanding in the happy outcome, Portia must force their consciousness on him and allow Bassanio his chance to grow. In Venice she creates one more scene, the preparation for her final play in Belmont; she stages Bassanio's conflict between his two loves and benefactors by demanding the ring. Bassanio can no longer evade or escape: in order to be true to his friend, he must betray his wife. With the ring that he sends after Balthasar he completes his fall from grace. Again Portia has forced the word into act in order to teach the actor its consequence.

In Belmont, Lorenzo and Jessica strike the minor chord that

now prevails under the changeable moon. Their flight from
Venice, each hazarding life, property, and self for the other,
presaged the marriage of Portia and Bassanio. Now in counterpoint—the mirror of separate states seeking harmony—they
talk of reckless, impulsive lovers: Troilus, Thisbe, Dido, Me-
dea, Jessica, Lorenzo. The theme of Bassanio's play has
sounded. Into a discourse of the betrayed, hunted, and abandoned, Jessica and Lorenzo fit themselves, sublunary lovers in
a briefly held paradise. In contrast they see what lies above
them:

> How sweet the moonlight sleeps upon this bank!
> Here will we sit, and let the sounds of music
> Creep in our ears. Soft stillness and the night
> Become the touches of sweet harmony.
> Sit, Jessica. Look how the floor of heaven
> Is thick inlaid with patens of bright gold.
> There's not the smallest orb which thou behold'st
> But in his motion like an angel sings,
> Still quiring to the young-ey'd cherubins;
> Such harmony is in immortal souls,
> But whilst this muddy vesture of decay
> Doth grossly close it in, we cannot hear it. (V. i. 54–65)

The only transition between the body's decay and the soul's
eternal life is the magnetic power of perfect art, the musical
note that makes animals return to their prelapsarian state, the
metaphor that organizes around it a world of play:

> For do but note a wild and wanton herd
> Or race of youthful and unhandled colts,
> Fetching mad bounds, bellowing and neighing loud,
> Which is the hot condition of their blood,
> If they but hear perchance a trumpet sound,
> Or any air of music touch their ears,
> You shall perceive them make a mutual stand,
> Their savage eyes turn'd to a modest gaze,
> By the sweet power of music; therefore the poet

Did feign that Orpheus drew trees, stones, and floods;
Since nought so stockish, hard, and full of rage,
But music for the time doth change his nature.
The man that hath no music in himself,
Nor is not moved with concord of sweet sounds,
Is fit for treasons, stratagems, and spoils;
The motions of his spirit are dull as night,
And his affections dark as Erebus:
Let no such man be trusted. Mark the music. (V. i. 71–88)

Orpheus, the prototype of the artist, can create in his auditors, animal or human, a sense of the harmony that resides in the heavens: planets quiring to cherubins, singing the sweet harmonies of the music of the spheres. Music is a metamorphosing force; it changes the nature of those who hear it. Like play, it mediates between the perfect world of the spirit, from which humans are exiled, and the imperfect world of the body, "this muddy vesture of decay." Yet the musician's art—and the player's as well—lasts only as long as he performs, and then the world falls by gravity back into savagery and dullness.

So Portia, her understanding of mutability experienced in Bassanio's equivocal generosity, returns to Belmont with relativity as the subject of her discourse: "Nothing is good, I see, without respect" (V. i. 99). Yet she turns the negative note in Lorenzo's observation on the body's muddy vesture of decay to positive force by emphasizing that in a relative world the good is known only in terms of the bad—the crow and the lark are equal singers when they are not closely attended, the nightingale a seemingly great singer because he sings in the dark when no other bird offers his harmony: "How many things by season season'd are / To their right praise and true perfection!" (V. i. 107–108). When Bassanio enters, completing her metaphor of the relativity of day and night by calling her the sun that makes the night day, the grace of his generosity plays relatively against the betrayal it produced. In play, the Bel-

mont in Venice was revealed and affirmed. Now the Venice in
Belmont—Bassanio—must be revealed to himself for himself
to correct.[8]

While Portia and Bassanio watch, the play begins with Nerissa challenging Gratiano on the subject of the rings they ex-
changed. The subject of the quarrel is the ring's value, Gratiano
asserting that it was "a hoop of gold, a paltry ring / That she
did give me" (V. i. 147–48), denigrating the poetry of its message—"Love me, and leave me not"—and generally assessing
its value in worldly terms. But Nerissa prevents him from reviving the Venetian value system by declaring that the ring's
value was not material but symbolic, and so beyond Gratiano's
terms of value. Because it represented faith and loyalty in love,
it was as invaluable as the lead casket.

The play, of course, is staged to educate Bassanio. Never before has his will to succeed been checked or his gambler's
principles questioned. Habitually, Bassanio floods the world
with energy, relying on it to right all wrongs and bathe all
wounds. Now he must hold back in the knowledge that he is
audience to a scene that he, too, will be playing. He must observe it closely, study it, learn from it; he must be inwardly
quiet enough to absorb others' reactions. Although Bassanio
has reversed his material position in life with Antonio, managing Portia's money and enjoying the limits of worldly power
and prestige, he has not enacted Antonio's nature. It is time for
him to experience life within the lead casket, to be a cipher.

Portia, who like Hal can simultaneously playwrite, witness,
and act, begins to move the scene towards a didactic end:

> You were to blame, I must be plain with you,
> To part so slightly with your wive's first gift,

8. James E. Siemon, "*The Merchant of Venice*: Act V as Ritual Reiteration," *Studies in Philology*, LXVII (1970), 201–209, views this last act as repeating the play:
Lorenzo and Jessica as hero and heroine, the ring as "merry bond," and its loss as
"airtight" case. This time the play is resolved, not with Shylock's undissipated hostility, but "in charity and love, in reconciliation" (p. 208).

> A thing stuck on with oaths upon your finger,
> And so riveted with faith unto your flesh.
> I gave my love a ring, and made him swear
> Never to part with it, and here he stands.
> I dare be sworn for him he would not leave it,
> Nor pluck it from his finger, for the wealth
> That the world masters. (V. i. 166–74)

As Portia carefully creates an expectation in her audience, Bassanio begins to see his gift to Antonio's savior in another light. With Gratiano as his surrogate, he is able to view himself from outside himself. Bassanio responds to Portia's commentary with an aside, an indication that he is aware of a reality outside the immediate one, as the duality of human consciousness after the Fall begins to dominate the scene. Bassanio considers a lie, but rejects it because the facts of his guilt are patent (V. i. 186–88). He is faced with the conflict between his behavior in Belmont and in Venice, and he cannot swerve from it.

Portia has checked his spontaneous outward motion and put him on the defensive; she has made him squirm. But it is still too soon to be merciful. The man who is too miserly to give of himself or his goods must be stripped and then given all, and the man who is too eager to give must suffer others to give away freely what he considers his before they return it to him:

> Let not that doctor e'er come near my house.
> Since he hath got the jewel that I loved,
> And that which you did swear to keep for me,
> I will become as liberal as you,
> I'll not deny him any thing I have,
> No, not my body nor my husband's bed. (V. i. 223–28)

Portia does not spring to an easy peace. When Bassanio moves from an honest confession to a charming plea for mercy, swearing by her "own fair eyes" (V. i. 242), she will not have it:

> Mark you but that!
> In both my eyes he doubly sees himself,

> In each eye, one. Swear by your double self,
> And there's an oath of credit. (V. i. 243–46)

Bassanio's first oath, made on the mutual image of self to self, was undone in his desire to return to Antonio the love and life that his friend had ventured for him. Any oath that excludes Antonio is therefore unacceptable. Portia and Bassanio have reached the end of their ability to reconcile.

When Antonio enters the picture, voluntarily staking his soul on Bassanio's faith to Portia (V. i. 252), the unification of Portia, Bassanio, and Antonio is complete. The new oath is indeed sworn by a "double self," as the two men fuse in Portia's eyes. Both have a fuller understanding of human nature; both are able to mingle the joyous promise of life with its griefs and sins. In play each member of the triad has become the other, and the conflicts among them dissolve.

Portia has accepted the role bequeathed by her father. Witnessing the manner and results of the play he staged to keep her free of the acquisitive and the proud, she has turned that lesson into a way of life suitable for the leader of Belmont. She has transformed her knowledge into art and has created the mysterious harmony that effects harmony, revealing Venice to itself, uniting the split identities of her world, restoring Antonio's goods, rooting Lorenzo and Jessica again in their paternal society. Above all, however, Portia's art rests on her understanding of human imperfection as it searches restlessly under the burden of a dead man's will, or a heavy debt, or a mutable moon, for absolute freedom from the imperfect. For the Player-Queen, the imperfect is the material for art, mutability the ground for play, and play the music that opens the spirit to eternal harmony. Like all Shakespeare's constructive players, Portia forms, from within the drama that she inhabits, the shape it ultimately takes—the shape of comedy, which is the shape of human redemption.

CHAPTER IV

The Middle Comedies:
Imminent Chaos

Shakespeare's middle or satiric comedies, represented in this study by *Troilus and Cressida* and *Measure for Measure*, explore the problems that face a corrupt society when leadership is unsure of itself. These plays, so puzzling that their classification has become a critical battle, deal with the imminence of chaos in human life, a chaos that extends over all human efforts—politics, war, love. The world of the flesh is exaggeratedly real in both dramas and the escape from it difficult to attain. In *Troilus and Cressida*, the failure of enlightened leadership from either Hector or Troilus among the Trojans or Agamemnon or Ulysses among the Greeks turns over the playing of both communities to the diseased visions of Pandarus and Thersites. When no Player-King steps forward to play his world into harmony, the stage is left for the Adversary, who forces it into his image. Pandarus desires the gratification of his own hungers in vicariously stage-managing the love of Troilus and Cressida; Angelo succumbs to his own lust and almost stamps it indelibly on the city he had wanted to save. But the plays move in two different directions. *Troilus and Cressida* never frees itself from the physical world and so ends with its disease worsening and threatening to spread through Pandarus to its audience. *Measure for Measure*, on the other hand, is a play world saved from within by the rapidity of Duke Vincentio's learning experience, which he then extends to the citizens of Vienna. Both dramas experiment with the imbalance caused when play, the medium between the worlds of the spirit and the flesh, is misused for strictly material ends.

Troilus and Cressida:
Play Corrupted

In *Troilus and Cressida*, no retreat exists on either side of the battlefield for a person who feels the need to withdraw from his assigned role. No secret space nurtures a Player-King. Although the characters pride themselves on their hidden loves—Troilus' for Cressida, Achilles' for Polyxena—their passions are open secrets. Crisis and self-doubt do not drive any of the characters to self-surrender; the duties of war and the will to pleasure hold them fixed in staged roles that they will play to the death.[1] War proceeds by error and mismanagement to its fated conclusion because no leader has educated himself in play; none therefore can educate his community through play. Love brings in its wake no ecstatic experience of movement out of self and unity with another, which when enacted restores Eden briefly to exiled humanity; rather, the corruption of the human love impulse to the cloyingly physical—the most fallible level of experience—traps the play's misguided lovers in the finite gratifications of sex. At the root of the corruption is the misuse of play that occurs when the playwriting for a community is usurped by the Adversary—here that poet of the flesh Pandarus—and the play viewing by the scabby gaze of the cynic Thersites, who comments in the audience's stead on the events before him.

In the early comedies, a rapport between audience and players spreads the harmonies of triumphant love. In *Henry V*, the culmination of the histories, a careful imaginative unity between drama and audience engages a world in the willing reenactment of community. But in *Troilus and Cressida*, the

---

1. Harry Berger, Jr., "*Troilus and Cressida*: The Observer as Basilisk," *Comparative Drama*, II (1968), 134, notes this "exposure and the self-consciousness it produces." Most of the characters, says Berger, "seem somehow conscious of performing, observing, and being observed. . . . [They have an] uneasy awareness of being constantly on display, living a theatrical existence" (p. 131).

widening circles of play, emanating from within the drama to its audience outside, are systematically impeded. First, the drama is presented to us at a remove by a Prologue who asks only for our judgment and not for our participation: "Like or find fault, do as your pleasures are, / Now good or bad, 'tis but the chance of war" (Prologue. 30–31). We are not asked to piece out the players' imperfections with our thoughts.[2] The imperfect is the milieu of *Troilus and Cressida*, the quest for cosmic stability abandoned and, in its place, the delineation of the world of "broils." The Prologue's opening diction, a parody of epic elevation, falls suddenly with relief to the casual tone of familiar address:

> In Troy, there lies the scene. From isles of Greece
> The princes orgillous, their high blood chaf'd,
> Have to the port of Athens sent their ships
> Fraught with the ministers and instruments
> Of cruel war. Sixty and nine, that wore
> Their crownets regal, from th'Athenian bay
> Put forth toward Phrygia, and their vow is made
> To ransack Troy, within whose strong immures
> The ravish'd Helen, Menelaus' queen,
> With wanton Paris sleeps—and that's the quarrel.
>   (Prologue. 1–10)

With the extremes of diction, we are forced to see the mythic struggle of ancient heroes simultaneously exaggerated and deflated.[3] The split thus created, which is reinforced by the unflatteringly public nature of private feelings, wills the actors on stage to assume postures of self-parody, acting out the passions of heroic diction within the framework of mundane and blemished motives. The Prologue's business, to create a sepa-

2. Berger comments on the opposite effects *Henry V*'s Chorus and *Troilus and Cressida*'s Prologue have on their audiences. The Prologue "assumes nothing about, and demands nothing from, the audience." *Ibid.*, 125.

3. Derick R. C. Marsh, "Interpretation and Misinterpretation: The Problem of *Troilus and Cressida*," *Shakespeare Studies*, I (1965), 186, has also used this passage to establish irony as the mode that "persists throughout the play."

ration between the play and its audience, is a necessary limit
to the art of viewing the drama presented. We must not be
tainted by the nature of what we see, and so our judgment,
rather than our imagination, is engaged in the mutual art of the
drama.

In addition to the split resulting from the Prologue's negative exposition of value, a surrogate audience is introduced
within the drama to block further the natural movement of
play from within to without. Thersites, the unteachable and
unredeemable, thwarts the audience's imaginative unity with
the playwrights within the play. He spies on Ulysses' attempts
to win the war; he observes Pandarus' climactic play scene—
the revelation of Cressida to Troilus. Always he stands between the audience and the actors, the perfect spectator for
the Adversary's play. As he comments and reviles, Thersites
reduces all the elevated passions he observes to bestiality, presenting as the outermost voice within the drama the futile maneuvers of a death-bound world.[4] Not until the last scene in the
drama is the audience allowed to entertain, and then only
briefly, any sympathetic connection with the world of *Troilus
and Cressida*.

> Troy—"Yon towers, whose
> wanton tops do buss the clouds"

In the center of Troy, a city dubiously graced by the living
Queen of Love, resides Pandarus, the go-between. Whether
teasing a boy servant, tormenting Troilus, or adoring Cressida,
he embodies the city's moribund ethical code. Troy has become a place where the spiritual values behind the physical
human world have died by attrition. Priam is old and listens to
his sons, chiefly Hector, who, while aspiring beyond the physi-

---

4. Theodore Spencer, *Shakespeare and the Nature of Man* (New York: Macmillan, 1942), 113–15, describes Thersites as a "reviling and denigrating chorus to the
whole action," commenting on the themes of war and love alike.

cal world, fails to play his aspiration to his people. The official
channels of communication, used maximally as play by Henry
V and Portia, are dead; and as a result a parasitic underground
has come into being, thriving on the decay of imaginative authority and usurping its function. With Helen comes wanton
pleasure-seeking, the split between the ideal of love and the
act of love, that demoralizes the military wholeness of her pro-
tectors. And with her an artist-in-residence, Pandarus, has
emerged with the raw energy to produce and maintain the
play acts which further pollute the city's integrity. Between
the war assaulting the walls from without and the decay of
leadership debilitating the fibers from within, Troy is an open,
defenseless body, a stage where no one acts any but the single
dimension of a given role. Values go unperformed in the culture, the human thirst for perfection ignored. Lacking the
guidance of a Player-King, Troy falls into the hands of Pandarus, and the body's apologist shapes its forms.

The initial failure comes from Hector. Outside the circle of
amorous encounters, never directly seen with Pandarus or
with Helen, he is even at the beginning of the drama the man
who will meet death surrounded and alone. Hector is unwilling to confront honestly the decay of his city's chivalric ethic,
based on true love and just war, and so is unable to correct it.
Like the untutored Bassanio, he avoids facing the realities of
fallen human nature and so, because he lies to himself, he
loses the power to overwhelm the influence of the bawds and
whores. He retreats systematically to an unproductive solitude, going into battle like Hotspur with his cause resting on
his personal strength. His most public play is his love challenge to the Greeks, but it is a call to single combat. In council,
too, he nullifies himself. Although he argues against keeping
Helen, he never mirrors back to his opponents, Troilus and
Paris, the hypocrisy and self-seeking they are guilty of: Troilus, who fights sporadically because the cause bores him, and

Paris, who fights when he is not enjoying Helen.

Yet after the debate touches on the origins of the war, consonant with the Trojan sense of honor, and continues to the now doubtful position of keeping the costly prize, Hector relents in one moment of willful blindness:

> Paris and Troilus, you have both said well,
> And on the cause and question now in hand
> Have gloz'd, but superficially, not much
> Unlike young men, whom Aristotle thought
> Unfit to hear moral philosophy.
> The reasons you allege do more conduce
> To the hot passion of distemp'red blood
> Than to make up a free determination
> 'Twixt right and wrong . . .
>
>   yet ne'er the less,
> My spritely brethren, I propend to you
> In resolution to keep Helen still,
> For 'tis a cause that hath no mean dependance
> Upon our joint and several dignities. (II. ii. 163–71, 189–93)

Hector's rigidity, the first mark of a worsening disease of the will, irrationally reinforces the paralyzing hold corruption has on Troy. Without play, there is no capacity for harmonious change, and Hector's impotence to communicate to others the vision he holds ever more singly and mortally leaves the imaginative life of his city in the hands of the pestilential Pandarus.

From his initial dramatic appearances in the play, the first with Troilus and the second with Cressida, Pandarus betrays the Adversary's mind—a thirst for comfort and gratification that denies any selfless act: "Will this gear ne'er be mended?" (I. i. 6). He pursues power in the pleasure of having a young man woo him. He lays his wares before Troilus, as he revels in his ability to rouse him to exclamations of passion and pain. He shares in full his kinswoman's facility at teasing and pouting:

Pan. She's a fool to stay behind her father, let her to the
Greeks; and so I'll tell her the next time I see her.
For my part, I'll meddle nor make no more i'th'matter.

Tro. Pandarus—

Pan. Not I.

Tro. Sweet Pandarus—

Pan. Pray you speak no more to me, I will leave all as I
found it, and there an end. (I. i. 80–88)

Troilus' wooing excites him; Cressida's sexuality delights
him. By adoring her, his niece, he can love himself. He talks
bawdily to her and accomplishes his purpose in getting her to
speak of her own sexual nature, listing the wards at which she
lies. Pandarus needs to believe her more beautiful than Helen,
for in her he can create his own symbol of decadence and take
his place at the heart of the Trojan love play. In bringing the
affair of Troilus and Cressida to consummation, Pandarus plays
with the surrogates of the city's most renowned lovers and discovers the satisfaction of manipulating a potentially spiritual
passion to a purely physical end. He did not create Paris and
Helen, but he can form the love of Troilus and Cressida after
their pattern.

With Paris and Helen, the models his art holds up for emulation, Pandarus is a willing accomplice, taking pleasure in
their attentions like a toady to movie stars. The lady of the
Trojan cause and the Greek dream titillates him, caresses him,
woos him to sing the theme song she has brought to Troy. Paris
finally convinces him to perform by telling him that he has
broken the music and must restore it: "Nell, he is full of harmony" (III. i. 52–53). Paris recognizes Pandarus' artistic gift,
the talent of the corrupted artist who, instead of communicat-
ing a vision of harmony to his community, sings the praises of
their corrupted lives, reinforcing their self-love in his distorted
mirror. What stimulates the flesh is the subject of the song:

"Love, love, nothing but love, still love, still more!
   For O, love's bow
   Shoots buck and doe.
   The shaft confounds
   Not that it wounds,
But tickles still the sore.
These lovers cry, O ho, they die!
   Yet that which seems the wound to kill,
Doth turn O ho! to ha, ha, he!
   So dying love lives still.
O ho! a while, but ha, ha, ha!
O ho! groans out for ha, ha, ha!—hey ho!" (III. i. 115–26)

The ribaldry inspires Paris to declare the chain of events from
thought to act that has become the mode in Troy: "hot blood
begets hot thoughts, and hot thoughts beget hot deeds, and
hot deeds is love" (III. i. 129–30). This revelatory contact with
Troy's heroine aids Pandarus in setting the stage for his own
cast of lovers.

Yet Troilus and Cressida are not merely passive victims of
Pandarus' play; they share in two extremes the malady of their
city. Each feels deeply the incompleteness of life, a sense of
aching unfulfillment that unites them to each other and suggests the opening phase of the Player-King's education. Unfortunately, it also makes them susceptible to their roles in
Pandarus' seemingly idyllic play. Cressida, from her first appearance, accepts the forms of Pandarus' art as she betrays her
desire to manufacture her public image, thus separating picture from self. She is passionately fond of Troilus, yet she will,
like Pandarus, seem to be stubbornly in need of prolonged
wooing. She believes that the act of love, once performed,
means the cessation of desire:

But more in Troilus thousandfold I see
Than in the glass of Pandar's praise may be;
Yet hold I off. Women are angels, wooing:

Things won are done, joy's soul lies in the doing.
That she belov'd knows nought that knows not this:
Men prize the thing ungain'd more than it is.
That she was never yet that ever knew
Love got so sweet as when desire did sue.
Therefore this maxim out of love I teach:
Achievement is command; ungain'd, beseech;
Then though my heart's content firm love doth bear,
Nothing of that shall from mine eyes appear. (I. ii. 284–95)

Her opinion of herself and of love sheds light on her coy sensuality as she admires the warriors passing before her. It tells of her lack of self-confidence, of her inability to see herself except on a stage where she plays the sexual role that must invoke its counterrole in a lover. Worldly wisdom though she speaks, her philosophy betrays a nullity at the root of her being. Once love is consummated physically, she sees nothing left but the finite dimensions of her body. Her vision of the world is not redeemed by glimpses of the spirit shining through the mortal dullness of life. Like Helen and Paris, she subscribes to the idea that love is hot thoughts leading to hot deeds, and beyond that lie only rejection and solitude.

Yet there is no other direction for her love to take but towards physical consummation. Although she complains that Pandarus will tease her unmercifully, she enjoys the moment of meeting Troilus and playing her role to the utmost before him and their scene-arranger. At that moment, she relaxes her aloof posture to confess that she loved Troilus long before she agreed to their assignation, that she was simply "hard to seem won" (III. ii. 117). And later, returning to her role as sex object and tease, she changes again to attribute her confession to guile:

> Perchance, my lord, I show more craft than love,
> And fell so roundly to a large confession,
> To angle for your thoughts. (III. ii. 153–55)

Her desire to be infinitely desirable is uppermost in Cressida's mind at all times. Yet the understanding that such an absolute seems incapable of fruition keeps her insecurity gnawingly active. The scene is already set for the later role she will perform with Diomedes before the eyes of her former lover and the diseased gaze of Thersites.

Troilus shares with her the awareness of his role as lover and the yearning for a gratification that is permanent. He, too, despairs of finding it in worldly love. He retreats to the literary formulae of the languishing suitor in the single pursuit of Cressida, searching for fulfillment in the lie of imitating an imitation of life. Like Richard II, his verbal powers of metaphor far exceed his ability to play out the vision of universal connections on which they are based. Instead he blindly restricts all his talents and ambitions to the aim of becoming Cressida's lover:

> Tell me, Apollo, for thy Daphne's love,
> What Cressid is, what Pandar, and what we:
> Her bed is India, there she lies, a pearl;
> Between our Ilium and where she resides,
> Let it be call'd the wild and wand'ring flood,
> Ourself the merchant, and this sailing Pandar
> Our doubtful hope, our convoy, and our bark.
> (I. i. 98– 104)

Instead of using his love to withdraw from his world's corrupt play, he submits himself to the guidance of love's tritest material metaphors—his mistress a pearl, himself a merchant—and so into the hands of Pandarus, his convoy; the bark steers him according to its will. Thus are those noble and generous impulses that Ulysses recites from Aeneas' description corrupted.

Troilus is so far beyond his ability to see clearly and to control his fate that when the meeting with Cressida is at last arranged, he comes to her in Pandarus' company dreaming only of the physical lust in which he has drowned spiritual love:

I am giddy; expectation whirls me round;
Th'imaginary relish is so sweet
That it enchants my sense; what will it be,
When that the wat'ry palates taste indeed
Love's thrice-repured nectar? Death, I fear me,
Sounding destruction, or some joy too fine,
Too subtile, potent, tun'd too sharp in sweetness
For the capacity of my ruder powers.
I fear it much, and I do fear besides
That I shall lose distinction in my joys,
As doth a battle, when they charge on heaps
The enemy flying. (III. ii. 18–29)

Love built on the potent, almost magical union of souls within the flesh is infinite in itself and a blessing on the world it helps to shape. But like Cressida, Troilus bases his love on the desire for the pleasures of the flesh alone, and in doing so confronts the materialism of love in the limitations of sensuality. He despairs of extending the body's pleasure indefinitely; he separates the imaginary relish from the deed. The imagination, so firmly allied to the cosmic harmony from which humanity is excluded in its fallen state, glimpses the hidden dimensions of a perfect world. But the body can dance only imperfectly what the imagination grasps.

When the lovers meet—Cressida believing she errs in giving in to the physical embrace and Troilus fearful that his sense will become cloyed with sensual pleasure—they play before Pandarus the love scene that is also a death scene. It is Troilus who finally verbalizes their predicament:

This is the monstruosity in love, lady, that the will is infinite and the execution confin'd, that the desire is boundless and the act a slave to limit. (III. ii. 81–83)

In the world where the gap between a person's spiritual potential and his actual weakness is not bridged by the play enactment of a vision, love is the most monstrous of contradictions and the greatest source of personal failure. The next day's knocking at the door only reflects the inevitable. Physical separation destroys physical love.

As Troilus takes his leave of Cressida before handing her over to Diomedes, his worst fears begin to take definite form. He has always known that the lust he felt, even before its consummation, had limits. About to be deprived of Cressida's presence, he begins to project the possible end of their love, bidding her repeatedly to be true to him. When she bridles at the implicit suggestion of her fallibility, asking whether he in fact believes she will prove false, he answers:

> No,
> But something may be done that we will not,
> And sometimes we are devils to ourselves,
> When we will tempt the frailty of our powers,
> Presuming on their changeful potency. (IV. iv. 93–97)

Troilus experiences the wrenching duality of Adam's fall from grace. His powerlessness to create a world where he and Cressida can love as Portia and Bassanio do, not oblivious to frailty but cognizant of it and using it to create the miracle of harmony, gives over to death the love that from the first was guided by death. Instead of creating his own play and bringing within it his love and his community, Troilus, like Hector, has strengthened Pandarus' hold over the Trojan art form. Never to become, only to seem—such is the fate of the city where the warrior Hector and the lover Troilus relinquish the power of play, where Helen reigns as inspiration and Pandarus creates the formal praises of her influence.

Ulysses and the Halted Engine of War

Pandarus is the playwright of his society's corrupted love vision, his aim to comfort and perpetuate the decadence caused by the division of act from ideal. He makes Helen his pattern for all excellence and weaves around her his imitation of love.

Although the Greek world is barren of Helen and her corrupting sensuality, its aim is the victory that will regain her; and it
will embrace her surrogate, Cressida, to gratify temporarily its
desire for the original Queen of Love. Despite the armed tents
and brutalized warriors produced by thwarted sensuality, the
Greek installation's frustrated war effort mirrors the Trojan paralysis. Enlightened leadership is as lacking among the attackers as it is among the attacked. While Pandarus works to bring
love to a physical end in sex, Ulysses operates among the
Greeks to bring malice, envy, and cruelty to physical fruition
in murder and victory. The aim of both playwrights is practical
and fleshly. On both sides of the conflict, there are efforts to
resist the motion towards completing the stalemated war.
Helen, Menelaus' wife, sustains herself and her value to the
Trojans by perpetuating the war, and Achilles, Polyxena's lover,
maintains his position as the last hope of the Greeks by refusing to take the decisive final step. As long as these cultural
axes keep separate the two worlds of Troy and Greece, the
love and war cultures perpetuate themselves indefinitely. The
Greeks as well as the Trojans lack the patterning power of a
true Player-King.

That Agamemnon's leadership is inadequate to unite his
community is apparent from his first speech to the Greek council. Instead of focusing his own efforts on the human scene of
division, like Henry V who could unite the warring states
within his own realm to defeat the French, Agamemnon accepts the lack of success by attributing it to the gods:

> Nor, Princes, is it matter new to us
> That we come short of our suppose so far
> That after seven years' siege yet Troy walls stand,
> Sith every action that hath gone before,
> Whereof we have record, trial did draw
> Bias and thwart, not answering the aim
> And that unbodied figure of the thought

> That gave't surmised shape. Why then, you princes,
> Do you with cheeks abash'd behold our works,
> And call them shames which are indeed nought else
> But the protractive trials of great Jove
> To find persistive constancy in men? (I. iii. 10–21)

Unlike Hector, who refuses to accept human imperfection and mutability, Agamemnon embraces them as fixed limitations on the Greek effort. Rather than resolve the problem, he excuses it as destined inaction. But such blind acceptance precludes the possibility of a person's trying to affect his fate by playing it as he would like it to be. While Nestor "applies" Agamemnon's discourse in figurative language, working from idea to metaphor but not from metaphor to action, the Greek army remains fixed in the paralysis that only human play can cure.

Since the Greek general has failed indeed to be the "great commander, nerves and bone of Greece" (I. iii. 55), Ulysses assumes the position of community leader and exposes the underlying cause of the war's failure. He cites the correspondences between the heavens and the earth, between the cosmic state of order and human imitation of it in order to explain the sense of impending catastrophe. Like Venice, the Greek camp has become a cannibalistic social unit. "Degree being vizarded,"

> Then every thing include itself in power,
> Power into will, will into appetite,
> And appetite, an universal wolf
> (So doubly seconded with will and power),
> Must make perforce an universal prey,
> And last eat up himself. (I. iii. 119–24)

Like Richard II who was warned that the insatiable appetite for more lands, wealth, power would at last turn on himself, like Shylock who allowed his material lust to fulfill itself in his desire for flesh, so Agamemnon and the Greeks will, after loosing the wolf of appetite, become its victims. Ulysses, in his statement of cosmic correspondence, speaks with the transcendent understanding of a Player-King. Yet his words alone, accepted by Agamemnon who asks that they be seconded with a prescription against the disease, cannot effect a change without a performance of them. Nor will Ulysses follow their import when he begins to administer his medicine.

He sees Achilles and his mime Patroclus taking over the play form of their community:

> With him [Achilles] Patroclus
> Upon a lazy bed the livelong day
> Breaks scurril jests,
> And with ridiculous and awkward action,
> Which, slanderer, he imitation calls,
> He pageants us. (I. iii. 146–51)

This form of imitation has provided the Greek host with a corrupt mode of play, and the disease spreads outward from the scurrilous mime to the receptive community. Agamemnon becomes the strutting proud commander whose inflated words fall into inappropriate sentences. Nestor becomes the coughing, spitting, palsied old bore. Not satire, which instructs, but travesty, artistic imitation limited to exaggeration and ridicule, shapes the Greek vision. When Ulysses' exposition is interrupted by Hector's challenge, the theoretical problem becomes practical. Ulysses, with his eye still on victory, uses the occasion to bring his understanding to performance.

Achilles' weakness resides in his belief in Belmont's silver casket. He is as he is reflected in the eyes of the men who surround him—an effective warrior, a culture hero, a touchy beloved. To unite Achilles with his now inactive warrior's role, Ulysses stages a play, its aim the disillusionment of Achilles with himself through the seeming indifference of his public to him. In order to create a thoroughly consistent art form, Ulys-

ses uses Ajax to replace Achilles in the role he formerly played
for the Greeks, much as a stage manager would remove a temperamental actor from the lead and substitute an inferior but
willing one. The play progresses as Ulysses lines up the Greek
actors and parades them past Achilles. At first the prima donna
of the host maintains his role—he rejects them. But when Agamemnon does not stop to inquire whether he will speak, and
when Nestor, Menelaus, and Ajax reinforce the rejection and
create a palpable atmosphere of unconcern and·disdain around
him, Achilles can no longer maintain himself as he was. The
problem appears to be a simple conflict between what he believes he is and what is reflected back to him from his audience:

> I do enjoy
> At ample point all that I did possess,
> Save these men's looks, who do methinks find out
> Some thing not worth in me such rich beholding
> As they have often given. (III. iii. 88–92)

Ulysses' "source" has taken the play life of a Player-King and
reversed it, so that instead of moving from within a person to
outside him, it starts with the result—the applause—and reflects back inward to the man, who does not otherwise know
who he is.[5]

Although Ulysses' lesson works on Achilles as he intends it
should, the play will fail to achieve any lasting results. Achilles
will ask whether his deeds are then forgotten, reaching immediately for the dangling compliment that Ulysses had so un-
expectedly turned on Ajax, but even though he hears that he

---

5. Peter Ure, *Shakespeare: The Problem Plays* (London: Longmans, Green,
1961), 38, notes Ulysses' practical reversal of his philosophy in dealing with the
respective ranks of Achilles and Ajax; he comments on the plan's ultimate lack of
success. Francis Fergusson, *Shakespeare: The Pattern in His Carpet* (New York:
Delacorte, 1970), 205–206, also sees a shadow cast over Ulysses' degree speech by
the trickery he engages in with Achilles.

cannot expect his role and reputation to continue beyond his enactment of them, he will not ultimately come to the fight because of Ulysses' play. Not only will the play still fail to catch the hero in its nets, but it will further create another negative side effect in making Ajax assume Achilles' role as yet another warrior who must be wooed and won. Ulysses has not succeeded in enlightening the Greeks to the cosmic meaning behind their roles; he has merely intensified their attachment to the worldly praise that affirms the shallowest playing of those roles. Ulysses, the source of wisdom among the Greeks, belies his understanding as he playwrites to cure Achilles' pettish arrogance. He fails to perform, and so to communicate affectively, that wisdom to his society.

In the midst of the Greek host, watching all its ineffectual activities and pricking the bubbles of the great, stands the clown, Thersites. Like all clowns, he is privileged to speak what he sees as the truth and to take his chances on being beaten for it. At first he is Ajax's constant companion, feeding off stupidity. When Ajax is given Achilles' role, Thersites switches to the former hero and jibes at his condition. Having the complementary function of the playwrights Pandarus and Ulysses, he, as audience, reverses the espoused values of his society and mirrors back into the play a deflating vision of boils and scabs. He is the participating audience within the play, at first attached only to the Greeks, but later the witness for the play-within-the-play that brings Trojan and Greek together under the moonlight where they witness the dissolution of spurious harmony.

Immediately after the elevated council scene, Thersites enters and brings with him the physical deflation of greatness:

> *Ajax.* Thersites!
> *Ther.* Agamemnon, how if he had biles—full, all over, generally?

Ajax. Thersites!
Ther. And those biles did run—say so—did not the general
run then? Were not that a botchy core?
Ajax. Dog!
Ther. Then would come some matter from him; I see none
now. (II. i. 1–9)

It is Thersites who keeps before us at all times the animal nature of the players he observes—their diseases, their brutalized feelings, their resemblances to the lower creatures they
have descended to:

> With too much blood and too little brain, these two may run mad,
> but, if with too much brain and too little blood they do, I'll be a
> curer of madmen. Here's Agamemnon, an honest fellow enough,
> and one that loves quails, but he has not so much brain as ear-wax;
> and the goodly transformation of Jupiter there, his brother, the
> bull, the primitive statue and oblique memorial of cuckolds, a
> thrifty shoeing-horn in a chain, hanging at his brother's leg—to
> what form but that he is, should wit larded with malice, and malice
> fac'd with wit, turn him to? To an ass, were nothing, he is both ass
> and ox; to an ox, were nothing, he is both ox and ass. To be a dog,
> a moile, a cat, a fitchook, a toad, a lezard, an owl, a puttock, or a
> herring without a roe, I would not care; but to be Menelaus, I
> would conspire against destiny. Ask me not what I would be if I
> were not Thersites, for I care not to be the louse of a lazar, so I
> were not Menelaus. (V. i. 48–66)

Thersites, the natural son of his society, credits himself with
more brains than all the Greek army together. Here he tasks
his own perverted imagination with finding play transformations suitable to the chief causes of the war—the cuckold and
his brother. Lower than a man, lower even than the higher
animals, Menelaus stands, a disgusting beast who has transformed the high aim of war into an argument over a placket.
And it is Thersites, too, who helps to unite the two simultane-
ous plays going on within Troy and the Greek camp by rele-
gating both cultures to disease: "and war and lechery confound

all!" (II. iii. 75). Standing between the audience and the play, he prevents the taint from reaching outward. By turning blood into brain, even a diseased brain, the audience is removed from affectively helping to perpetuate the Trojan war. None of Ulysses' efforts to restore harmony to his army can touch Thersites, who remains always outside, thumbing his nose at those within.

Both Trojans and Greeks, then, share the same plight. To war or love, they respond the same way, partially and physically. Pandarus plays to share the thrills of a first love; Ulysses plays to activate the army whose dragging feet prolong the interminable war. The success of either camp is stifled by its self-protecting need to maintain the stagnating status quo. Thersites, usurping the audience's function, blocks both plays from fulfilling themselves outside the drama. Only when the two self-contained communities mix to share their diseases does the stalemate break. When Troy comes to Greece—Cressida to her father, Hector to Achilles, and Troilus to Cressida—the two plays finally meet to culminate in the next day's mortal combat.[6]

The Marriage of Love and War:
"A juggling trick—to be secretly open"

Every art selects its material from the spectrum of the possible and patterns the lives it encompasses to given postures and selected ends. The Player-King's art differs from the Ad-

6. Norman Rabkin, "*Troilus and Cressida*: The Uses of the Double Plot," *Shakespeare Studies*, I (1965), 265–82, cross-references the love and war plots in the play according to the themes of value and time. All the characters, Rabkin states, "have been transformed by a process over which none of them has control. That process is time, a time presented so consistently in organic terms that one comes finally to understand its inevitability" (p. 280). Time, a product of the Fall, devours those who are not given the glimpse of eternal truths; the characters in this play seem helpless before it. For a closely reasoned argument on the relativity of value in the play, see W. R. Elton, "Shakespeare's Ulysses and the Problem of Value," *Shakespeare Studies*, II (1967), 95–111. Elton views the world of *Troilus and Cressida* as a marketplace rather than a stage.

versary's in its principle of selection. Having experienced as a
cipher the full potential of human life and its inherent limits,
the Player-King forms his play around the cosmic pattern that
renders his audience-subjects' seemingly haphazard experiences meaningful. He creates a metaphor consonant with the
network of metaphor that postlapsarian vision can only glimpse.
Neither the Trojans nor the Greeks possess such a leader.
Their artists strive instead to enhance the reflection of their
community's fallen state.

Troy and Greece go to battle vizarded and separate. Each
community holds itself apart from the other, living its obses-
sions within the protective confines of its own play. As long as
they remain isolated from one another, their individual plays
hold the actors within them captive to their given roles. But
when they meet, unvizarded, they serve each other as a reality
on which the inadequate illusions of their respective plays
will break. For Troy, the unmasking will reveal and destroy
the weakened fibers of a formerly strong vision of love and
honor. For the Greeks, it will concretize horrifyingly the rooted
cruelty of an empty, self-reflecting egotism.

On the decision to exchange Cressida for Antenor, the plays
of love and war begin to clash. The first indication that a dual
perspective is beginning to replace the protective, isolated
unit of each camp is the presence of verbal irony. The initial
encounter between Trojans and Greeks comes with Diomedes
as he enters the walled city to fetch Cressida to her father. He
and Aeneas and Paris greet each other in an ironic exchange as
their disparate worlds come into jarring contact:

> *Dio.*   Our bloods are now in calm, and, so long, health!
> But when contention and occasion meet,
> By Jove I'll play the hunter for thy life,
> With all my force, pursuit, and policy.
> *Aene.* And thou shalt hunt a lion that will fly
> With his face backward. In humane gentleness,

Welcome to Troy! now, by Anchises' life,
Welcome indeed! By Venus' hand I swear,
No man alive can love in such a sort
The thing he means to kill, more excellently.
                                        (IV. i. 16–25)

The hunter's hand of the Greek and the Venus-kissing hand of
the Trojan meet in deadly love. Paris shrinks the irony to its
verbal essence, the oxymoron: "This is the most despiteful
gentle greeting, / The noblest hateful love, that e'er I heard
of" (IV. i. 33–34). The interchanges begin, starting with Cressida's journey from one side to the other and continuing
through Hector's single combat with his cousin, the part-Tro-
jan Ajax. Cressida's visual taste for warriors in Troy is enlarged
to tactile satisfaction as she kisses her way through the Greek
ranks, acting out her own and her city's ills. Ajax is taught
blood love in Hector's decision not to fight to the death, Ajax
admitting that he would not have acted so honorably.

Hector, the gallant but mute leader of the Trojan army, meets
the Greeks on their own ground. Visored earlier, Hector now
stands exposed to the soldiers whose faces he has never seen
on the field of battle. Paralleling Cressida's line of introduction, Hector greets each Greek appropriately, mingling talk of
love and war with each. To Menelaus he mentions Helen, who
still swears by Venus' glove, but is met with the cuckold's
"Name her not now, sir, she's a deadly theme" (IV. v. 181).
Menelaus' degradation is one end of physical love. Ulysses,
whom he has met before, Hector greets with the remembrance
of the war's beginning. Ulysses responds with the images of
love that mark the destined end of Troy:

Sir, I foretold you then what would ensue.
My prophecy is but half his journey yet,
For yonder walls that pertly front your town,
Yon towers, whose wanton tops do buss the clouds,
Must kiss their own feet. (IV. v. 217–21)

But the meeting with Achilles is the most bitterly mingled in tone. With looks of almost sensual love, Achilles views Hector "limb by limb." Extending beyond words to touch, the proud warrior whose image has been destroyed within his own ranks lovingly and viciously examines his vehicle for redemption: "Tell me, you heavens, in which part of his body / Shall I destroy him—whether there, or there, or there?" (IV. v. 242–43). Although Ajax bumblingly restores the hospitable tone to the encounter, the end of this union of plays has been foretold. The land that kisses the skies will end by kissing the earth as Hector, isolated and spent, is mutilated at the command of Achilles.

The climactic mixture of Troy and Greece occurs in the carefully staged scene between Diomedes and Cressida. As audience, secretly positioned to view the encounter, Troilus watches with Ulysses. Behind him, and between the formal audience and the now detached participant, stands Thersites to comment on what he views. At no time is the audience in a position to hear Troilus' agony expressed without further hearing it reduced to the general disease of Thersites' tongue. Not even the wily Ulysses, so full of plots and plans, stands untainted as he unwittingly participates in Thersites' shaping theme of corruption. The meeting of Cressida and Diomedes continues Pandarus' play with only the actors changed. As Cressida attempts to reenact her Trojan style of love, so successful with the man who bears the name of his city and its weakness, she meets the hardened, no-nonsense manner of the Greek warrior: "I do not like this fooling" (V. ii. 101). Needing to be reassured of her attractiveness and fearful of losing Diomedes, Cressida gives in to his demands for an assignation and an end to flirtatious courtship. Secretly open to Diomedes, Cressida relents with an acknowledgment of the weakness she knows is hers:

Troilus, farewell! one eye yet looks on thee,
But with my heart the other eye doth see.
Ah, poor our sex! this fault in us I find,
The error of our eye directs our mind.
What error leads must err; O then conclude,
Minds sway'd by eyes are full of turpitude. (V. ii. 107–12)

The given assumptions of a play produce its inevitable end. Without a controlling vision to guide and direct human life, the play is doomed to the error that leads to further error. When the eye commands the spirit and the physical world becomes the end of all yearning, the spirit ceases to exert any control over mortality. Cressida is governed by the eye, desiring only gratification of her urge to be the beautiful woman worshipped or at least desired by an important man. And so she walks further and further away from the only possible way to achieve her dreams: to enhance her physical beauty with the wisdom of the spirit. Her end is no less than her fear: "Ay, come—O Jove!—do come.—I shall be plagued" (V. ii. 105). She descends by gravity into the physical diseases that grow on sexual love.

As Cressida fully enacts the results of her limited vision, Troilus with Ulysses at his side watches the culmination of his own failure. The man of imagination who allows that imagination to be controlled for him by the corrupted vision of another can only become what his role leads him to be. For the first time, Troilus is removed from the stage of the play. Because he never had the wisdom to hide from the Trojan myopia and become a cipher in his society, the objectivity of his position cannot illuminate him. Instead of willingly relinquishing his role, he has been forced to abandon it. The vision he sees, therefore, brutally enlightening as it is, arouses in him only the self-destructive instinct to eliminate the source of his perception. As he watches, he tries to dissociate himself from the play he is witnessing: "I will not be myself, nor have cognition / Of what I feel; I am all patience" (V. ii. 63–64).

The opposite of Cressida, Troilus will not allow his eyes to govern his spirit. Instead of being able to bridge the worlds of the flesh and the imagination, he divides them in two, his reaction to the secret openness a carefully argued denial of his senses:

> This she? no, this is Diomed's Cressida.
> If beauty have a soul, this is not she;
> If souls guide vows, if vows be sanctimonies,
> If sanctimony be the god's delight,
> If there be rule in unity itself,
> This was not she. O madness of discourse,
> That cause sets up with and against itself!
> Bi-fold authority, where reason can revolt
> Without perdition, and loss assume all reason
> Without revolt. This is, and is not, Cressid!
> Within my soul there doth conduce a fight
> Of this strange nature, that a thing inseparate
> Divides more wider than the sky and earth,
> And yet the spacious breadth of this division
> Admits no orifex for a point as subtle
> As Ariachne's broken woof to enter. (V. ii. 137–52)

Troilus' imagination could not unify the world because he had assumed it was one, and now that Cressida's perfidy forces on him the rending vision of duality—the human vision that resulted from the first sin—he is broken. His series of hypotheses rests on a basic misconception: beauty need not have a soul if it is merely physical, the beauty apprehended by the eye. Cressida has separated what he had thought was inseparable, and Troilus cannot hold together the dividing world. The enlightenment that he as audience is given will drive him only to the acts of desperation that will end one part of his division. He will fight Diomedes and in the bargain fight to destroy himself. Untutored by a Player-King, unable himself to be one,

Troilus will seek the end of his anguished vision of human failure in death.

Troilus' realization, however, is denied the full range of the audience's imaginative sympathy because behind him stands Thersites, watching and philosophizing. It is Thersites who uses the term that best describes the strange series of play circles, a play-within-a-play-within-a-play: "A juggling trick— to be secretly open" (V. ii. 24). In the outward-moving play circles—from Cressida and Diomedes to Troilus and Ulysses; from the least self-aware characters, who are the eternal actors, to the pattern-conscious former actors turned audience—Thersites is the stopper. It is his diseased images that begin to pervade the comments of the participants: Troilus' "O withered truth!" (V. ii. 46), Cressida's "I shall be plagued" (V. ii. 105). Together in his purely cynical vision mingle the wounds of war and the diseases of lechery. He brings together the false-playing of Pandarus and Ulysses, the plays for pleasure and self-delusion, and the play for material gain.[7] As audience, he is a negative parallel to Henry V's community of spectators, uniting in himself the thematic thrust of the drama and willing its inevitable end. Without Thersites, *Troilus and Cressida* might have emerged as tragedy, but with him it remains firmly in the ironic mode. All faith and beliefs are shattered before the leitmotif of focused disease—the mortal end of a mortal state:

> Lechery, lechery, still wars and lechery, nothing else holds fashion. A burning devil take them! (V. ii. 194–96)

The pitiful enactment of the drama's concluding scene occupies brief moments on the stage. Hector, despite the warnings of the supernatural from Cassandra and the natural from An-

---

7. Fergusson, *Shakespeare: The Pattern in His Carpet*, 209, notes that "Pandarus' pandering to the lust of Troilus and Cressida is ironically parallel to Ulysses' pandering to Achilles' morose vanity; he and Ulysses both take satisfaction in the cleverness of their 'policy,' and both find at last that it fails, and earns 'ill opinion.'"

dromache, goes to battle. Achilles will puncture his flesh with spears as he had punctured it earlier with his eyes, realizing in act what he had before rehearsed in play. Troilus, after receiving Cressida's letter and separating again what he once viewed as united in spirit—"Words, words, mere words, no matter from the heart; / Th'effect doth operate another way" (V. iii. 108–109)—girds his body for the battle with Diomedes for Cressida's sleeve. They will throw themselves on each other again and again, but without reaching any decisive climax. Throughout the battle, Thersites, the witness to the final play between Troy and Greece, deflates the desperate acts that could so easily be viewed as courage and honor, reducing the Greeks to animals—the mouse Nestor, the dog fox Ulysses, the mongrel Ajax, the cur Achilles—and the Trojans to whores and whoremasters. Unable to engage in any of the action since he is self-cast as the constant observer, Thersites convinces Hector he is unworthy to fight and later excuses himself from battle with Margarelon on the grounds that two sons of whores cannot fight for a whore without tempting judgment. Thersites the bastard—his community's natural exile—usurps the vision of his world from the audience.

The battle ends with Achilles' whorish victory over Hector, which follows Hector's murder of an unknown warrior for his fine armor: "Wilt thou not, beast, abide? / Why then fly on, I'll hunt thee for thy hide" (V. vi. 30–31). Hector had abandoned his authority over his brothers when he was touched by the counterfeit honor of keeping Helen; now the latent dishonor of that abrogation of responsibility becomes manifest as the mere appearance of worth and nobility prompts him to an unworthy and ignoble action. Even though he knows the Greek is a coward who flees from the great Hector, he hunts him to death for his hide, acting out not his own but Thersites' degraded view of human nature. Hector's inability to rally his own community behind him by supplying it with a unifying, enacted vision of honor results in the loss of that vision even for himself and finally ends in his dying alone, disarmed, and dishonored.

In the final moments of the drama, Pandarus, who has been absent from the scene since the consummation of Troilus' and Cressida's passion, steps before the audience again. After Thersites has unified the drama in his images of corruption, Pandarus can regain the stage to point out the obvious lesson that Troy's loss is the Greeks' gain. Both camps are again one in Helen and her gift. For the first time, the drama extends outward directly to its audience, the Greeks and Trojans reaching out as Pandarus invites the observers to see and recognize their image in the vicarious dealer in flesh. Troilus has turned on Pandarus and wished shame and ignominy heaped on his name. Pandarus philosophizes about his end:

A goodly medicine for my aching bones! O world, world, world! thus is the poor agent despis'd! O traders and bawds, how earnestly are you set a-work, and how ill requited! Why should our endeavor be so lov'd and the performance so loath'd? What verse for it? What instance for it? Let me see:

> Full merrily the humble-bee doth sing,
> Till he hath lost his honey and his sting;
> And being once subdu'd in armed tail,
> Sweet honey and sweet notes together fail.

Good traders in the flesh, set this in your painted cloths:

> As many as be here of Pandar's hall,
> Your eyes, half out, weep out at Pandar's fall;
> Or if you cannot weep, yet give some groans,
> Though not for me, yet for your aching bones.
> Brethren and sisters of the hold-door trade,
> Some two months hence my will shall here be made.
> It should be now, but that my fear is this,
> Some galled goose of Winchester would hiss.
> Till then I'll sweat and seek about for eases,
> And at that time bequeath you my diseases. (V. x. 35–56)

In the last words of the drama, Pandarus summarizes the images and themes that made his play a disaster of flesh. In this pandering society, where the artist engages himself in the business of fleshly comfort and abrogates his responsibility to ally it to spiritual vision, the will is still infinite but the execution confined; the desire is boundless, but the act a slave to limit. Even victory for the Greeks has its limit. Their prize for victory is Helen. Such is the nature of the world Pandarus apostrophizes. In character, he fits his rejection to verse, just as he fitted his song of love to Helen's gift, and in it lies the lament of the flesh's inevitable decline to the animal—a galled goose of Winchester—and the mortal—the groans and tears of disease. The eyes that saw only the material world clearly are now also mortal and too diseased to see it at all.

Ulysses discoursed on the correspondences that define the sympathetic universe; Hector affirmed honor as a touchstone for human life. But Ulysses vainly deserted his wisdom for an immediate response from Achilles, and Hector repudiated his principle for temporary fraternal harmony. Both fail to perform as Player-Kings, leaving Pandarus, the Adversary, and Thersites, his cooperating audience, to contain *Troilus and Cressida* and its characters within their corrupt play circle. When Pandarus ingratiatingly communicates with the audience at the drama's end, he widens the circle.[8] With Pandarus and audience in direct contact, the threat of his contamination is made shockingly evident, as he, black priest, includes its members in his sealing of the senses in death. Should the disease of a corrupted imagination catch, it will extend outward to the culture observing it. If an English audience can will the perpetuation of Henry V's reign of play, it can also will the contamination of the misplaced efforts of the Trojan Pandarus.

8. Berger, *"Troilus and Cressida,"* 133, has also called attention to this mingling of audience and play: "The audience which the play has 'created' is the audience to whose pleasures it now pretends that it must pander. This fictional or second-world audience is finally called onstage from the stews and the pit, and there it plants the flag of a worsening world on the former ground of Troy."

Presented thus negatively, ironically, *Troilus and Cressida* is a warning to the time-servers and the bawds. The world where no Player-King lives becomes self-devouring and cannibalistic, willing itself at last into the grave.

Measure for Measure:
Duke Vincentio and the Redemption of Play

Duke Vincentio's Vienna strongly resembles Hector's Troy. Disease flourishes and bawds are kings. Brothels have extended their corrupting influence from their immediate patrons to the community's youth. The pervasive atmosphere of sensuality has either eroded potential virtue or rigidified and alienated it. Claudio and Juliet descend to perverting love's communal end in marriage and legitimate children; Isabella chooses to bury herself in the isolation of convent life.

In the natural order of influence, the ruler of any land is responsible for the initiating metaphor that forms his reign. Yet Vienna's Duke is free from the sins of his city. Like Hector, his failure emanates not from his personal character but from his public inaction. Because he has maintained his virtue and wisdom separate from his public presence, he has allowed human fallibility to fulfill itself in sin. But, unlike Hector, he does not delude himself into believing that all is well as long as he is well. As Vincentio moves quickly in the first scene to resolve his problem by staging a lesson for himself, he allies himself with Hal and Portia, Player-King and Queen.[9]

9. Previous references to and studies of *Measure for Measure* that discuss the play-within-the-play construction are G. Wilson Knight, *The Wheel of Fire* (Rev. ed.; London: Oxford University Press, 1957), 73–96; Harold S. Wilson, "Action and Symbol in *Measure for Measure* and *The Tempest*," *Shakespeare Quarterly*, IV (1953), 375–84; Francis Fergusson, "Philosophy and Theatre in *Measure for Measure*," *Kenyon Review*, XIV (1952), 103–20; Righter, *Shakespeare and the Idea of the Play*, 176; Josephine Waters Bennett, *"Measure for Measure" as Royal Entertainment* (New York: Columbia University Press, 1966). Fergusson has gone farthest before Righter and Bennett into the internal drama of *Measure for Measure*, establishing the audience's view of the play, and particularly of Act V, as a "double vision" (p. 114). The last act concludes what Fergusson calls "one of the important theatre-poetic themes," "life itself as a dream or masquerade," in which the characters are forced to cast off

The difference between his position and theirs, however, is crucial to the mixed nature of the genre he creates from within the drama. Portia did not don the legal robes of Venice's savior until after she had been tutored by her father's play; Hal emerged from hiding into the full responsibility of England's governance only after he had discovered the limits of disguise and withdrawal with the aid of the Chief Justice. Vincentio, on the other hand, is already in power and therefore isolated without a guide in his apprenticeship to play. As a result, his drama becomes a breathtaking race against time. If the city is to be saved from its geometrically accelerating fall to destruction, he must quickly learn to instigate and embody the metaphor of redemptive play. He must overcome his resistance to public display and confront the need to act out the principles that will redeem his world from inhumanity and chaos.

Disguise

⚔ As the drama opens, we find Vienna's Duke about to disappear from his realm, his motives and destination unclear. Haste dominates the scene, preventing questions and precluding refusals. The Duke's character and, by inference, the character of his rule are exposed both by his sudden withdrawal and by his shy refusal to be accompanied: "I'll privily away. I love the people, / But do not like to stage me to their eyes" (I. i. 67–68). His love of privacy and the corollary distaste for courtly show he will later reiterate to the friar:

---

their masks (p. 117); Fergusson sees the Duke as a projection of Shakespeare. Righter explores the theatrical techniques of the internal play, regarding disguise in the dark comedies as "a state of negation and symbolic death, an image of nothingness" (p. 176). She concludes from her study that these plays represent a period of disillusionment for Shakespeare, particularly with the theater, noting that the actions and characters of *Measure for Measure* evade the Duke's efforts to control them. Bennett assigns the role of Duke Vincentio to Shakespeare in the play's performance before the court, thus reinforcing Fergusson's thesis, and explores the concentric circles of players moving from the actor-Duke in the center to the witnessing, image-conscious James. Shakespeare becomes the playwright and star of his company, skillfully managing his "stage puppets" (p. 153) in the festive spirit of Christmas.

My holy sir, none better knows than you
How I have ever lov'd the life removed,
And held in idle price to haunt assemblies
Where youth, and cost, witless bravery keeps.

(I. iii. 7–10)

Like Antonio, the Duke is proud of the "complete bosom" that
will not be pierced by love's "dribbling dart" (I. iii. 3, 2). He
makes his alienation from his people and from love a virtue,
just as Isabella takes pride in embracing the strict vows of the
convent. As Duke, Vincentio does not permit the closeness of
human contact because it deprives him of the distance he finds
needful for his philosophical pursuit. We have Escalus' word
later that the absent ruler is "one that, above all other strifes,
contended especially to know himself" (III. ii. 232–33). In his
quest for personal, private identity, however, the Duke has ignored his community's need for a leader to serve as nexus and
generator of all metaphors, and thus ignored his public identity.

Yet in his search for self-knowledge, he has felt even before
the opening of *Measure for Measure* the need to connect himself to human nature intimately, to abandon temporarily the
severe isolation of his official presence. We learn later from
Mariana that the Duke has donned disguise before. He has
not, however, reached the awareness of his problem that would
help him to bridge the gap between educating himself and
educating others. By fixing his play life to the broad view of
human possibility that a person learns in disguise, Vincentio
has lost contact with the principles of just government. He has
allowed the laws that protect people from themselves and
from each other to lie unused. Still fluidly in the process of
becoming, he can too easily see all vices as potentially his own
and will not condemn others for them.

As duke of his city, however, he cannot remain in a state of
unlimited sympathy. His refusal to judge his people has al-

lowed them to sink deeper into their fallen natures. As Hal learned from the Chief Justice, play must become a medium for enlightening others as well as a therapeutic acting out of personal burdens. It must teach others by giving them the wider view that the player has achieved in expanding his own consciousness. And in order to teach, a leader must finally limit his own pursuit of vision to the dimensions of a single role. He must be like Portia, a combination of Bassanio and Antonio. The Duke, moving between a given role that he feels uncomfortable playing and a congenial disguise that he can adopt only sporadically, reveals both parts of the Player-King's nature, but they are not yet fused into one. He has not connected the surrendering of his social identity to the public performance of the wisdom acquired through it. "If to do were as easy as to know what were good to do, chapels had been churches, and poor men's cottages princes' palaces." As Duke, Vincentio is a dealer in words, a still pool of wisdom, and his community suffers for it.

When he begins in Act I to move towards resolving his conflict, he is not yet aware of the root of his city's problem, although he has recognized the connection between his own method of governance and Vienna's increasing corruption. The situation is critical: he cannot think himself out of his trap, and some new approach, whether it works immediately for better or worse, is necessary for Vienna's health. And so, Duke Vincentio resorts to the Player-King's technique for opening and exploring a problem. He withdraws from the limited perspective of the one role he has not been able to manage and sets a play in action. He stages a comparison between himself and Angelo, whose reputation for virtue, even if fugitive and cloistered, has interested him before. He must know whether Angelo's virtue can stand the test of use and whether it is more suited to reign and administer justice than his own crowd-shy, forgiving nature. Although he is wary of Angelo's supposed perfection, his need is not only to expose his surrogate's latent weaknesses but also to learn from any virtues that power will strengthen in him. In his play, he withdraws again to the role of friar—a part that exposes him to the world's secrets yet protects him from their taint. From the crowned head of Vienna, ineffectual and insecure, Vincentio becomes a religious, allowing himself in this disguise to act out all his ducal lacks, and so to cleanse himself of them in preparation for resuming temporal authority should it be warranted. The friar can also witness as audience the results of the test. From this play-within-the-play that he has set in motion, two possible results can occur. Either the Duke will discover in Angelo the ideal ruler, or he will lay bare the wants in character that produce a poor ruler and thereby train himself to resume the crown. Either result will force him out of his dilemma into a permanent and delimited role.

The Surrogate

Duke Vincentio's choice of Angelo to occupy his seat of authority is not casual. Angelo lives out the Duke's most secret wish—to remain outside the clamor of public opinion. Yet the Duke knows that it is a weakness to stay selfishly isolated from people whose lives need guidance, and the aura of suspicion surrounding Angelo's reputation for stern virtue strengthens that assumption. The Duke has had occasion to doubt Angelo specifically in his dealings with Mariana as well as generally in his unwillingness to bring his principles out of doors. The two men's resemblance to one another, however, is clear. When Vincentio explains to Escalus the arrangements he has made for Angelo to rule Vienna in his absence, he uses the terms of play that suggest an identity transformation:

> For you must know, we have with special soul
> Elected him our absence to supply,
> Lent him our terror, dress'd him with our love,

And given his deputation all the organs
Of our own pow'r. (I. i. 17–21)

Angelo is the Vincentio who might have been had Vincentio
not been born to power and raised to affirm the public good.
Partly as a test of his own desire to absent himself from his
public role, then, the Duke bids Angelo to "be myself." The
surrogate takes on the character of an alter ego, and the test of
his character an implied option for the tester.

Unlike the Duke, who has been forced into adopting disguise by his predisposition to solitude and his consequent
need to escape public life, Angelo has never been a player. He
has never had cause to question himself nor has he ever desired to increase his store of human experience. When Angelo
regards his image, he sees perfection. And so where the Duke
was too lenient, Angelo is too strict: the man who does not
doubt himself cannot doubt his judgments of others. Because
he does not assume human frailty in himself, he cannot see the
frail as human. And because he has never seen through eyes
other than those of Angelo the virtuous man, he is incapable
of understanding human passion and its consequent suffering.
His evil begins as the Adversary's failure of imagination.

The first effects of his governance occur in Claudio's arrest
on the charge of fornication. Claudio is convinced that the new
ruler is using him as an example, and he is right. No matter
how much Escalus pleads for Claudio as a young man of good
family about to lose his life for a crime committed under exten-
uating circumstances, to Angelo Claudio is still only a criminal, the actor of a fault, a forfeit to the law. Juliet in labor is the
"fornicatress" who should be provided with as little comfort as
is decently given an animal. Duke Vincentio's pattern of justice—to find the flaw residing in himself and so to use mercy
against the offender—Angelo entirely rejects. Escalus pleads
with him to imagine himself in Claudio's position, but Angelo

spurns the unfamiliar leap into play by asserting the validity of appearance:

> What's open made to justice,
> That justice seizes. What knows the laws
> That thieves do pass on thieves? 'Tis very pregnant,
> The jewel that we find, we stoop and take't,
> Because we see it; but what we do not see
> We tread upon, and never think of it. (II. i. 21–26)

The law, in fact, cannot know that thieves pass on thieves, nor can it know anything—it is an abstract medium requiring the human interpretation of a Henry V or a Portia. In allying himself with that unyielding principle, Angelo denies his own humanity; he cannot accept the inevitable imperfection of an ideal current among living people. The limitation of Angelo's rule, even if it stopped short of his tyrannical use of power with Isabella, would still spell disaster for all the fallible souls within his control:

> If you head and hang all that offend that way but for ten year together, you'll be glad to give out a commission for more heads. If this law hold in Vienna ten year, I'll rent the fairest house in it after threepence a bay. If you live to see this come to pass, say Pompey told you so. (II. i. 238–43)

But Angelo's rigid adherence to the abstract qualities of virtue at the expense of their human embodiments cannot stop short of tyranny. A man who has grown accustomed to thinking of the absolute, single and indivisible, cannot see any breach of perfection as correctible. When he encounters temptation, therefore, it is without the grace of human pity, even self-pity. Isabella, a votary of St. Clare, appears before him. She emanates the hard glitter of perfection; she speaks in weighted, reasonable language; she argues from the ideal to the real. She is Angelo in female form. For the first time confronted with an image of himself in another body, Angelo feels a stirring. The

man who could not feel love for another falls prey to love of
self. He is moved. But he cannot be moved, not even from a
single decision, without the monolithic structure of his being
crumbling. If he once sways from his affirmation—"Look what
I will not, that I cannot do" (II. ii. 52)—he becomes prey to all
change. Isabella, cutting through the impenetrable guard of
Angelo's pride of self by approaching him through a mirror,
opens him to the disease spreading like an epidemic through
Vienna: "She speaks, and 'tis / Such sense that my sense breeds
with it" (II. ii. 141–42). Sense breeds sensuality in the man
who has never before experienced contact with another human being. And as sense suddenly gives way to its other aspect, Angelo becomes aware of duality. He is opened to
questions that he has never before raised: "The tempter, or the
tempted, who sins most, ha?. . . ." "What dost thou? or what art
thou, Angelo?" (II. ii. 163, 172). From assertion to question,
from confidence to self-doubt, from studied gravity to reckless
passion—Angelo traverses these distances in the moments following Isabella's exit, and by the time she reappears, he has
succumbed to the corruption of the flesh.

The disease begins with a split in his will that will change
his life's style from singleness to duplicity:

> When I would pray and think, I think and pray
> To several subjects. Heaven hath my empty words,
> Whilst my invention, hearing not my tongue,
> Anchors on Isabel; heaven in my mouth,
> As if I did but only chew his name,
> And in my heart the strong and swelling evil
> Of my conception. The state, whereon I studied,
> Is like a good thing, being often read,
> Grown sere and tedious; yea, my gravity,
> Wherein (let no man hear me) I take pride,
> Could I, with boot, change for an idle plume,
> Which the air beats for vain. (II. iv. 1–12)

As the crack between *should* and *will* widens, Angelo feels the tedium of his former limitation. All the dangerous monotony of life for a man who traps himself in one role reveals itself as Angelo cannot raise the strength of will to resist his starved human need to become another. Even the spiritual promise of heaven becomes gross food chewed in the mouth. Prayer and thought separate from invention and conception, the activities of the imagination now put to use and opposed to reason.

As the shift from spirit to flesh nears completion, Angelo reaches out for the physical sign of his new state—the idle plume, a new costume. Vanity conquers him—love of the world, love of the flesh—both rooted in love of the insatiable self. While that self gratified its need for eminence by identifying itself with the angels, Angelo was safe in his stillborn virtue. But when Isabella appears, brighter than angels in her human virtue, he cannot help wanting to possess that self as his own. The desire to possess draws him into the human arena where, untrained, he slips past the relative and falls into the absolute, seeing in his desire alone the loss of salvation. As he encounters Isabella again, the perception of duality will transform his language and method into ambiguity and double-dealing: "I can speak / Against the thing I say" (II. iv. 59–60). And when his intention is finally revealed, he will use his new perception to protect himself from Isabella's accusations:

> Who will believe thee, Isabel?
> My unsoil'd name, th'austereness of my life,
> My vouch against you, and my place i'th'state,
> Will so your accusation overweigh,
> That you shall stifle in your own report,
> And smell of calumny. I have begun,
> And now I give my sensual race the rein.
> (II. iv. 154–60)

Angelo, his mind and speech now marked by duality, his motives fleshly and selfish, has become an Adversary.

The Duke's other, his surrogate in power, has fulfilled the expectations of the player Vincentio. Once the Duke confronts the weakness of a virtuous man who has never acted out his virtue, never encountered human nature in its variable forms, never acknowledged that his blood runs like any man's, he has eliminated one source of doubt in his power. If disguise has helped the Duke overcome the Angelo in him, then disguise and the play it sets in motion must be affirmed. It is no accident that Isabella will also prove irresistible to the Duke, just as it is no accident that Angelo has been living out the Duke's secret desire. The Duke must understand and absorb Angelo into himself, as Hal did with Falstaff; the Player-King must know all forms of play.

In finally testing the Angelo within him, Duke Vincentio prepares himself to accept the full consequences of his own role as leader of Vienna. Now at least he knows that disguise extends a person's education, that his desire for permanent withdrawal from other people was a potential evil and not a sign of virtue. Still, however, he must learn how to put his discovery into full use in governing Vienna, and this he must learn not as audience but as actor, as tested not tester. He must learn what is wrong with the Duke by discovering what is wrong not only with Angelo but also with the Friar.

The Failure of Words

In his encounters with the actual people who reside in his realm, the Duke learns to see feelingly that the "complete bosom" and its words are a wall between himself and those souls he must guide. First with Juliet and Claudio—the victims of his muffled rule—then with Pompey and Lucio—the exemplifications of his city's vices—Duke Vincentio learns that wisdom cannot remain verbal. Even in his expository device for staging the play that becomes *Measure for Measure*, the Duke's reliance on words creates discord and disharmony.

To gain Angelo's consent for the trial he is preparing, he expounds the doctrine of use:

> Spirits are not finely touch'd
> But to fine issues; nor Nature never lends
> The smallest scruple of her excellence,
> But like a thrifty goddess, she determines
> Herself the glory of a creditor,
> Both thanks and use. (I. i. 35–40)

As a summary of the philosophy of rule, the lines suit the occasion. But they do not communicate need for the action they are intended to prompt. Angelo responds with a feeling close to panic as he and Escalus meet to determine the extent of their powers and duties. The Duke must bridge the separation between word and act by unlocking the passions within himself and perfecting them in play as exempla for his people.

Even as Friar, the Duke's tendency to preach erects barriers around him. On entering the prison that all Vienna will visit before the city is redeemed, he meets Juliet in labor. He seizes the opportunity to foster virtue and proceeds to catechize her on the fine points of shame and sin:

> *Duke.*　　　　　　but lest you do repent
> 　　As that the sin hath brought you to this shame,
> 　　Which sorrow is always toward ourselves, not heaven,
> 　　Showing we would not spare heaven as we love it,
> 　　But as we stand in fear—
> *Jul.*　I do repent me as it is an evil,
> 　　And take the shame with joy. (II. iii. 30–36)

His remarks do not move Juliet to further understanding or to full repentance. Within seconds her verbal acquiescence turns to a cry of despair as she curses the lives she would willingly forego, both her own and her unborn child's.

The Duke's failure with Juliet, however, does not jar him into realization because he moves hastily away, anxious to reach Claudio. To him he unfolds sonorously and at length the wisdom of rejecting the world and its illusory pleasures. Structured by heavily parallel syntax, his language creates an unreal world of logic, balance, and symmetry. Claudio responds in the same intellectual, cool, and dispassionate tone: "To sue to live, I find I seek to die, / And seeking death, find life. Let it come on" (III. i. 42–43). Yet the lecture on life's fundamental baseness, on the dissolution of valor and nobility before the terror of death, does not penetrate the mind's surface response. When he leaves Claudio, the Duke is assured that he has communicated the proper philosophy of life to a man engaged to death. Only when he becomes audience, secreted within range of the scene between Claudio and Isabella, does he learn the limitation of his own preaching, of words' unpenetrating bluntness when compared to passion's sharp need. What the Duke has told Claudio, Claudio himself enacts in his base plea for life. Before "the soft and tender fork / Of a poor worm" (III. i. 16–17), his bravery melts into desperate fear. He has heard from the Friar that:

> Thou art not thyself,
> For thou exists on many a thousand grains
> That issue out of dust. (III. i. 19–21)

But it does not move him to deny the world until at last he begs to live on Isabella's prostituted body. Nor does the Friar's observation that human nature is as uncertain as the moon penetrate the fear of death until Claudio finds himself metamorphosing into a parasite.

The Friar, overhearing the scene where passion releases itself from words to act out its worst desires, finds himself witness to the power of play. He sees his words transformed into gestures, his barren, unused wisdom given life and power as it is demonstrated feelingly. The verbal lesson is now affective as Claudio responds to his own debasement with full horror:

Let me ask my sister pardon. I am so out of love with life that I
will sue to be rid of it. (III. i. 171–72)

The impulse to vice cannot be quelled by words, nor can a
leader who does not comprehend the necessity of exposing
passion to itself before correcting it rule a fallen humanity.

The pace of the drama begins to quicken; the Duke has
hardly enough time after this, his first learning experience, to
prevent Angelo's intrigue from achieving its end—the infec-
tion of Isabella and with her the total corruption of Vienna.
But he has learned not to step in, announce himself, and de-
claim the words of justice and truth. Instead he reaches for the
vehicle that will permit Angelo to release his passion and consequently to cleanse himself of the obsession that bars his redemption. He reaches for Mariana and for the play that will
return her fidelity and love to Vienna.

Mariana is an ideal substitute for Isabella, not merely because she was contracted to Angelo, but because she is Isabella's counterpart in virtue. Both women isolated themselves
from Vienna because Vienna could no longer support their
principles, neither Mariana's lyrical feeling nor Isabella's unyielding reason. Both were rendered vulnerable by a brother.
Yet both react to the ensuing assaults on their principles by
reaffirming them: to Angelo's sudden breach of faith, Mariana
responds with lasting fidelity; to Angelo's threatening and ir-
rational lust, Isabella responds with stubborn and indomitable
purity. In arranging for the substitution of Mariana for Isabella
in the garden, Duke Vincentio is working towards restoring
love as the basis for sex by directing an offstage play-within-a-
play that, when exposed on stage, will tutor all Vienna. He is
arranging for Angelo to become Claudio in play. Mariana and
Isabella need one another to fulfill themselves, and the city
needs the principles of both women to create a new mode for
living—a controlled art where feeling is shaped by reason and
reason softened by feeling.

Pompey's appearance, descending upon the Duke like another blow, pierces his objectivity further. No longer rationally aloof nor desiring to be so, the Duke experiences rage. Like Portia, he must *feel* as well as *know* human failure. Here before him is a seller of the poison that is paralyzing his city's moral nerves:

> Fie, sirrah, a bawd, a wicked bawd!
> The evil that thou causest to be done,
> That is thy means to live. Do thou but think
> What 'tis to cram a maw or clothe a back
> From such a filthy vice; say to thyself,
> From their abominable and beastly touches
> I drink, I eat, array myself, and live.
> Canst thou believe thy living is a life,
> So stinkingly depending? Go mend, go mend. (III. ii. 19–27)

He has just observed Claudio sink to wishing himself a bawd rather than die. He has learned how Angelo would willingly sell his principles to gratify his lust. Now with Pompey, he sees the bestiality in all their lives summed up in one. He is no longer the Duke who could wink benignly at violations of the law; he has begun his journey back to power: "Correction and instruction must both work / Ere this rude beast will profit" (III. ii. 32–33). Instruction alone will not suffice; the experience of correction must feelingly work on the animal life in human nature. His refusal to judge has given Vienna to the Pompeys. In feeling justifiable rage, the Duke has shaken free his will to rule, no longer with words that protect his distance, but with the passion to create form out of the straying lives he governs.

His new feeling life is not complete, however, without a personal direction provided by a personal passion. Angelo's outrageous injustice, Claudio's weakness, Pompey's impudence are followed immediately by Lucio and his slurring references to the Duke who "had some feeling of the sport" (III. ii. 119).

This unblushing vice, the Pandarus willing to usurp the Duke's reign over his play community, forces into the open the connection the Duke has all along feared. Lucio reasons that a corrupt populace presupposes a corrupt ruler, and consequently attributes to the Duke the very flaws Lucio himself owns on his petty scale: lechery and ignorance. As the Duke sees how viciously his own crowd-shy rule can be distorted to excuse the vices of a Lucio, he feels both the desire for vengeance and the need to vindicate himself from the charges. He feels outrage, injustice, frustration—and the accompanying need to vent himself of those emotions, which have now penetrated so deeply his "complete bosom." The passion for justice has released him from his diffidence and turned him into the active player who can redeem his city.

By his quick substitutions in Act IV—his countermoves to Angelo's shifting duplicity—the Duke begins to proclaim himself worthy of his throne. With his new awareness of life as gesture and act, of redemption as enactment and expiation, he finds that he can stage himself to the people's eyes. All of Act IV is a preparation for his new art form, which he will carry in triumph into Vienna from the city gates where all acts meet their consequences. If corruption is a preliminary to chaos and the death of the human spirit, then cleansing is a preparation for rebirth and harmony. Still as Friar, but showing his ducal seal to the Provost to signify his willingness to exercise his institutional power, Duke Vincentio gathers into his play all the actors who must learn from his new vision, those who see themselves as sinners and those who see themselves as victims. He himself is both. No actor other than he knows the full scope of his play-within-the-play. Each is ignorant of the one fact that will test his worthiness to be saved. Angelo does not know that he slept with his lawful wife; Isabella does not know that her brother was saved; not Angelo nor Isabella nor Mariana nor Lucio knows that the Friar is indeed the Duke. On the ignorance of his actors rests the possibility of redemption for each individually and for Vienna collectively. Now with both the method and the passion informing it, the Duke readies himself to resume his authority and bring justice as play to a people starved for moral guidance.

The New Mode

✎ Act V is *Measure for Measure*'s second play-within-a-play.[10] The first, Duke Vincentio's test, ran uncontrolled until the Friar abandoned his objectivity and entered the play's action. The second is a controlled condensation of the first, its intent to arouse in its actors a passion for order and to structure their newly freed wills around a harmonious life. He must release all the victims of blind governance from prison in order to effect this metamorphosis; he must bring his play vision to the actors within his play. He must shift perspectives so quickly and whimsically that no one actor knows anything except his own ignorance of the play. He must create a scene of chaos and uncertainty so entire that all participants communally desire order. Vienna's complete immersion in its dark lusts, in the prison so commonly inhabited, must occur before the Duke can raise his people to the level of communal awareness that Henry V owns from his accession to the throne. The only way for a ruler to assume the throne of a Player-King is to bring to his people the play that will enable them to act out their burdens and release them into the context of a greater order. Once

10. Bennett, *"Measure for Measure" as Royal Entertainment*, 125–37, has analyzed Act V as a typical five-act Elizabethan play. William B. Bache, *"Measure for Measure" as Dialectical Art* (Lafayette, Ind.: Purdue University Press, 1969), 59–64, has treated Act V as a reenactment of the play preceding it. He discusses the play as conforming to the Shakespearean pattern of prosperity, destruction, and recreation established by E. M. W. Tillyard, *Shakespeare's Last Plays* (London: Chatto & Windus, 1938). Bache comments: "The society at the beginning of *Measure for Measure* is one of false prosperity, of 'seeming'; it is divorced from actual life. And the movement of the action is in the direction of making the world more consonant with true life, with human reality. The characters are corrected and instructed" (p. 11).

out of the dark prison of self where no patterns of connection exist to build harmony from monody, all Vienna—Angelo, Lucio, Isabella, Claudio, the Duke himself—is free to deny the division of neighbor from neighbor, of a person from his better self, and to embrace the mystery of marriage's two becoming one. In order to open the prison, the Duke stages and enacts a complex pattern of disguise and revelation based on the principle that only ignorance checks pride, helplessness power, and play egocentrism.

As the play opens, the Duke has resumed his original seat of authority in the company of Angelo and Escalus. Only the ambiguity of his words reveals that he is other than what he has always been, hasty in withdrawal and shy of judgment. The play begins, then, with an enactment of the state of Vienna's governance that mirrors the problem with which *Measure for Measure* began. For Angelo, the first scene represents a continuance of the Duke's policy of hiding, which made it possible for corruption to grow unchecked. He feels safe. Even Isabella's entrance with her cry for justice cannot budge him from his newly formed adherence to vice and injustice. But just as passion moved him before to abandon his pursuit of perfection, so passion will move him again to repent his tyranny. In order to excite that passion, however, the Duke must cast Angelo into the turmoil from which his villainy sprang by again shifting the ground beneath his feet. With Isabella, he is still in the company of the now familiar surface of his crime. He merely continues along the path of his obsession, disposing of her accusation as the result of an unsettled mind and accepting her arrest as necessary to his self-preservation.

For Isabella, however, this first scene is a test of far-reaching importance. Confronting Angelo and Vincentio playing their old selves, she finds she must prove her reason in order to be heard. She must asseverate the structure of sense in an atmosphere of doubt, where rational connection has ceased to lay

claim to any ear but her own. From her first devotion to the
convent's strict isolation, Isabella has been a solitary figure in
Vienna. Her quickness to give up her cause to Heaven, the
only remaining arbiter of virtue and reason, as Hamlet does in
the final moments of his play, demonstrates her despair of finding the structure for her virtue within human society. In the
play, she is forced to assert herself over the dark lies and
power-protected deeds of corruption:

> *Duke.*   By mine honesty,
> If she be mad, as I believe no other,
> Her madness hath the oddest frame of sense,
> Such a dependancy of thing on thing,
> As e'er I heard in madness.
> *Isab.*   O gracious Duke,
> Harp not on that; nor do not banish reason
> For inequality, but let your reason serve
> To make the truth appear, where it seems hid,
> And hide the false seems true.
> *Duke.*   Many that are not mad
> Have sure more lack of reason. (V. i. 59–68)

With every cause to dissolve into the incoherent mutterings of
passion, Isabella maintains her reason and reaches out to assume the Duke into her sense of order. If all Vienna is insane,
then reason must sound like madness. But when her attempt
to restore the city fails, when the Duke—knowing that he has
not yet caught Angelo's conscience and cannot catch it by reason alone—rejects her plea, Isabella returns to her former
isolation:

> And is this all?
> Then, O you blessed ministers above,
> Keep me in patience, and with ripened time
> Unfold the evil which is here wrapp'd up
> In countenance! (V. i. 114–18)

The Duke knows that the mind's reaction to reason rests superficially on top of the will's desire for self-gratification and survival. He knows, too, that only in play is that will released to act itself out.

The second scene of his play, therefore, functions to tear from Angelo the security of his seemingly total comprehension of his actions, and so to put him in doubt as to their consequences. Friar Peter, standing for Friar Lodowick, denies Isabella's charge and introduces Mariana, hidden beneath a veil. Mariana's passion, now consummated, is unveiled as submission to a husband she knows has treated her cruelly, but whom she loves beyond logic. Upon Angelo's bidding, she literally unveils and presents him with the end of his intent: his lust turned to lawful love by the grace of an artful play in which he was an unwitting actor.

At the revelation, Angelo's control over the situation—and consequently his self-control—begins to slip. If Mariana is indeed the woman he lay with in the garden, then his crime is equivalent to Claudio's. Rather than confront the possibility, he moves to impede any further revelation:

> I did but smile till now.
> Now, good my lord, give me the scope of justice,
> My patience here is touch'd. I do perceive
> These poor informal women are no more
> But instruments of some more mightier member
> That sets them on. Let me have way, my lord,
> To find this practice out. (V. i. 233 –39)

Again mirroring the full extent of injustice under his old rule, the Duke gives Angelo the power to deal with the accusers and exits from his authority. Like Portia, the Duke has given his Adversary the chance to repent or else to follow his obsession to its end. In order to restore Angelo to a full communal

life, the Duke must reactivate the passion that led him to demand Isabella's chastity and to order her brother's execution
despite her apparent compliance. He must put into his hands
once more the ability to tyrannize over the weak, to bend all
wills to his own.

In the shifting levels of perception and in the identity transformations, the Duke has already brought the situation to a
new head. It remains for him as Friar Lodowick to take his
stand on the other side of justice's bench and speak what he
knows is truth. Only he can bear witness not only against Angelo but also against the Duke. His search for personal identity
and public justice forces him to indict himself and the empty
throne of power:

> But O, poor souls,
> Come you to seek the lamb here of the fox,
> Good night to your redress! Is the Duke gone?
> Then is your cause gone too. The Duke's unjust
> Thus to retort your manifest appeal,
> And put your trial in the villain's mouth
> Which here you come to accuse. (V. i. 297–303)

Combining within his now transformed self the reason of Isabella and the passion of Mariana, the Friar moves to destroy
first in words what he will later carry through in acts:

> My business in this state
> Made me a looker-on here in Vienna,
> Where I have seen corruption boil and bubble,
> Till it o'errun the stew; laws for all faults,
> But faults so countenanc'd, that the strong statutes
> Stand like the forfeits in a barber's shop,
> As much in mock as mark. (V. i. 316–22)

The horror with which the truth is greeted marks the degree
to which justice has been deprived of enactment in Vienna. In
response to an honest passion for reform based on a total per-

ception of the city's condition, the Friar is greeted with a flurry of defensive assaults from Escalus, from Angelo, and, most of all, from Lucio. The well-meaning upholder of order to whom the truth is slander, the duplicitous surrogate who uses order to protect himself from exposure, and the time-server who can use any breach of order to raise his estimation—all are enemies of the Duke's unfolding vision. But it is Lucio's rude hand that uncovers the new Duke, just as Lucio had earlier forced Vincentio to acknowledge that he was capable of a personal passion for vengeance. It was Lucio's barbs that finally pierced the Duke's disinterested quest, and it is Lucio's assault that tears away the cowl. From his status as audience, a "looker-on" in Vienna, the Duke has discovered the grim fate of those who merely assume that justice will be measured by truth. Now uncovered, he is no longer the unwilling actor of his title nor the horrified but helpless audience, but the man he discovered could play out in his own person the quest for harmony and order.

Assuming his dukedom with the full desire to deliver justice to his people, Vincentio turns to Angelo. He has stripped away from him the protective robes of office, the role he used to effect his desires. And through the play, he has also stripped away the limitations of Angelo's vision, which was based solely on his own appraisal and guarded by self-confidence. Angelo must acknowledge himself publicly as a sinner and ask to be judged as he judged Claudio, whose sin he repeated in the garden:

> O my dread lord,
> I should be guiltier than my guiltiness,
> To think I can be undiscernible,
> When I perceive your Grace, like pow'r divine,
> Hath look'd upon my passes. Then, good Prince,
> No longer session hold upon my shame,
> But let my trial be mine own confession.

Immediate sentence then, and sequent death,
Is all the grace I beg. (V. i. 366–74)

For the first time Angelo sees himself through other eyes and so ceases to be an Adversary. In the agony of revelation he begs for death, the only cover left for his shame and the natural consequence of his identification with Claudio. But a sentence of death would simply extend Angelo's assumptions about human nature; it would admit that vice is correctable only by destroying the body it inhabits. Such justice is not in the spirit of play, which dictates not only the revelation of justice but also the pursuit into life of the revealed harmony on which justice is based. A fate other than death awaits Angelo.

The exposure and enlightenment of Angelo, however, is not the only function of the Duke's play. In order to bring into focus the gifts of both Isabella and Mariana, the Duke must discover whether Isabella's reason can be moved by compassion. Only the Duke knows that Claudio is still alive and that under no code of justice can Angelo be executed. Yet he still maintains that illusion before Isabella, now weaving his play to give her the scene to enact not only virtue but also feeling. First, he must know whether the series of rejections to her pleas for reason and justice, ending on the threat of personal harm, have damaged her tie to reason and justice. And second, he must know whether her coldness to the cries of passion, from both Claudio and Angelo, are rooted in virtue or indifference.

Mariana, exiled so long from the city in need of her unswerving fidelity, turns her strength to Isabella and begs of her the seconding voice that will again unite the city under a governance of lawful passion controlled by reason. Unaware of the Duke's actual plans for her husband, Mariana begs Isabella to help effect forgiveness for Angelo and for all of frail human nature: "They say best men are moulded out of faults, /

And for the most, become much more the better / For being a little bad; so may my husband" (V. i. 439–41). She invites Isabella to be an active part of the frail human race.

But the Duke counters Mariana's pleas with constant references to Claudio, supplying Isabella with a clear motive for injustice under the guise of legal right:

> *Duke.* He dies for Claudio's death.
> *Isab.*   Most bounteous sir:
> Look, if it please you, on this man condemn'd
> As if my brother liv'd. I partly think
> A due sincerity governed his deeds,
> Till he did look on me. Since it is so,
> Let him not die. My brother had but justice,
> In that he did the thing for which he died;
> For Angelo,
> His act did not o'ertake his bad intent,
> And must be buried but as an intent
> That perish'd by the way. Thoughts are no subjects,
> Intents but merely thoughts. (V. i. 443–54)

The Duke prompts her to be legally just; Mariana prompts her to be merciful. Isabella tries to mediate between the two by kneeling beside Mariana for Angelo's pardon and by presenting her arguments for that pardon in rational, legal terms. Her logic holds if the question of Angelo's guilt rests solely on his supposed execution of Claudio. But it does not alter the fact that Claudio died for the same crime that Angelo committed with Mariana. Isabella lends her intellect to Mariana's purely emotional plea, but that intellect alone does not conquer the obstacles to Angelo's conviction on the charge of fornication.

Yet it is not Isabella's ability to reason that is being tested, because Angelo's life is not at stake. The Duke will not execute Angelo on the law he helped him break. The question is rather the extent of Isabella's humanity, and she responds to that question with new self-knowledge. In acknowledging herself the cause of Angelo's temptation, she accepts her own human frailty. The tempter is an accomplice in the sin of the tempted. More important, by presenting her argument in play terms—look on Angelo as if Claudio were alive—she negates the grounds for legal vengeance and pleads for Angelo as if he were Claudio. In the play test, she has proven herself a player and, as such, worthy of her own rise to power as the Duke's wife. Isabella, Mariana, and Angelo have been returned from their isolation and brought into full communal harmony by the Duke, who in his search for a solution to his own problem of rule discovered the principle of governance through play. The final mystery of rebirth can now occur as Claudio, the first victim of Vienna's decay, is restored to full life and to the marriage he had so undervalued.

For Lucio, the last remaining sinner to be exposed, the Duke stages his final test, this time a light-hearted reinforcement of the principles he has been inculcating. On sentencing Lucio to marriage, whipping, and hanging, he arranges for Lucio finally to have the stage that he has been usurping as heckler throughout the drama. Yet all Lucio can manage is:

> I beseech your Highness do not marry me to a whore. Your Highness said even now I made you a duke; good my lord, do not recompense me in making me a cuckold. (V. i. 514–17)

And the Duke, under his new form of play justice, requites him with the exact replica of Vincentio's own decision to accept his responsibilities. In arousing the Duke's passion and in exposing him beneath the Friar's cowl, Lucio forced the Duke to return to the responsibility he had so long delayed accepting fully. In return, the Duke forces responsibility on Lucio by marrying him to the whore who bore his child. The greatest whoremaster of a city of brothels shoulders the burden of legitimizing lust through marriage. And so in Lucio the fallen virtue of Vienna is given its rebirth in a lawful, communal institution.

The new harmonies brought to Vienna manifest themselves legally, politically, domestically, socially. They are the new metaphors of play's "let it be so" and the new acts of a people and leader willing to fulfill the metaphors. Marriage, the insistent motif of Act V's play-within-the-play, is the firmest manifestation of the belief in metaphor. It is based on the mystical principle that two people can become one not only in body but in spirit and mind as well. With the Duke freed from his reluctance to playwrite and to act for his people, Vienna can release its own imprisoned will and begin to form around the notes of harmony. The Duke has won his race against time and accomplished what was impossible in Troy. He has delivered his city from moral chaos and imminent destruction to art—that is, to justice, reason, and the informing passion they control. He is a man who has learned to stage himself, and *Measure for Measure* is his vehicle for absorbing and teaching the lesson that life, like just government, is good play.

CHAPTER V

The Tragedies: Failure of the Player-King

ᴥ When a Player-King achieves his reign by the end of his drama, the world that he leaves to his audience is a reconstruction of elemental harmony—a synergetic organism. Because he has played through the varieties of being, he has achieved a view broad enough for him to act as a function of the divine will in bringing good out of evil. As he learned, so he teaches—by broadening the human experience through play. Henry V, Portia, and Duke Vincentio teach the divine nature of justice and love by allowing their world to act out those principles. The Adversary always threatens to upset the Player-King's balance by restricting human nature to his own image; but Falstaff, Scroop, Cambridge and Grey, Shylock, and Angelo are all controlled and brought into balance because another player has acted as the selfless medium of enlightenment. In *Measure for Measure*, that synergetic harmony is achieved in the nick of time; in *Troilus and Cressida* it is never achieved. The former is finally comedy; the latter an ironic drama that eludes easy categorization. *Troilus and Cressida* escapes tragedy because the audience is not allowed to participate sympathetically in the potentially tragic ends of Hector and Troilus, who have both failed their world by refusing to act out their visions. Hector breaks solitude only to surrender his vision; Troilus allows his love to be staged by an artist of the flesh.

The tragedies pursue the imminent disorder of the middle comedies to a mortal conclusion in which the audience does participate. Hamlet, Lear, and Macbeth in particular release their torments on the audience in soliloquy as they struggle with pressures from within and without. The heroes of the tragedies are isolated, and the Adversaries are stronger than any potential Player-Kings. Hamlet, who attempts to reconstruct his society, fails to complete his apprenticeship in play before the forces of Claudius usurp his world and hunt him into the open.

Lear, a worldly man who values words more than acts, becomes a player unwillingly when he gives his defining role—king—over to the management of his daughters. He gave them all, but he did not think he was venturing all he had. In fact, he gave the worldly signs of dominance—power and wealth—to those daughters who valued them as he did; they are the Adversaries both within him and outside him. In Edmund, the Adversary's mentality is given its clearest rational exposition. When Lear is no longer king, no longer even father, he seeks his self-definition in madness—a disguise that disrupts the mind's habitual patterns and allows a person to see himself and the world from a fresh perspective. Lear confronts injustice in play trials, in widening metaphors that attempt to link humanity and nature. Edgar, too, travels the road of self-surrender. As Tom o'Bedlam he learns the principles of discovering meaning in play by watching Lear; and later, disguised as the peasant, he uses his discovery to stage his father's recovery from despair.

Macbeth himself destroys his place in society and his world's harmony by murdering for power and thus playing the Adversary's role. He listens to the witches—again a principle within him and outside him—who he believes are casting him in a play of supernatural authorship. But his deduction that the world is indeed patterned by the black arts forces him to isolate himself from himself, allowing the hand to do what the head would deny. His end is despair—the only possible feeling left to a man who has killed his spiritual part and allowed himself to act out only the physical remains.

The world of *Othello* is also dominated by a successful Adversary, Iago, who playwrites Othello's marriage into disillusionment and solitude, thus reversing the magnetic force of love until all becomes nothing. Othello, despite his transcendent imagination, limits his faith to outward signs, accepting the Adversary's staged revelations as accurate charts of the world. All plays controlled by the Adversary limit human possibility to the gold and silver caskets at Belmont, and their result is death and folly.

Coriolanus is unwilling, despite frequent opportunities and the lack of an Adversary, to take on the robes of any man but himself. He isolates himself, refusing to play out his candidacy or his alienation. This persistent refusal to extend his consciousness to other forms of humanity makes him a symbol, a god, a beast—but not a man. He creates his own enemies as he forces others to break all identification with his heroic image.

Antony and Cleopatra, both brilliant actors whose roles suit themselves to one another, do not extend their vision to the world they partially rule. In each other, they find completion, denying the base elements of earth and water as they ascend phoenix-like to a supernatural world. They fail the mutable world they play in by leaving it in Caesar's materialistic hands. The harmonies that Antony and Cleopatra discover draw them into a world where mutability ceases; they do not transform through play the world of flux, which becomes dung without their brilliance.

The tragic world, then, is isolating, material, and mortal. It restricts human possibilities; it closes the self to other selves.[1]

1. Matthew N. Proser, *The Heroic Image in Five Shakespearean Tragedies* (Princeton: Princeton University Press, 1965), 3, discusses tragedy as the result of a "discrepancy between the main character's self-conception and his full humanity as it is displayed in action." The tragic hero, then, collaborates with the Adversary since he himself limits his humanity to a public *persona* and self-dramatizes it: Brutus plays the patriot, Macbeth the manly figure, Othello and Coriolanus the warriors, Antony and Cleopatra the hero and heroine. "The image [that the hero adopts and plays], in short, is a kind of metaphoric simplification." Proser's study explains the

The potential Player-Kings—Hamlet, Antony and Cleopatra, Lear—are destroyed by their inability to project a forming spiritual vision. They learn to discern evil but not to transform it into goodness. Their attempts are too weak or too late, and they leave the cosmic pattern to assert itself without human direction. The mysterious elation of the tragic end relies heavily on this surrender of human control and on the divine grace that takes over as a consequence. In one sense, the ends of tragedy and comedy are the same—the restoration of harmony—but the exploration of heroic knowledge and ignorance and the aching sense of loss that occur in tragedy differ from the consonance with the universal order that prevails at the end of a Player-King's comedy. Tragedy ends with a chastened humanity submitting to the divine will; comedy with an awed, wondering humanity molding itself in the shape of the divine will.

Hamlet: "Or I could make a prologue to my brains, They had begun the play"

Prince Hal's father is a usurper, his entire future tainted with the blood of the past. Portia is entombed by her father's will until her active other self returns her to life. Richard II is unpowered, unwived, unanointed. Vincentio watches his Vienna turn syphilitic under his rule. For each of these characters, only one possible road remains open: to shatter the given social role and become a cipher, the receptive state in which all identities can be played.

Hamlet too begins his life on stage in an agony of loss. He has been exiled from all the sureties that he had known in life. His separation from his former self is the most extreme of all in its focus on the familial roots of identity. Not only is a greatly

---

peculiar weakness of the tragic hero that makes him highly susceptible to the Adversary's machinations.

respected father dead, but a mother has denied his past life further by remarrying hastily, exposing herself for the first time as a fallen, sexual being. The feeling of betrayal is intensified by her choice of a husband: an uncle whose reputation for virtue and grace was dubious until his accession to the throne. Hamlet's denial of his mother and her marriage leads him to a psychic alliance with his father, and so with the dead. The drama's first moments show Hamlet tied to a role played in solitude and in the eye of death.[2] He is in the potentially fruitful dormancy of the Player-King's first reaction to self-doubt—a strawberry growing beneath the nettle. In order to reach maturity, he must be allowed to play through that darkness into his own light, which he can then shed on his society. Hamlet, however, is hemmed in at the very outset of his drama by the two forces that have caused his dilemma and that demand not withdrawal, but participation in their world: the court of his mother-aunt and uncle-father and the ghost of his late natural father.

Dramatically, he is presented between the two. Even before the audience sees Hamlet, it has watched the specter of his father drift across the night. And in the next scene, before the audience hears Hamlet identify himself in speech, it has observed the court life of Denmark under Claudius' rule. Caught between a death that seems more real than life and a life parasitically rooted in death, Hamlet will attempt his self-definition in the solitude of play. Henry V, Portia, and Duke Vincentio all succeed in playing through potential tragedy and bringing a new comic form to their societies. Richard II, however, falls victim to his own bad timing and dies with his vision unrealized. Hamlet, too, will become a victim of time, the two forces

2. G. Wilson Knight's famous reading of *Hamlet*, in *The Wheel of Fire*, 17–46, as the disease of death walking in the midst of life is accurate to Hamlet's opening frame of mind. It is also true that he does not recover from that disease in time to avert the disasters that he represents from the play's beginning. Knight does not note, however, that the life in the play is built on deception and must be corrected.

working against him exposing and crushing him before he can ripen into a Player-King.[3]

The Two Enemies: Murderer and Victim

Hamlet's first appearance in his drama occurs in the midst of a colorful court presided over by the now King Claudius, a man apparently of reasonable temperament, disposed more to peace than war, and intent upon the unanimous approbation of Denmark. He knows that his marriage seems a breach of propriety, but he perseveres in his largely successful attempts to bury all censure:

> Therefore our sometime sister, now our queen,
> Th'imperial jointress to this warlike state,
> Have we, as 'twere with a defeated joy,
> With an auspicious, and a dropping eye,
> With mirth in funeral, and with dirge in marriage,
> In equal scale weighing delight and dole,
> Taken to wife; nor have we herein barr'd
> Your better wisdoms, which have freely gone
> With this affair along. For all, our thanks. (I. ii. 8–16)

Denmark is on the brink of war. Claudius, in emphasizing the military position of his country, reinforces the motives behind the court's decision to approve this marriage. All those oxymorons—mirth in funeral, dirge in marriage—appear unnatural, according to Claudius, only because of the unnatural state of war, which turns night into day with preparations against invasion.[4] Claudius has capitalized on the power vacuum cre-

---

3. Wolfgang Clemen, *The Development of Shakespeare's Imagery*, 106, 108, points out the qualities of Hamlet's imagery that demonstrate his potential as a Player-King: "[It] shows us that whenever he thinks and speaks, he is at the same time a visionary, a seer, for whom the living things of the world about him embody and symbolize thought" and also a close observer of "trades and callings, objects of daily use, popular games and technical terms." Hamlet, therefore, is a man whose mind encompasses both the physical world and the spiritual world, a prerequisite mentality for the man who can bring both together in play.

4. Harry Levin, *The Question of "Hamlet"* (New York: Oxford University Press,

ated by King Hamlet's sudden death and the consequent fears of the Danish court over the weakened country. He publicly displays himself in his role as king as the stabilizing force of reason, so consoling to the anxious: "You cannot speak of reason to the Dane / And lose your voice" (I. ii. 44–45). Like Bullingbrook, his guilt divides his nature in two as he acts out a role that denies its origin in the passions that gave rise to murder. Rationality moves with cordiality and grace when Claudius deals with supporters like Polonius and Laertes, but its appearance transmogrifies into harshness when he confronts the one resistance to his new role—Hamlet.

From the way Hamlet looks and dresses, the way he speaks and is spoken to, we know that he has alienated himself deliberately—and in the eyes of his mother and step-father perversely—from the court. Prompted by the need to negate his mother, whose love and grief for his father Hamlet had accepted as genuine and permanent, he rejects the appearance of things. Hamlet recognizes in the oxymorons that surround him the tendency of picture and word to separate from self and act, always common when an Adversary controls the drama. In response to his mother's query, "If it be [that death is common], / Why seems it so particular with thee?" (I. ii. 74–75), he answers:

> Seems, madam? nay, it is, I know not "seems."
> 'Tis not alone my inky cloak, good mother,
> Nor customary suits of solemn black,
> Nor windy suspiration of forc'd breath,
> No, nor the fruitful river in the eye,
> Nor the dejected havior of the visage,
> Together with all forms, moods, shapes of grief,
> That can denote me truly. These indeed seem,

1959), 49–51, examines the antithetical nature of the play as it condenses into oxymoron, especially as it appears in the language of the double-dealer Claudius.

For they are actions that a man might play,
But I have that within which passes show,
These but the trappings and the suits of woe. (I. ii. 76–86)

His awareness of false play, disguise, and seeming in men's,
and especially in women's, lives manifests a spiritual thirst for
the union of *seems* and *is*. Hamlet himself has tried to merge
the two by refusing to doff the mourning clothes fitting and
honorable for a son to wear for a father only two months dead,
and so refusing to follow the lead of the court.

Claudius responds to this black figure with guilty anger,
subdued partially by the need to appear equable. Hamlet represents the tie with his past crime that blocks his future success. Because Claudius must false-play Denmark as if all that
appears proper and reasonable were in fact so, he attacks Hamlet's grief as irreligious, unmanly, simple-minded:

> Fie, 'tis a fault to heaven,
> A fault against the dead, a fault to nature,
> To reason most absurd, whose common theme
> Is death of fathers, and who still hath cried,
> From the first corse till he that died to-day,
> "This must be so." (I. ii. 101–106)

In the conscience of the man who has murdered a father, this
reasoning must hold. But for Hamlet, who reacts not to guilt's
self-excusing rationalizations but to paternal and royal attack,
it is a signal to retire further into solitude. Claudius, anxious to
believe that Hamlet has fallen into his mode, accepts Hamlet's
terse answer to Gertrude's request for him to stay—"I shall in
all my best obey you, madam" (I. ii. 120)—and leaves the
stricken man alone on stage.

Hamlet's solitude, now physical, only carries to its logical
end the dark loneliness of the man in black amidst gay colors,
in grief amidst relief and joy. The danger of that isolation,
which other Player-Kings have faced—Portia in the lead cas-

ket, Vincentio in his friar's robes, Richard II in his prison cell—
is the permanent exile from life. And Hamlet, like Richard II,
passively accepts his withdrawal, not fighting to return to life.
His death would complete the lesson that what seems true in
him is true:

> O that this too too sallied flesh would melt,
> Thaw, and resolve itself into a dew!
> Or that the Everlasting had not fix'd
> His canon 'gainst self-slaughter! O God, God,
> How weary, stale, flat, and unprofitable
> Seem to me all the uses of this world! (I. ii. 129–34)

Rather than play in the hope of redeeming the time, as Hal
did, Hamlet too easily sinks into Antonio's state of inactive
melancholy. His wish to melt also functions as an escape from
his debilitating obsession with his mother's hypocrisy and its
effects on his view of life. Yet this obsession, blocked by the
divine will from fulfilling itself in suicide, reduces him forci-
bly to the man who holds his tongue and refuses to act, to that
death-confronting cipher who suddenly knows not the man he
was but only the blankness of what every man could be.

Claudius and his court, with their probings and demands,
constitute one of Hamlet's enemies in his search for personal
fruition. The other is a more difficult figure for Hamlet to resist—the figure of his father with whom he identifies in his
denial of a world that has become an unweeded garden. From
his first appearance, the Ghost epitomizes military as well as
supernatural strength. He wears the armor of his victorious
campaign against the Poles; he appears in "fair and warlike
form" (I. i. 47). He will speak to none of the men on watch, but
stalks the night, which the threat of Fortinbras' invasion has
turned to day. The renowned elder Hamlet has come to call on
the living for aid in a new campaign and, as the night watch
rightly guesses, will address himself to his son only.[5]

When Hamlet must face his father and the murder hidden beneath the seemingly natural death, the time for his personal quest begins to run out. The Ghost wants his son only as an arm among the living to avenge his murder:

> *Ham.*   Speak, I am bound to hear.
> *Ghost.*   So art thou to revenge, when thou shalt hear.
>
> (I. v. 6–7)

Under the invocation of filial love and natural feeling, Hamlet's father demands from his son an even greater act than his step father's and mother's demand for obedience—vengeance. He extracts from Hamlet the one promise impossible for him to give willingly without destroying his own and his world's precarious balance: the promise to emerge into an act of judgment before he has learned through play the nature of justice. The Ghost demands Hamlet as his surrogate for the posthumous last act of his life's play. His is a revenge tragedy, and the postures commanded are those indigenous to it: passions that transcend reason and border on madness.[6] Yet Hamlet's personal quest leads him to another play, where guilt is punished within the guilty, where sinners confront and redeem their sins in themselves—the quest of the Player-King. For Hamlet

---

5. Concerning the Ghost, there are a number of theories, summarized in Robert H. West's *Shakespeare and the Outer Mystery* (Lexington: University of Kentucky Press, 1968), 56–68. If the Ghost is from a Christian purgatory, why does Shakespeare make him vengeful? If he is from a pagan underworld, why are there references to the last rites of the Catholic Church? If he is a devil, why is he concerned for Gertrude? West concludes that the uncertainty about the Ghost is functional, that it is designed to awaken an uneasy feeling in the audience and so give the apparition dramatic life. The Ghost's concern for Gertrude, however, is suspect. In saving her from Hamlet's painful mirror, he has done her a disservice in Christian terms. See Eleanor A. Prosser, *Hamlet and Revenge* (Rev. ed.; Stanford: Stanford University Press, 1971), 97–143, 197–201.

6. John Holloway, *The Story of the Night: Studies in Shakespeare's Major Tragedies* (Lincoln: University of Nebraska Press, 1961), 29, emphasizes Hamlet's awareness in his soliloquies that it is the role of revenger he is being called upon to play, and that he is preoccupied with that role: "a recognizable 'part,' undertaken by him with what might almost be termed a preordained course and end."

the simple, military solution is not enough, yet he is now pledged to accept it, the values it rests on, and the form it operates through.[7]

"Remember me," Hamlet's second cue to action, leads him to the state of mind in which he puts aside the black coat of grief and embraces the compromising disguise of madness. He writes it down in his tables "that one may smile, and smile, and be a villain!" (I. v. 108). He plays falconer and hawk to the friends he has now left permanently behind him. At once he has become the ruling figure possessing superior knowledge— falconer—and the bird of prey he controls—hawk. Both reason and passion exist simultaneously within him, both control and servitude. His faith in human nature is gone forever; the former friends must swear, and on his sword, not to divulge what has occurred. And nowhere can Hamlet escape the Ghost, who moves to control his actions, who burrows here and there underfoot, always prompting, always pressing for his own.

Hamlet's escape lies in the antic fit, which can seem acqui-

---

7. Irving Ribner, *Patterns in Shakespearian Tragedy* (London: Methuen, 1960), 65–90, sees Hamlet's problem as a schism between the act demanded of him and the state of mind required to fulfill the act righteously. Thomas McFarland, *Tragic Meanings in Shakespeare* (New York: Random House, 1966), 33, fixes Hamlet's problem in the Ghost's demand for his son's total being: "To honor the 'then and elsewhere' of the ghost's claim, which, made in the explicit context of a father's summoning up of past love and duty, is a claim upon nothing less than a son's defining sense of self—to honor such a claim, Hamlet must give up, not goods, no matter how rich, nor youth, no matter how bright, nor friends, nor approval, nor any of the other treasured affects of existence—rather, Hamlet must give up the movement of existence itself." This demand leads to Hamlet's destructive identification with his father, from which he never successfully extricates himself. Levin, *The Question of "Hamlet,"* 57, also notes that "to avenge his father would, in effect, be to step into his father's shoes." Mark Rose, *"Hamlet* and the Shape of Revenge," *English Literary Renaissance*, I (1971), 135, 138, also views Hamlet as tethered by a will other than his own, by his father, "the figure who represents the dignity of man," casting Hamlet "in a limited, hackneyed, and debasing role." Rose asserts that Hamlet's problem is aesthetic. It is not that he abhors murder, but that he does not like the style demanded of him. Farrell, too, in *Shakespeare's Creation*, 170, sees the Ghost's manipulations as destructive for Hamlet: "His program makes no provision for healing Denmark or Hamlet. The Prince must desire nothing for himself, no ambition or passionate love, no dream of renewal."

escence to his father's demands by mimicking the revenger's passion and opposing the seeming rationality of Claudius, make his mother's request for obedience irrelevant, and still be a protective covering to his own developing awareness. In this disguise of madness, he can win time to find his own way in the chaos of conflicting obligations. He recognizes his dilemma in terms of time: "The time is out of joint—O cursed spite, / That ever I was born to set it right!" (I. v. 188–89). The play with the cast of father, mother, and uncle has begun against Hamlet before he has even begun to "make a prologue to [his] brains."

Claudius' Surrogate Adversaries:
Polonius, Rosencrantz and Guildenstern

⚓ The world of Denmark, where something is rotten and natural time is perverted, is run by the man who has committed himself to the proposition that what *seems* must remain the mode of communication. For Claudius, unnatural murder must seem natural death. Reason must seem dominant over passion, and human corruption must seem practical wisdom. Denmark, then, is a play world whose form is an extension of the Adversary's mind, encouraging within it the hypertrophy of self-interest.

When Hamlet resists accepting this play form, Claudius begins to probe further into the reasons for his willfulness; but because he has instigated a form universally accepted by his court, he does not need to confront Hamlet directly. Within his control are others who, in their own self-interest, will do the job for him. Such is Polonius; such are Rosencrantz and Guildenstern. They become the gadflies of Hamlet's solitude, disguising themselves and their motives, baiting him verbally, staging plays in which he is to reveal himself. Hamlet, desperately in need of time spent alone pursuing his own wisdom, must repeatedly break his inner preoccupation to fend off the guileful attacks of his enemies. Not only, then, does Hamlet have to cope with the assumptions of the revenge play previously begun by Claudius and King Hamlet; he now has to cope with the present offshoot of that play in the figures of the former player, Polonius, and the two amateurs, Rosencrantz and Guildenstern.

Polonius' art, like that of Pandarus, abets the interest of worldly power. Under Claudius, Polonius' self-congratulating, smug nature blossoms. He fits himself to all the uses of the king and plays for the approval of a regime whose justice he never questions because the question is irrelevant to his gratified vanity. He has just enough insight into play as heuristic learning to make him an excellent stalking horse for Claudius and a danger to Hamlet. A man whose self-value is rooted in the opinions of others, Polonius perverts his small talent by using play in the service of Claudius' seeming. His art is another form of the Platonic lie; like Falstaff's, it rests on the old plots and stylized characters of drama—the prodigal son, the fiery youth, the love-sick wooer. Even though his initial insight into the nature of a problem is inaccurate, his pressure to play out his insight produces the setting in which truth could be exposed. First with his son and then with Hamlet, Polonius playwrites the scenes of truth-catching, always with the motive of finding out how things are in order to keep them as they should seem.

On Laertes' leave-taking, Polonius bombards him with the proverbs of worldly experience, which, like "All that glisters is not gold," fail to educate unless they are enacted. Recited against the pressure of a waiting ship, his verbal lecture is as silly as it is ineffectual. But Polonius is not just a doddering, long-winded old fool. His instructions to Reynaldo include the play techniques of disguise and plot—Reynaldo is to seem other than what he is and use the deceptive plot of an acquaintance inquiring after Laertes—but for the purpose of eliciting Laertes' true behavior in Paris: "See you now, / Your bait of falsehood take this carp of truth" (II. i. 59–60). Polonius' aim is not to engender what he considers proper deportment in his son, but to catch him in the act of improper conduct. His view of what is proper for a young man abroad characteristically includes all the vices that the social world he inhabits winks at—drinking, fencing, swearing, quarreling, drabbing. If Laertes is so engaged, his behavior provides Polonius with material for future lectures even while he slyly accepts the faults as part of the wild youth he wishfully remembers in himself. Polonius as a playwright, like Pandarus, is interested in boosting his own ego by watching others—here his son—perform the very acts that he wishes he could enjoy.

With Hamlet, Polonius' play pursues a different end, although it is still motivated by the need for gratification. The question at court that dominates all other issues is Hamlet's madness, its origin, and its effects. The man who can resolve that question will certainly win the appreciation of the monarchy, and with such honeyed bait, Polonius cannot resist employing his talents to uncover the truth. He was willing to spy on his son to boost his own ego, and he is equally willing to use his daughter in order to spy on Hamlet. Triumphant before Claudius and Gertrude, Polonius proposes the play that will reveal the roots of Hamlet's madness.

In this scene, Polonius employs his best rhetoric, which, like his style of playing, is imitative and bookish. His aesthetic is based on ornament and elaboration. The rhetoric of linguistic elaboration arithmetically increases the number of like statements but never geometrically multiplies them into metaphor. The result is tautology:

> My liege, and madam, to expostulate
> What majesty should be, what duty is,
> Why day is day, night night, and time is time,
> Were nothing but to waste night, day, and time;

Therefore, since brevity is the soul of wit,
And tediousness the limbs and outward flourishes,
I will be brief. Your noble son is mad:
Mad call I it, for to define true madness,
What is't but to be nothing else but mad?
But let that go. (II. ii. 86–95)

The imminent danger of Polonius' speech patterns lies in his forgetting altogether, as he does with Reynaldo ("And then, sir, does 'a this—'a does—what was I about to say? / By the mass, I was about to say something" [II. i. 49–50]), the communicative end of words. He needs Reynaldo and Gertrude to bring him back to the "matter," where his means and ends again mesh to move him forward. In his own dusty notions of motivation, he presents to Hamlet's anxious parents the letter to Ophelia and flourishingly announces that Hamlet has obviously become a victim of unrequited love. To prove it further, he will stage the play in which all will become evident to the eye. He has studied Hamlet's habits, especially his solitary walks, a necessary prerequisite to using him in his play, and gives the time, place, and nature of the encounter he will stage.

Before he can put into effect his plan to "loose" Ophelia on Hamlet, however, he meets Hamlet in just such a preoccupied walk. For the first time the two men, who operate throughout the drama as each other's critics (Polonius has just passed judgment on Hamlet's "the most beautified Ophelia"), clash head on. Polonius ventures to "board" Hamlet, to pry him out of the solitude that Hamlet deeply needs and push him into speech. The exchange between them epitomizes the different aesthetics of the two artists. Polonius is a categorizer, a shallow imitator of old forms, and ultimately a rational man in a rational court who has glimpses of truth beyond his own capacity to experience it. Hamlet, full of the double consciousness that is essential to play, where a man can play at playing, verbally dances around the heavy-handed probings of Polonius:

> Pol.   Will you walk out of the air, my lord?
>
> Ham.   Into my grave.
>
> Pol.   Indeed that's out of the air. [*Aside.*] How pregnant sometimes his replies are! a happiness that often madness hits on, which reason and sanity could not so prosperously be deliver'd of.
>
> (II. ii. 206–11)

Even though Polonius is simply a nuisance to Hamlet, an easy tool for his ironic reversal of roles where the seeming madman is the bearer of wisdom and the seeming wise man a tedious old fool (II. ii. 219), Hamlet must spend precious time in fending him off. Claudius' chief tormentor robs him of solitude.

Like Polonius, Rosencrantz and Guildenstern work to destroy the secretive dormancy of their former friend. Polonius is just leaving when they appear, full of another kind of rhetoric, the rapid repartee of youthful friends addicted to displays of wit. But this rhetoric, too, is alien to Hamlet in itself and dangerous in its disingenuous probings of Hamlet's state of mind. The two visitors seize on Hamlet's "Denmark's a prison" (II. ii. 243), turn it to questionings of ambition, and between them verbally pummel Hamlet until he cuts short the conversation with a "Shall we to th' court? for, by my fay, I cannot reason" (II. ii. 265). Hamlet, a more experienced player who must play for mortal stakes, ferrets out with ease their reasons for the seemingly free visit, thus again exposing the real beneath the apparent; there is something too forced in their joking and too probing in their casual questions.

The extent to which he knows that he is being used is evident when, after his mousetrap has been staged before the court, Hamlet begs Guildenstern to play a recorder. When

Guildenstern refuses on the grounds that he does not have the skill, Hamlet replies:

> Why, look you now, how unworthy a thing you make of me! You would play upon me, you would seem to know my stops, you would pluck out the heart of my mystery, you would sound me from my lowest note to the top of my compass; and there is much music, excellent voice, in this little organ, yet cannot you make it speak. 'Sblood, do you think I am easier to be play'd on than a pipe? Call me what instrument you will, though you fret me, yet you cannot play upon me. (III. ii. 363–72)

A human being is like a musical instrument, potentially full of harmony and "excellent voice." But the person who desires to make music from so delicate and complex an instrument must know the mystery of playing. Hamlet is apprenticed to the art, knowledgeable enough to see and reject the amateurish attempts being made to play on him, and, through the staged scene of confronting Guildenstern with the recorder, he enacts his knowledge. They can fret him, as Polonius does, by breaking his silence, but they cannot play upon him.

Polonius' play also fails to elicit the complex music of Hamlet's madness. In Polonius' prurient, self-projecting worldliness, he has assumed that love is the root of Hamlet's distemper, just as Rosencrantz and Guildenstern have focused on ambition as its probable cause. In Claudius' play world, the human desire to make the world an extension of the self is given total freedom. For Hamlet, this genre of the Adversary is a protection. Since a person who cannot understand a consciousness other than his own cannot learn the nature of another, the cipher of a society can rest safe in his own play world. The seeds of the future rest in Hamlet's madness, and no attempt by either Polonius or by the Rosencrantz-Guildenstern team can expose the ripening seed before it begins to sprout. Polonius' obvious and stylized stagecraft, his use of the peeking eye behind the arras, is as ineffective in producing response as Rosencrantz' and Guildenstern's seeming friendliness.

It is to Ophelia that Hamlet expresses the full anger of his disillusionment. At the moment, he is struggling with the player's awareness that all human faults are his:

> Get thee to a nunn'ry, why wouldst thou be a breeder of sinners? I am myself indifferent honest, but yet I could accuse me of such things that it were better my mother had not borne me: I am very proud, revengeful, ambitious, with more offenses at my beck than I have thoughts to put them in, imagination to give them shape, or time to act them in. What should such fellows as I do crawling between earth and heaven? We are arrant knaves, believe none of us. Go thy ways to a nunn'ry. (III. i. 120–29)

In the corrupted world that he lives in, Hamlet's experience of human possibility includes the faults of Claudius, Polonius, the Ghost, and Rosencrantz-Guildenstern. He has internalized the pride, vengefulness, and ambition of those worldly men who pursue personal gratification. The dormancy that produces the vision on which the Player-King builds the future with words and acts has effected in Hamlet a close understanding of hidden vice. One by one his former friends and his relatives have betrayed him, and in order to understand their motives, Hamlet has in play made them his own. He takes on himself all the vices of his rotten Denmark, making himself the focus of all the Adversary's self-bound metaphors.

Not only has his mother failed Hamlet, but now Ophelia too gives herself over to Claudius through her father and becomes a weapon turned against him. And so he makes her the symbol of frail womanhood:

> I have heard of your paintings, well enough. God hath given you one face, and you make yourselves another. You jig and amble, and you lisp, you nickname God's creatures and make your wantonness your ignorance. Go to, I'll no more on't, it hath made me mad. I say we will have no moe marriage. Those that are married already (all but one) shall live, the rest shall keep as they are. To a nunn'ry, go. (III. i. 142–49)

Women, too, engage in the false disguises that make a mockery of spiritual inclination. They disguise their faces and their minds; they transform their husbands into horned beasts. Not only are men at fault, but women as well; and Hamlet is all men and Ophelia all women. The good seem wicked, and the wanton good. Such is the world of false-seeming in which the two potential lovers—lovers like Portia and Bassanio, who could bring harmony to their discordant world—are forced by the eyes upon them to abandon the mutual self for the isolated self. Like Barnardo and Francisco, Hamlet and Ophelia disappear separately into the dark. Hamlet's anger at Ophelia is directed at her innocence of false-seeming and her obedience to a corrupt order. She becomes, then, all women—and particularly the woman corrupted by her world who then furthers the corruption by passing it on to her children. The darkness swallows the potential for a new harmony based on love.

Claudius' world of seeming has made possible the self-expression of other seemers. The Adversary reigns over a land of corruption, vice, and self-interest. Although Claudius himself never emerges from behind his mask of rationality and good-nature to confront Hamlet, his own forms have made it possible for others to do it in his stead. Both Polonius and Rosencrantz-Guildenstern stage the plays designed to catch Hamlet unaware and make him reveal himself to them. Hamlet, however, is a far more accomplished player than his enemies. He can keep them at bay and check all their attempts to play upon him, but the persistence of their efforts disrupts his solitude and forces him to spend his time parrying with them. They are like hunting dogs for Claudius, and Hamlet must dispose of them before he can reach their master. They attempt with their barking to drive the prey into the clearing where the real hunter can aim to kill. Ineffectual as their individual plays are, they keep Hamlet constantly on the run.

Hamlet's Progress

⚔ Throughout the studied attempts of Claudius' play-surrogates to wrest from him the secret of his madness, Hamlet continues to search for his own voice and his own road out of the darkness. Unfortunately the pressure on him mounts to the point where it exceeds his self-protecting need to stand apart from his society until he has found the answers to his inner questionings. In his interview with Ophelia, during which he focuses on her all the hypocrisies of women and on himself all the vices of men, and in his scene with Guildenstern, in which he stages the lesson that a human being is a complex and delicate instrument whose harmony can be released only by the skilled player, Hamlet breaks out of his isolation to play to the society some pieces of his new wisdom.

His central revelation occurs in his Mousetrap, and through it Hamlet uncovers himself and his knowledge of all the court's vices and sins, principally Claudius'. The surrogate Adversaries, however, have done their work; Hamlet's solitude has not yet produced the vision that connects his society's mortal lives to the patterns of the universe. He can mirror his world in play, but he cannot playwrite it into harmony. Left at the end of the Mousetrap is a devastatingly final vision of corruption and passion that does not alleviate either threat. Hamlet has been driven to reveal himself by the proddings and disguises of the seeming world, but too soon. He has not answered his own questions about the aims of life and art before he is forced to use one to explain the other.

The series of movements that prompts Hamlet to abandon disguise and reveal himself in play begins with the news that the tragedians of the city have arrived at Elsinore. Hamlet, from having been interrogated, becomes interrogator, asking why the actors whom he has always delighted in are now forced to travel the road to find an audience. In matters of play and art, Hamlet does not shy away from dialogue. He learns that an innovation in theater and not a decay in the players' quality has dimmed their popularity. Companies of children acting in private theaters and producing personal satire have forced the professional actors to the road. Hamlet shows a great deal of interest in this conflict among professional actors because it illuminates his own conflict. He too has experienced a decay in taste in his own land, where his stepfather's image in small is worth good sums of money to the very people who would have grimaced at his face before he was king. Hamlet is also concerned about the playwright's use of the children to proclaim against their own succession. Those who put satiric words about adult professionals into their mouths are using the children against their own future. So Hamlet is used by the generation preceding him to right its errors and settle its disputes and consequently to cut him off from his own future as a fully matured player and king.

With the players themselves, Hamlet feels at ease. No longer lost among a rapidly growing number of poor players—spies disguised as friends, fools as wise men—Hamlet greets, in the form of these actors, his own aesthetic view of decorum. He asks for a speech from one of the company's unpopular offerings, a play

> well digested in the scenes, set down with as much modesty as cunning. I remember one said there were no sallets in the lines to make the matter savory, nor no matter in the phrase that might indict the author of affection, but call'd it an honest method, as wholesome as sweet, and by very much more handsome than fine.
>
> (II. ii. 439–45)

In contrast to Polonius' efforts, which are full of self-conscious rhetoric and affectation, Hamlet applauds the play in which matter and manner blend so thoroughly that the writer himself seems absent from it. A play to Hamlet must be honest, wholesome, and handsome, direct in its intent, natural and integrated in its parts, and beautiful as an artistic unit.

Just as the theatrical debate and the child actors' part in it reflect on his own situation, so too does the speech that Hamlet selects for the players. It deals with the unnatural murder of a good king and the consequent death of the Trojan world—a world to which Englishmen felt mythically connected. The main figures are Pyrrhus, the murderer; Priam, the victim; and Hecuba, his wailing wife:

> "Unequal match'd,
> Pyrrhus at Priam drives, in rage strikes wide,
> But with the whiff and wind of his fell sword
> Th' unnerved father falls. Then senseless Ilium,
> Seeming to feel this blow, with flaming top
> Stoops to his base, and with a hideous crash
> Takes prisoner Pyrrhus' ear." (II. ii. 471–77)

The consequences of the death of so mythic a father and king are universal throughout Troy. An act as grievous as Pyrrhus' to the harmonious structure of a world must have consequences as deep as human nature can feel. Even he, bent on destruction, must for a time give over his next action as he listens to the discord. His sword "'seemed i' th' air to stick'" (II. ii. 479). He becomes a figure from a static art form, "'a painted tyrant?'" (II. ii. 480): "'And, like a neutral to his will and matter, / Did nothing'" (II. ii. 481–82). We see motion arrested, frozen to static gesture, in a man at once willing and unwilling to commit a murder so outrageous to the world's wholeness. But the break in movement is only temporary. "'A roused vengeance'" (II. ii. 488) for his father Achilles stifles all remorse, and Pyrrhus' sword takes its blood to the universal horror of the gods:

> "Out, out, thou strumpet Fortune! All you gods,
> In general synod take away her power!
> Break all the spokes and fellies from her wheel,
> And bowl the round nave down the hill of heaven
> As low as to the fiends!" (II. ii. 493–97)

The strumpet Fortune must be blamed for the murder, and the gods must see her consigned to hell for her part in the rending scene.

At this point Polonius, not drawn into the art because he

does not see himself in it, objects to the length. Hamlet squelches the outburst—"he's for a jig or a tale of bawdry, or he sleeps. Say on" (II. ii. 500–501)—and demands that the player move on to Hecuba. Hamlet cannot forego the third side of the triangle, the immediate sufferer of the destructive play of murderer and victim. It is Hecuba, the universal mother with " 'all o'er-teemed loins' " (II. ii. 508), who with her clamor can bring all passion to remorse and move heaven to tears.

Pyrrhus is the most stereotyped of Adversaries. The impulse to universal destruction is in him a purpose black as the night (II. ii. 453), ready to be born from inside the Trojan horse—the chief example of false-seeming in mythology. For Hamlet, the reenactment of this primary example of the Adversary's power produces an ambivalent reaction. The father Priam is his own father, destroyed by the Adversary Claudius. Yet Hecuba, the wife and mother, is Gertrude, not only the wife of King Hamlet but of Claudius as well, and the arrested motion of Pyrrhus' sword above the head of Priam represents Hamlet himself neutralized between desire and action. Should he arm himself with a revenger's sword, he too will be the murderer of a king and stepfather. He too will be a Pyrrhus, an Adversary who can unstring the possible harmony of his world.

Hamlet's soliloquy following this illuminating play shows him caught between his two needs: the first to avenge his father and complete his role in the old revenge play, and the second to know that what he does is right and proper for himself and for his society. Cued by the player's tears for Hecuba, Hamlet laments his own inaction in a greater cause:

> What would he do
> Had he the motive and the cue for passion
> That I have? He would drown the stage with tears,
> And cleave the general ear with horrid speech,
> Make mad the guilty, and appall the free,
> Confound the ignorant, and amaze indeed
> The very faculties of eyes and ears. (II. ii. 560–66)

Before him is an example of the power of play to present to its audience an image of itself so clearly that all eyes and ears will be drawn into the speaking vision presented to them. Hamlet does not assert that the player, had he Hamlet's motives, would take his sword and kill the offender. He asserts that the player would present the picture before the actors of the original offense and produce affectively in that audience the vision of truth that leads to redemption for the redeemable. He would teach them through his own performance.

It follows logically, then, that Hamlet, an apprentice player of great quality, would leap into the art he believes in so profoundly and do for others what this play has done for him. All the self-recriminations past, Hamlet faces the issue squarely:

> About, my brains! Hum—I have heard
> That guilty creatures sitting at a play
> Have by the very cunning of the scene
> Been strook so to the soul, that presently
> They have proclaim'd their malefactions:
> For murther, though it have no tongue, will speak
> With most miraculous organ. I'll have these players
> Play something like the murther of my father
> Before mine uncle. I'll observe his looks,
> I'll tent him to the quick. If 'a do blench,
> I know my course. The spirit that I have seen
> May be a dev'l, and the dev'l hath power
> T' assume a pleasing shape, yea, and perhaps,
> Out of my weakness and my melancholy,
> As he is very potent with such spirits,
> Abuses me to damn me. I'll have grounds
> More relative than this—the play's the thing
> Wherein I'll catch the conscience of the King. (II. ii. 588–605)

Hamlet is caught between two interpretations of his own inaction. He can see it as a cowardly refusal to do what he should, or he can see it as an important hesitation before an act that must be proven just. The first reading of his actions holds no force for him. After he accuses himself of cowardice, he calls himself an ass and sets his brain to the real issue—to prove to himself that the murder requested of him will not be the act of a Pyrrhus. Hateful as Claudius is to him, Hamlet is more interested in making the guilty mad, in catching his conscience, in presenting to him the image of himself, than in the act of revenge. Through play, Hamlet believes he can accomplish all that he must to please his father, his society, and himself. He can fix Claudius' guilt as real and not the illusion of a devil tempting him to senseless destruction; he can demonstrate the justice for an act of murder; and, most important, he can rid the society from which he has alienated himself of the guilt and hypocrisy that make it a world of seeming. There is one necessary condition of his play's ultimate success, however. If he is successful in making mad the guilty and appalling the free, he must then assume the leadership of his community and destroy or convert the Adversary in its midst.

Even though Hamlet has not completed his apprenticeship to play—he is still not possessed by the vision of possible harmony in his world—his next soliloquy demonstrates that he has changed meaningfully from his first appearance in the play. Before his confrontation with his father's ghost, Hamlet's view of life's turmoil was personal and despairing—"O that this too too sallied flesh would melt, / Thaw, and resolve itself into a dew! / Or that the Everlasting had not fix'd / His canon 'gainst self-slaughter!" (I. ii. 129–32). His preoccupation with his mother's betrayal had turned his personal world into an unweeded garden possessed by the corrupted and corrupting. In black garb, firmly allied to his father, Hamlet desired the end of his obsessive vision of human frailty, an end he saw possible only in death. But from the time of his interview with the Ghost, Hamlet has in solitude and soliloquy reached beyond his personal crisis into the realm where all people experience the brunt of evil.

From considering his own suicide, Hamlet passes to the

broader question of existence. He has finally found the proper question:

> To be, or not to be, that is the question:
> Whether 'tis nobler in the mind to suffer
> The slings and arrows of outrageous fortune,
> Or to take arms against a sea of troubles,
> And by opposing, end them. (III. i. 55–59)

In the broadest terms of human experience, Hamlet questions the comparative nobility of passive acceptance of grievous fortune—the Fortune so recently given the responsibility for the death of Priam—and of active assault on fortune with death as the possible result. He no longer poses the question of life in personal terms. In his disguise, Hamlet has become aware that his problems are everyone's problems. The play world, which allows the possibility of one becoming all, has instilled in Hamlet a keen perception of his plight as common to all men. He is no longer Hamlet, the son of a murdered father and a hypocritical mother; he is anyone faced with vices that surround and wound him, confronting the ultimate question—to be, or not to be.

The extent to which Hamlet's present thoughts include the plight of others is evident in his list of fortune's slings and arrows:

> For who would bear the whips and scorns of time,
> Th' oppressor's wrong, the proud man's contumely,
> The pangs of despis'd love, the law's delay,
> The insolence of office, and the spurns
> That patient merit of th' unworthy takes,
> When he himself might his quietus make
> With a bare bodkin. (III. i. 69–75)

It would be better, he concludes, not to be, were it not that we may face worse ills after death than we face in life. He has depersonalized and made broadly applicable the feelings that he had expressed earlier in his "O, that this too too sallied flesh would melt" soliloquy. In his role as cipher, Hamlet has experienced all fortune's wounds, although they are not all his as Hamlet, Prince of Denmark. He has seen injustice where it lurks for other people in other situations, not only those that are narrowly his own. Because human beings do not know the place they flee to, they are caught in the plight of being, fearful of taking the action that will end their troubles. And so, if it is cowardice that prevents Hamlet from following his father's command or from making his own end, it is a human cowardice based on a human philosophical doubt. The play of Priam's murder has helped to extend his own consciousness to other people, so that his conclusion is inclusive rather than restrictive:

> Thus conscience does make cowards of us all,
> And thus the native hue of resolution
> Is sicklied o'er with the pale cast of thought,
> And enterprises of great pitch and moment
> With this regard their currents turn awry,
> And lose the name of action. (III. i. 82–87)

Indeed, what stops a person from performing an action of great pitch and moment is what keeps Hamlet still in his dormant state, short of becoming a Player-King. Even though the play he engages in is based on the ability of one person to become all, he still formulates his human possibilities in terms of either/or: either to be or not to be, either to suffer or to take arms. Not yet can he find it in himself to transform his world into play's neither/nor–both/and: neither to be nor not to be; to be by not being; to suffer and not to suffer by taking and not taking arms. Although he is not responsible for the revenge play bequeathed him, Hamlet, like the Adversary Bullingbrook, is caught between two art forms—one a haunting past, the other a wishful future. And so he moves to the Mousetrap, which will expose the corrupt to themselves, without the full understanding of what to do with the results that he achieves. Hamlet, still caught in his mind's either/or, has found the way to make mad the guilty, but he has not yet found the way to make them free.

The Mousetrap

In leaping at the opportunity to demonstrate his own awareness and thus unburden himself of the vices and guilts that he carries within himself for his whole society, Hamlet moves prematurely into play. His art becomes the medium for personal release but not the medium of social redemption. His play strips from Denmark the guise of seeming and presents it with a moving picture of what it really is. In order to make that vision the vehicle of permanent change, Hamlet must then step into power, pick up the strands of awareness, and create his society's vision in play. But he does not. He is satisfied with the immediate gratification of watching the emotional effect of his play on Gertrude and especially on Claudius, not realizing that to reveal himself beneath his disguise without rendering the Adversary powerless is to write his own death. All that Hamlet's play accomplishes, then, is to expose the raw nerves of passion beneath the seeming rationality of the court and to turn those passions against him.

Aesthetically, Hamlet handles his play with care. His admonitions to the players before the Mousetrap's performance assume the play's wholeness and a desire to keep all parts subservient to it. The speeches are to be delivered smoothly, with natural emphasis. Hamlet, in opposing the style of acting that tears a passion to tatters (III. ii. 9–10), expresses his disapproval of an acting style that imitates acting and not nature. He speaks against the Platonic lie where the performance is an imitation of an imitation. Passion, as he well knows, is in nature mingled with rational conduct. He wants a performance through which all will realize "that one may smile, and smile, and be a villain" (I. v. 108). Nor should passion be expressed too tamely, for then the disguise stays on and the revelation of the state of feeling is not communicated to the audience:

> for any thing so o'erdone is from the purpose of playing, whose end, both at the first and now, was and is, to hold as 'twere the mirror up to nature: to show virtue her feature, scorn her own image, and the very age and body of the time his form and pressure.
>
> (III. ii. 19–24)

At the heart of Hamlet's philosophy of play is the concept that the player creates images of himself and his society in order to mirror back to an audience's conscience—its center of feeling and judgment—the vices that need correction and the virtues that need strengthening. Play is an instrument of correction, a mirror of conscience, and a revitalizer of ideals. It establishes the patterns of human life in order to bring them closer to the perfection of the prelapsarian pattern, in which a person is no longer trapped and isolated within himself like the Adversary but free to see through the eyes of others not what *seems* but what *is*. Passion and reason must be mingled in play because through passion the audience can experience the feelings of others and through reason judge them.

Hamlet's concern for his play—the playwright's careful supervision of his art's performance—brings to him a sense of release and fulfillment that eases the burden of keeping his own passions hidden. Before the play begins, he freely, even gaily, expresses himself in the terms of play to the people around him who matter most. First he affirms Horatio's freedom from a corrupting imbalance of passion and reason:

> and blest are those
> Whose blood and judgment are so well co-meddled,
> That they are not a pipe for Fortune's finger
> To sound what stop she please. Give me that man
> That is not passion's slave, and I will wear him

In my heart's core, ay, in my heart of heart,
As I do thee. (III. ii. 68–74)

In Horatio, Hamlet finds the man who is immune to obsession.
The passions that produced the revenge tragedy that Hamlet
is forced to act in—and so forced to shape his own passions
to—are not Horatio's. Fortune, that strumpet responsible for
Priam's death and the fall of Troy, cannot play on him. Only in
Horatio can Hamlet find the perfect human mixture of reason
and passion that places a person above the vicissitudes of daily
events.

In turning from him to the King, who has entered, Hamlet
responds literally to the innocuous question "How fares our
cousin Hamlet?":

Excellent, i' faith, of the chameleon's dish: I eat the air, promise-
cramm'd—you cannot feed capons so. (III. ii. 93–95)

Hamlet announces his principle of disguise. The tame, cas-
trated rooster eats his food from his executioner's hand; Hamlet is not that obedient neutral but rather the elusive chameleon
who disguises himself in the color of his habitat as protection
against a predator. His food is air, crammed with the promise
of release from hiding. With Polonius, Hamlet again brings up
the subject of playing, bringing to light Polonius' acting of
Caesar at the university. The two players, Polonius and Hamlet, have divided on the issue of loyalty—whether it rests in
the authority of government or in the freedom of the individual. The fate of Caesar, soon the fate of the man who takes
the role of Caesar on himself, is murder at the hands of a fellow
Roman. And with Ophelia, once his possible wife, Hamlet acts
out his disillusionment with women, again reaching into her
modesty for the seeds of lust that he assumes must be there.
She, too, he assumes, is in disguise. Before the Mousetrap begins, Hamlet confirms his appraisal of the real models on which
his portraits are based: Horatio, the ideal and balanced man;

Claudius, the predatory tyrant; Polonius, the arm of tyranny; Ophelia (and Gertrude in her), the shameless temporizer.

The play itself is about passion and self-interest. Its first purpose is to bring Hamlet's vision of his society's corruption to the view of the court, and so to put their own hypocrisies and failures before their eyes. In Hamlet's own pursuit of play, this purpose is strong. The second purpose, however, is equally strong, even though it is motivated by the Ghost through Hamlet—to bring into the open the secret guilt of Claudius and to confirm the Ghost's report of his murder. Hamlet sees his Mousetrap as ideally combining the two. But the play is a too-close imitation of the actual events of the elder Hamlet's death, thinly disguised as the murder of Gonzago. In his failure to restructure those events around the possibility of penitence and absolution, Hamlet dooms himself and his society to the old revenge form.

Within the play, Hamlet portrays all the villainies that surround him. Gertrude's hypocrisy, which Hamlet has extended to Ophelia, is exposed in the Player-Queen. Claudius' hidden villainy is brought to light in the murderer Lucianus. Hamlet is also the source of the Player-King's lines of wisdom, in which the whole court of pestering hypocrites lives:

> The violence of either grief or joy
> Their own enactures with themselves destroy.
> Where joy most revels, grief doth most lament;
> Grief joys, joy grieves, on slender accident.
> This world is not for aye, nor 'tis not strange
> That even our loves should with our fortunes change:
> For 'tis a question left us yet to prove,
> Whether love lead fortune, or else fortune love.
> The great man down, you mark his favorite flies,
> The poor advanc'd makes friends of enemies.
> And hitherto doth love on fortune tend,
> For who not needs shall never lack a friend,
> And who in want a hollow friend doth try,

Directly seasons him his enemy.
But orderly to end where I begun,
Our wills and fates do so contrary run
That our devices still are overthrown,
Our thoughts are ours, their ends none of our own.
(III. ii. 196–213)

The strange, unnatural mixture of grief and joy, present as a mark of Denmark's corruption, the Player-King points to as passions that are housed within each other in a fallen, ephemeral world. Fortune, the villainess of Troy, the ancient symbol of a fallen world, becomes the touchstone for corrupted human nature. Love, friendship, gratitude all fly when fortune leaves. Polonius, formerly the elder Hamlet's councilor, fled with all his loyalty to Claudius; Hamlet's hollow friends Rosencrantz and Guildenstern, when tried by the test of self-interest, turned into his enemies; Gertrude's love was given to the man who defeated her husband.

In the final couplet of the Player-King's speech, Hamlet has synopsized his own fate; for his thoughts, as profound and knowing as they are, do not create the end they intended in the play. Since Lucianus is Gonzago's nephew, not his brother, Hamlet has extended his double awareness of Pyrrhus as both Claudius and potentially himself into his own play. In acting out the murder, Hamlet as Lucianus is releasing himself from his own murderous impulses, thus dissipating the passions necessary for the disposal of Claudius.[8] He is experiencing a kind of premature catharsis. And by becoming both murderer and victim simultaneously—Pyrrhus and Priam, the elder Hamlet and Claudius—Hamlet has fulfilled his view of the

8. Ernest Jones, *Hamlet and Oedipus* (New York: Norton, 1949), 88–89, discusses another psychological reason for Hamlet's taking on the role of Lucianus by pointing out that his Oedipal tie to his mother would inevitably bind his sense of identity to Claudius. Levin, *The Question of "Hamlet,"* 88, sees the change as a preview of Hamlet's revenge more than as a reenactment of the murder. Yet this association of himself with Lucianus cannot have such simple psychological results for Hamlet.

world where anyone has within him the possibilities of everyone else's virtues and sins. Yet that vision fails to provide for
the Danish court and for Hamlet himself the necessary road to
communal harmony. The performance of Hamlet's awareness
lacks a pattern for the continuation of life. By taking on himself
the roles of both the sinner and the sinned against, he has focused all Denmark's ills on himself. He has placed himself in
the role of sacrifice, paving the way for Denmark's release
through his own death.

The missing culmination of Hamlet's vision, where play can
bring not only the revelation of evil but the full harmony of
goodness, creates a violent effect in the audience. It releases
the passions long pent beneath the rational-seeming court, but
it does not shape them to the end of harmony. Those passions,
not yet corrected of their self-interest, will turn on Hamlet just
as they turned on his father. This Mousetrap has embarrassed
the court and caused Claudius anguish, but it has also caught
its creator. Hamlet too is lured by the bait—release from his
burden—and he too is caught in the trap. In his joy at the
play's seeming success, Hamlet asks Horatio whether the play
would not win him fellowship in a company of players, and
Horatio answers, "Half a share" (III. ii. 279). Horatio is quite
right. Hamlet has not made himself complete, as he thought
he would, by the play. Gertrude is still unredeemed, as are the
serviceable Polonius and the treacherous Rosencrantz and
Guildenstern. Claudius falls to his knees, but only to rise more
steeped in his guilt than before and now armed with
knowledge.

Indeed, Hamlet's play has only hardened the guilty in their
vices. Because he has forced them to see themselves, they
now pursue their own ends in full cognizance of their flaws.
He has infected his audience with the passions they had previously denied. Hamlet has not managed to fuse his own obligations with his responsibility to the Ghost after all. They are
still separate, and both remain to be carried out. But in the

meantime, Hamlet has put off his disguise; Claudius knows what lurks beneath the seeming madness. When Hamlet, confident of his complete success, foregoes the opportunity to kill the King at prayer, he has sealed his own doom. He has finally cut himself off from his cycle of alienation, extension of being, and redemption by forcing himself out of the first phases into the last too soon. It is now Claudius' turn to take action.[9]

The passion beneath Hamlet's antic disguise also releases itself after the play. Hamlet, misguided in his belief that he has succeeded in his play, becomes overconfident of his ultimate success. He reveals himself further to Rosencrantz-Guildenstern with his recorder play; goes to his mother feeling within him the possibility of violence; foregoes the opportunity to kill Claudius at prayer in the confidence that he can pick his own time now that all is well. The passions that have been released in him do in fact culminate in action, not in front of the entire community for whom he should stage himself but before Gertrude alone. Following through on his artistic philosophy that to correct vice is to hold the mirror up to its face and let it see its own ugliness, Hamlet presents himself to his mother with just such an intent:

> Come, come, and sit you down, you shall not boudge;
> You go not till I set you up a glass
> Where you may see the inmost part of you. (III. iv. 18–20)

9. Francis Fergusson, *The Idea of a Theater* (Princeton: Princeton University Press, 1949), 126–33, has discussed Hamlet's play-within-the-play as "the basic vision of human action in the play," exposing all of its actors. It is "[Hamlet's] own black mass, his own parody of a rite." This view reinforces the idea that the Mousetrap's vision falls short of redemption, merely parodying redemptive play by fixing on the revelation of past sins without extending them into future, penitent action. In his Mousetrap, Fergusson states, Hamlet has—like Duke Vincentio and Prospero— used the theater improvisationally as a trap for Claudius' conscience and as a test of his own and the Ghost's vision. But Hamlet has stumbled on this method without clearly understanding what he has accomplished. "We are certainly intended to feel that Hamlet, however darkly and uncertainly he worked, had discerned the way to be obedient to his deepest values, and accomplished some sort of purgatorial progress for himself and Denmark."

At that point Polonius, secreted behind the arras where he is directing and observing his latest play, inopportunely breaks the illusion and cries for help, and Hamlet, his passions active, stabs him to death. Hamlet's only immediate response is "Thou wretched, rash, intruding fool, farewell! / I took thee for thy better. Take thy fortune" (III. iv. 31–32). Unlike Horatio's, Polonius' passion and judgment are imperfectly mixed and he becomes a pipe which fortune's finger has stopped. Polonius' death is Hamlet's first action in breaking down the circumvallation of Claudius' spies and moving one step closer to the source of Denmark's corruption.

But it is not the Ghost's revenge that concerns Hamlet most at this moment. Rather it is the root of his obsession, the one act that destroyed his personal world's order and made it a rank, unweeded garden—his mother's lustful marriage. Intent upon instructing and correcting that fault, and so beginning the redemption of his society where its degeneration began for him, Hamlet pursues his mother's self-image, destroys it, and presents her with the image of the real self hidden behind the seeming virtue. It is she who has committed

> Such an act
> That blurs the grace and blush of modesty,
> Calls virtue hypocrite, takes off the rose
> From the fair forehead of an innocent love
> And sets a blister there, makes marriage vows
> As false as dicers' oaths, O, such a deed
> As from the body of contraction plucks
> The very soul, and sweet religion makes
> A rhapsody of words. Heaven's face does glow
> O'er this solidity and compound mass
> With heated visage, as against the doom;
> Is thought-sick at the act. (III. iv. 40–51)

In her submission to Claudius, Gertrude has corrupted all the world. Through her sin, all women have fallen, all loves, all marriages. She has taken what is heaven-directed—the spiritual feeling between lovers—and plucked out its soul. The earth faces its doom again, as it faced it with the first frail woman's fall, and in shame and anger the face of heaven itself confronts the act. Hamlet echoes the player's speech on Hecuba: in her all that was virtuous in human love expressed itself until heaven answered; in Gertrude all that is weak and self-deluding acted itself out until heaven's visage heated "as against the doom." Gertrude was a motive for her husband's murder. Without her final compliance, Claudius' wickedness could not have acted itself out in the usurpation of crown and wife.

But in Hamlet's pursuit of Gertrude's redemption, he has again focused on the past without bringing hope for the future. His obsession has drawn him into its center, and there he dwells until his father's spirit enters, reminding Hamlet of his obligation and telling him to step between Gertrude and her fighting soul. Once more he grasps Hamlet's arm as his own, demanding his own last act and ignoring Hamlet's need to make it also the first act of a new play. He is not interested in Hamlet or in Gertrude, whose very salvation lies in her struggling with her soul and winning the struggle. Although Hamlet's plays tend to remain thematically fixed in the past's sins, he is struggling towards future redemption. The Ghost, however, is interested simply in his need for vengeance. When, at his request, Hamlet does speak kindly to his mother, she returns to her former hypocrisy, blaming Hamlet's words on his madness. In order to make her face her guilt, Hamlet must go back and reiterate her sins. The Ghost has led him astray from his purpose, separating again what Hamlet has striven to unite—his own pursuit of justice and redemption and his father's pursuit of vengeance. Hamlet has wanted to save the living half of his family; his father demands vengeance for the dead. Hamlet still strives to accomplish both, successful in moving Gertrude to penitence and a promise to sin no more. He has saved at least one corrupted being—for him, the most important one.

When his burst of passion, released by his play, is over, Hamlet again contemplates the body of Polonius. As Brutus killed Caesar, so Hamlet kills Polonius, unleashing the chaos of tyranny and murder. Hamlet has abandoned the safety of isolation and disguise in his Mousetrap and, with that play, has committed himself to action. The murder of Polonius is the first action he takes, and it draws him into the guilt of the world that he had wanted to keep at bay. Hamlet is now not only a victim of his society; he also partakes of its guilt:

> For this same lord,
> I do repent; but heaven hath pleas'd it so
> To punish me with this, and this with me,
> That I must be their scourge and minister.
> I will bestow him, and will answer well
> The death I gave him. (III. iv. 172–77)

With the failure of his play to cleanse the world, Hamlet takes on himself the task of destroying it; his will be the heated visage of doom. With Gertrude saved for heaven, he is willing to become scourge and minister, the man who will work at punishing the guilty in heaven's name but who will also answer for the deaths he deals. At the moment of the Mousetrap's performance, his self-education in play had reached an understanding of universal human frailty and of his own participation in that frailty. The Player-King also sees the universal human yearning for perfection and shapes it, using frail lives as his media. Hamlet's progress as a Player-King has been blocked before he reaches the latter stage. He has taken on himself the naked viciousness of the people around him until he cannot believe that any other facets of human nature exist. He has turned erring humans into either saved or damned souls.

Chaos Come Again

 Hamlet's play unleashes all the lurking passions in Denmark, both in himself and in his audience. It confirms Claudius as an Adversary, hardening his resolve to keep the gains he has won through murder and deception. It occasions Hamlet's murder of Polonius, thus clearing the stage of one surrogate Adversary, and it occasions, too, his indirect murder of Rosencrantz and Guildenstern, the two-headed other surrogate Adversary. It makes the populace rebellious, and it breaks Ophelia's hold on sanity.

Ophelia's innocence of the chasm between seeming and being produces madness when she is forced to face it in the events following Hamlet's wake:

> "How should I your true-love know
>   From another one?
> By his cockle hat and staff,
>   And his sandal shoon." (IV. v. 23–26)
> Lord, we know what we are, but know not what we may be.
>   (IV. v. 43–44)

In her madness, Ophelia epitomizes the destruction of all that was virtuous in her society. She metaphorically encompasses within her songs the conflict between true love and lust, between harsh reality and comforting appearance; and with the flowers that she bestows on each member of her audience, she presents the poisonous mixture that produced the tragic world she lives in—remembrance, thoughts, flattery, ingratitude, sorrow, and faithlessness. The violets—faithfulness—all withered when her father died. She has no one left to be faithful to; her own virtues died when there was no one to play them to.

When Hamlet's play did not culminate in the cleansing of Denmark, it dissolved the potential harmonies of life in a cacophony of individual passions. Claudius is troubled by insurrection among his people, but Hamlet is not there to guide them to Claudius' destruction. He has abandoned that role to Laertes, who shares his initial predicament. Laertes, a straightforward, unthinking man, is readily swayed by Claudius' apparent innocence and becomes what his father was before him—an easily directed actor whom Claudius fashions into a hunting dog. If anything demonstrates the justice of Hamlet's hesitancy to act immediately on the Ghost's cue, it is the consequence of Laertes' too-ready acceptance of the role of revenger. Claudius, too, is caught in the chaos that Hamlet has unleashed; it takes him an entire act to force his world back to the shape of his will. By the time Hamlet arrives back in Denmark, the force of the Adversary has turned against him with all his strength, knowing that Hamlet, naked of his disguise, is the enemy.

The first setting for Hamlet after his return from his death voyage is the graveyard where Ophelia is to be interred. There Hamlet finds the gravest philosopher of all, a man who responds literally to Hamlet's questions, the first person in the drama who does not play at being other than what he is:

> *Ham.*   What man dost thou dig it for?
> *1. Clo.*   For no man, sir.
> *Ham.*   What woman then?
> *1. Clo.*   For none neither.
> *Ham.*   Who is to be buried in't?
> *1. Clo.*   One that was a woman, sir, but, rest her soul, she's dead.
> *Ham.*   How absolute the knave is! we must speak by the card, or equivocation will undo us.
>
> (V. i. 130–38)

The gravedigger's resistance to understanding the motive behind Hamlet's questions produces a comic effect like that generated by the interview between Hamlet and Polonius. Both he and Hamlet are philosophers, intent on arriving at the truth behind words:

Ham.	How came he [Hamlet] mad?
1. Clo.	Very strangely, they say.
Ham.	How strangely?
1. Clo.	Faith, e'en with losing his wits.
Ham.	Upon what ground?
1. Clo.	Why, here in Denmark. (V. i. 156–61)

In all the drama's activity towards discovering the cause of Hamlet's madness, no conjecture comes nearer to the truth than the clown's absolute acceptance of it. His philosophical training comes from observing the great world in its remains; he has mastered firsthand the supremacy of reality over seeming.

For Hamlet, who has returned to Denmark marked for death and feeling the premonitions of it, he is a valuable tutor. Through the mystery of gravedigging, Hamlet sees what all the disguises and role-playing come to at last: the lawyer's quiddities, the landowner's fines, the lady's painting—all are resolved in a final justice. Rank and occupation are leveled before the clown's shovel. The issue is made personal for Hamlet with the discovery that the unfleshed skull tossed out of the ground is Yorick's, the jester who was Hamlet's childhood playmate:

> Where be your gibes now, your gambols, your songs, your flashes of merriment, that were wont to set the table on a roar? Not one now to mock your own grinning—quite chop-fall'n. (V. i. 189–92)

Under the tutelage of the natural philosopher—the gravedigger—on the one hand, and the learned philosopher—Horatio—on the other, Hamlet learns to accept the process of life into death. His attempt to find justice in his own world through his play failed him because he did not form it as a disinterested party, an unclouded medium for truth. Now, having lost the possibility for redeeming his world on this side of the grave, he learns a faith that justice will ultimately be done. The scene is highly medieval in its use of the motifs of *ubi sunt* and the dance of death, and it is a medieval sense of justice that Hamlet learns to accept. The judgment passed on the flesh is unswerving; Alexander's greatness may indeed be reduced to the loam stopping a bunghole.

On the heels of this revelation, Hamlet finds that the grave that lies open before him is Ophelia's. Like him, she fell victim to their world's corruption, but her insanity and death are Hamlet's responsibility. Polonius' death made him a full member of that murderous world. But after his confrontation with death in the graveyard, he can no longer bear the posturings of grief and the stylized words that come too easily to comfort the living.[10] He rejects all seeming, even innocent self-deception like Laertes', and is moved for the first time in the drama to state his identity in clear, unambiguous terms:

> What is he whose grief
> Bears such an emphasis, whose phrase of sorrow
> Conjures the wand'ring stars and makes them stand
> Like wonder-wounded hearers? This is I,
> Hamlet the Dane! (V. i. 254–58)

Another player has made the heavens stand still in his enactment of overwhelming grief, but Hamlet now has abandoned the player's stance. He no longer gives himself the title of prince or the title of madman, and he asks this death-oriented world as well to announce itself clearly here where all pomp and deceit drop away. He warns Laertes that while he is not

---

10. Rose, "*Hamlet* and the Shape of Revenge," 141–42, notes that Laertes is a model revenger of the sort that tears a passion to tatters and that this view of Laertes accounts for Hamlet's annoyed reaction to him, a reaction manifested by Hamlet's matching him hyperbole for hyperbole. With Osric later as well, Hamlet shows that he can still play any role he wishes, but chooses not to in order to give his own style to the act of vengeance required of him.

"splenitive and rash," yet he has something dangerous in him which is to be feared (V. i. 261–63). Hamlet, scourge and minister of heaven, son of a father murdered and a mother stained, potential redeemer of a world—all identities fall away. His grappling with Laertes in Ophelia's grave and the whole Danish court's pilgrimage to the graveyard rehearse the play to come. The time has arrived for death, nature's universal judge, to take in hand the vicious and the virtuous and to finish the task that Hamlet had begun but left uncompleted.

Hamlet's own attitude towards life and justice has changed markedly since he forced himself out of disguise into the Mousetrap. He has released the tensions of a too-burdensome vision of evil, freed himself from disguise, and killed the figures who stood between him and Claudius. He has not, however, changed the world, nor has he taken vengeance for his father's murder. He is still as impatient with seemers as ever, as he demonstrates with both Laertes and Osric, but he is no longer moved to the art of playwriting. He has used it, but he has failed it. His play-within-the-play is not in the fifth act, as is Duke Vincentio's, or in the first, as is Henry V's, but in the third. His form remained embedded in the old play he had inherited, and so it stopped short of bringing his world into cooperation with a greater harmony.

Because of that failure, he has abandoned the pursuit of human justice for a faith in eschatological justice. In telling Horatio of his disposal of Rosencrantz and Guildenstern, Hamlet asserts a master plot that supersedes all human machinations:

> Rashly—
> And prais'd be rashness for it—let us know
> Our indiscretion sometime serves us well
> When our deep plots do pall, and that should learn us
> There's a divinity that shapes our ends,
> Rough-hew them how we will. (V. ii. 6–11)

He has the specific issues before him clearly in focus. He understands that he has been "benetted round with villainies," that he has entered the scene after the play was begun: "Or I could make a prologue to my brains, / They had begun the play" (V. ii. 30–31).[11] He has personal warrant now for Claudius' death, and he strikes from his conscience both his intention to kill him and his indirect murder of Rosencrantz and Guildenstern: "Why, man, they did make love to this employment" (V. ii. 57). He lists Claudius' several sins and finds his own cause just. No longer pressured by time, since he has already been cut off from his own living redemption, he abandons plots and plays to assert that "a man's life's no more than to say 'one'" (V. ii. 74).

Hamlet's new mood is a quietude that is reasonable and dispassionate. With Horatio, he has made his claim to heaven, justified his cause and his personal actions, and left the resolution's time and place to the divinity that shapes our ends. When Osric arrives to circumlocute the news of the bet placed on a fencing match between him and Laertes, Hamlet begins by mirroring back Osric's absurdity (V. ii. 117–25); then, aware of the futility of trying to change the butterfly, his perspective changes to the gravedigger's, whose exact reading of words Hamlet adopts:

Ham.	What's his weapon?
Osr.	Rapier and dagger.
Ham.	That's two of his weapons—but well.

(V. ii. 144–46)

He forces Osric to define his words—"carriages," "impawn'd"— questions the definitions, and at last patiently lets him go. There hangs about Hamlet a new sense of peace derived from

11. Charles R. Forker, "Shakespeare's Theatrical Symbolism and Its Function in *Hamlet*," *Shakespeare Quarterly*, XIV (1963), 227, states: "[This] metaphor summarizes Hamlet's tragic predicament and indicates his progress through the drama—the symbolic advance from thought to action."

the faith that he can count on divine justice to use him in its own cause without his having to stir. He has sloughed off the awesome responsibility of establishing justice himself. From this new passivity, Hamlet speaks of the premonition that he acknowledges but will not obey:

> There is special providence in the fall of a sparrow. If it be now, 'tis not to come; if it be not to come, it will be now; if it be not now, yet it will come—the readiness is all. Since no man, of aught he leaves, knows what is't to leave betimes, let be. (V. ii. 219–24)

The grave has taught him that human glory is evanescent in the face of inevitable decay. No one can deny death or the special providence that uses it as assistant. Since Hamlet cannot create the divine pattern from within his play, providence—that ultimate creator and final audience—will assume the role of playwright.[12]

The final scene comes to fulfill an almost aching anticipation of the deaths that must occur. In contrast to the fumbles and hesitations that mark the preceding acts, it moves like clockwork. Hamlet continues to make his peace with life by apologizing to Laertes and calling him brother, blaming all his supposed errors on his madness—the disguise that marked his original quest for order in a vice-ridden world. Laertes' proud response, that he cannot accept Hamlet's apology as fulfillment of a matter of honor until he has authority for it, serves as a foil to Hamlet's own exploration of an uncharted land where no authority exists. Unlike Laertes, Hamlet has understood enough about the nature of evil both outside and within himself to rely on the simple act of humility over the strong

---

12. Harold Fisch, *"Hamlet" and the Word: The Covenant Pattern in Shakespeare* (New York: Frederick Ungar, 1971), 165, also views this last act as God's play: "The great stage play which is ultimately intuited by Hamlet and for which the grave-diggers provide us with the essential terms is no other than the covenant history of the world, considered as a great plan of Providence unfolding in a Biblical dimension of time and place."

voice of precedent.[13] Yet that dangerous something waits in
Hamlet. He is a man on the brink of the grave, a man who can
no longer bring any who adhere to him back to life. When Gertrude drinks to his fortune, she takes into herself the poison
meant for him. When Laertes "against [his] conscience" pursues Hamlet with the tainted foil, the poison turns back on
him. The Adversary can succeed in destroying his enemy only
at the cost of losing the world that they both struggled for. As
Gertrude dies and Laertes, dying, points the blame to the king,
Hamlet finally raises his hand to return to its originator all the
poison in the realm.[14] Stabbed by the envenomed sword and
choked with the poisoned wine, Claudius loses in an instant
his crown, his queen, his life, and his soul. Hamlet has caught
him in the full evil of his nature and proved indeed that a
"man's life's no more than to say 'one.'"

But the moment of his own possible return to life has also
passed. What remains is to make assurances that these deaths
will pass on to those still living as a story of justice. What Hamlet could not bring together in life—his father's demand for
vengeance and his own demand for justice—he unites in death.
He could not transform life into redemptive play and live in
his own creation, but he can give his life as play for others to
learn from. He has acted in a play that will

> Make mad the guilty, and appall the free,
> Confound the ignorant, and amaze indeed
> The very faculties of eyes and ears. (II. ii. 564–66)

13. Wendy Coppedge Sanford, *Theater as Metaphor in "Hamlet"* (Cambridge:
Harvard University Press, 1967), 32, 44, discusses Hamlet's play-acting as developing his understanding and defining himself to the point where he can act, but finds
his view of human nature in Act V so restricted to the evil he has been mirroring, so
"one-sided," that the world order will no longer tolerate him. However, he seems to
have resigned himself to that order's ultimate goodness.

14. Helen Gardner, *The Business of Criticism* (Oxford: Clarendon Press, 1959),
47, notes that Hamlet kills Claudius only when Claudius' guilt is exposed publicly,
so that he is clearly an executioner and not an assassin.

For this reason Hamlet needs Horatio to absent himself from felicity a while. Time closes in on his need to render his own cause before the "mutes or audience to this act" (V. ii. 335). In his last moments of life, Hamlet returns to his desire to hold the mirror up to Nature—"O, I could tell you—" (V. ii. 337)— but resigns himself to the fell sergeant, Death, and his story to Horatio, the only man living who could render it as Hamlet would wish. And Horatio complies with both the message and the medium:

> give order that these bodies
> High on a stage be placed to the view,
> And let me speak to th' yet unknowing world
> How these things came about. So shall you hear
> Of carnal, bloody, and unnatural acts,
> Of accidental judgments, casual slaughters,
> Of deaths put on by cunning and forc'd cause,
> And in this upshot, purposes mistook
> Fall'n on th' inventors' heads: all this can I
> Truly deliver. (V. ii. 377–86)

As Hamlet's Player King stated in the Mousetrap, "Our thoughts are ours, their ends none of our own" (III. ii. 213).

Given the temperament of a player and an extreme personal crisis, Hamlet embarked on the road common to Shakespeare's Player-Kings. But the play had begun before him, and he became enmeshed in the conflicting needs of his own and his parents'—especially his father's—fulfillment. Hamlet was a dutiful son. But in order for him to be a part of life in the full sense that a Player-King must be, Hamlet had to pursue his own ends independently of his father's. The pressure of time and the court, deeply enmeshed in Claudius' medium of self-interest, forced Hamlet to the performance of play before he had discovered a vision of the universe's ultimate health, and therefore before he was ready to affirm and shape life. In uniting himself in play with his father through the Player King and with Claudius through Lucianus, Hamlet resigned himself to act out the roles of both murderer and victim. The Mousetrap does not end with justice, but with death. Hamlet neither placed the arm of justice within his play nor did he assume it himself afterwards. As a result, his play merely unleashed the ugly passions beneath the world of seeming reason. It brought chaos to his world and necessitated the scene of carnage that finally ended it. Because Hamlet did not have the time to save himself and Denmark from destruction, time and its fell sergeant Death arrested him. Hamlet's last moments in the drama are devoted to resigning his individual desire to enact justice to a new faith in the ultimate power of harmony in the universe. This power, which transmits itself to all those who become part of the larger scheme of life by abandoning their narrow selves, he did not understand in time to inform himself and his world. The tragedy of Hamlet is based on the loss of the potentially greatest Player-King in Shakespeare, a prince who "was likely, had he been put on, / To have prov'd most royal" (V. ii. 397–98).

Coriolanus: The Tragedy of a Recusant Player-King

The forfeit to tragedy is often a character who loves certainty in an uncertain world, who dedicates himself to a personal wholeness that he guards from public erosion. Like Hamlet, Coriolanus was born into a world he never made; but unlike Hamlet, he does not know it. Coriolanus has replaced the relative world, which can be an unweeded garden or a place inhabited by a divinity that shapes our ends, with an ideal one of his own imagining, one he can happily defend from harm since it is his own creation. Because he lives within its confines, he never sees the need to educate, change, or save the one outside him; indeed he does not choose to see it at all.

During the course of the play, however, that other world announces itself in ways he cannot ignore: patricians are scorned by rabble; warriors' deeds are forgotten in peace; and his own friends and family demand compromise. But despite shifting times and loyalties, Coriolanus refuses to play in the world outside himself. Instead, he clings more tenaciously to the man he will always be—patrician, warrior, son; brave, superior, self-willed, intolerant—in the perfect world that never existed. He is a closed system, a static work of art that inspires awe rather than emulation, honest in Hotspur's manner and paradoxically corrupted by the same purity. Were it not for his innocence of duplicity, for his desire to master only his imaginary world rather than the real one, Coriolanus would be a Bullingbrook or a Shylock. But what he lacks is precisely the awareness of fallen nature—others' and his own. Because he does not accept the hypothesis that he is imperfect, he lacks sympathy for imperfection; because he is absolute, he cannot grow.

The drama that forms around him plays out his limited vision in its imagery and plot. The potential human forms, expressed first in metaphor and then in action, are all distortions: beasts, diseases, and fragments on the one hand, and gods, machines, and statues on the other.[15] Not merely the rabble—subject ever to Coriolanus' "kind word"—but Coriolanus himself frequently falls into the categories marked by predator and prey, parasite and host. To Coriolanus' exaggeratedly patrician

15. Clemen, The Development of Shakespeare's Imagery, 154–58, discusses these images of disease and bestiality surrounding the rabble and concludes that Shakespeare disliked the masses intensely. He notes, too, that Coriolanus is the focus of all discussion and action in the drama in his role as godlike hero. Clemen sees the two as simple contrasts, not accounting for the interrelatedness of these images. In Henry V, the common citizens are given great credit as soldiers because Henry is human in his dealings with them. Lawrence N. Danson, "Metonymy and Coriolanus," Philological Quarterly, LXII (1973), 30, perceives that "metonymy and synecdoche are figures of fragmentation and usurpation—of parts representing the whole and of the whole absorbing its parts—and that Coriolanus itself is a play about the relationship of the individual to the community, of the community to its constituent members, and of the association of man with man, and of man with the elements that compound him."

eye, the multitude are geese, hares, rats, minnows, curs, the beast with many heads, scabs, measles, boils; with their tribunes they fare little better—they are beasts whom nature teaches to know their friends. Coriolanus himself, however, receives the same manner of appellation from his enemies, the tribunes, who debate with Menenius whether he is a lamb or a bear, but refer to him in private as a sheep on whom they can sick the dogs of the commonalty.

Neither side knows which is the predator-host and which the prey-parasite. The citizens are convinced that all designs coming from the Senate have but one purpose: "If the wars eat us not up, they will; and there's all the love they bear us" (I. i. 85–86). And Menenius, the most vocal patrician, sees the rooted hatred that the people bear Coriolanus as similarly cannibalistic:

> *Men.*   Pray you, who does the wolf love?
> *Sic.*   The lamb.
> *Men.*   Ay, to devour him, as the hungry plebeians
>   would the noble Martius. (II. i. 7–10)

As in *The Merchant of Venice*, metaphoric cannibalism indicates a dangerously solipsistic world. But cannibalism is a concept that applies to this state of Rome only if the opposing factions consider one another human. The images they paint function rather to reduce the enemy to pests worthy of extermination or to cattle marked for slaughter.

Coriolanus alone is given another identity, as dehumanizing as the animal figures that sometimes depict him. When he is not a beast, he is a god—the divine creator of his own world. He has always embraced the image of his unnatural superiority—a Mars in war, an Olympian in peace. He has restricted his human life to the superhuman and the inhuman, never doubting that his blood, so visibly spilled on Rome's battlefield, is different from other men's. And this imagery of beast and god is not merely descriptive; it is deterministic. Since the metaphors supply a person with his possible selves, *Coriolanus*, fixed on images of life lower and higher than human, restricts the roles that anyone in the drama can enact to these.

Like the imagery, the plot that reflects Coriolanus is a closed and predetermined system. The occasions that could move him to embrace play and extend himself into the consciousness of others give him instead the occasions for rejecting any personal change. Again and again, he is given the chance to stop being himself and to become more, but each time the possibility arises, Coriolanus, in spite of public pressures, succumbs to the personal need to assert himself. Hamlet, although unsuccessful, demonstrates a craving to redeem his world and only too late becomes aware of time's victory over his efforts. He plays, but he plays in the past and cannot fulfill the future's need for a harmonic pattern to live by. Duke Vincentio picks up his lessons within seconds of his own and his city's demise and steps in to playwrite the action of *Measure for Measure*. But Coriolanus, given both time and opportunity, blinds himself to his own imperfections and categorically rejects his city's need for proper leadership. He is himself, and that, he believes, is all the city he needs.

His opportunities to enlarge his identity are marked by changes of clothing: first to the gown of humility as he stands for Consul; second to hat-in-hand before the enraged multitude; third to wanderer's clothing after his exile. Although each of his failures to change breeds change in the world around him, the turmoil occurs ironically because he has refused to change. In a dramatic world marked by assault from without and rebellion from within, where an entire society thirsts for a principle of form to guide it, Coriolanus—the only man capable of revealing that form—abrogates his responsibility as leader and, in his self-congratulating isolation, creates wider-spreading chaos. His is the tragedy of a man who will not extend his consciousness of self and so cannot understand humanity in any terms other than his own. Coriolanus, despite the opportunities, refuses to become a Player-King.[16]

Rome: The Enemy Within and the Enemy Without

Coriolanus' Rome, in peace or war, is ravaged by dissent. Like Henry IV's England, Rome knows only division wrought by an uncommunicative ruling class, figured notoriously in Caius Martius who, like Henry IV, is morbidly jealous of his prerogatives. Not guilt, however, but personal integrity closes him to public contact. A common man's humanity detracts from his own because he bases his not on the fallibility of all human nature but on the merits of his own nature—bravery and birthright. The essence of charity and justice taught by Portia, which lies in the ability to see oneself in others and to respond accordingly, he has denied in his rigid system of rewards based on merit. For Coriolanus, the act of single combat betrays not only his overwhelming denial of anyone else's worth, but also his self-imposed isolation from society. The same isolation caused Hotspur's and Hector's deaths. To Coriolanus either you are a patrician or you are a cur; he allows no Falstaff and no Francis to tutor him in the ways of common weakness.

As the play opens, Rome is suffering from a famine that threatens to wipe out much of the plebeian population. The drama's first words, uttered by a citizen, name Coriolanus as the cause of that starvation. Unreasonable as the accusation is, the citizens well know that this godlike warrior has only con-

---

16. Righter, *Shakespeare and the Idea of the Play*, 189, praises Coriolanus' inability to act other roles because she sees the images of play in *Coriolanus* as suggesting "futility and shame." They are so only because the fine art of playing as practiced by Henry V, Portia, and Duke Vincentio has been denied by Coriolanus and given over to people of limited vision—Menenius and the tribunes. See Proser, *The Heroic Image in Five Shakespearean Tragedies*, 135–41, 148, for a contrast to Righter's thesis. Proser understands Coriolanus' weakness as emanating from a self-definition too fixed in a public role and resulting in his inhumanity.

tempt for the ravages of hunger and disease in their midst; he has never known them nor will he accept them as his plagues. They belong to the common multitude; and he insists that no grain, which the citizens perceive the city has in store, should be meted out without the receivers' having proven their worth. What the citizens lack is an avenue of communication with the patricians—a voice—and since they lack it, their only recourse is open rebellion. Only one man at this point in the drama speaks to both patrician and plebeian—Menenius—and he, that "humorous patrician" who "loves a cup of hot wine with not a drop of allaying Tiber in't" (II. i. 47–49), speaks not out of concern but fear. Menenius, with his openly admitted weaknesses of temperament and age, has the ability to playwrite, as his tale of the belly demonstrates. He has not, however, the ability to make Coriolanus act in his tale, and so any salutary effects he creates are only temporary.

Besides, Menenius' organic system of government is contradicted by Rome itself. His motives for telling the tale are hypocritical; he wants merely to send the trades home, not to train them to participate in the affairs of state. No more than Coriolanus does he believe that Rome is theirs; they are perpetual nuisances to be fobbed off with parables that teach them submission. Yet in the heat of rebellion, Menenius is politician enough to understand the need for communication, and he chooses a play situation to create it. He begins with the metaphor itself—the belly accused by the body's other members of being a parasite in their midst—and proceeds to involve the citizens in the metaphor's working out, making the equation clear: the body is the social state. His premise is an argument that seeks to bridge the menacing chasm between Senate and populace by assuming that they are one. And by staging the play, he enacts that premise of bringing separate elements into a formal whole. The citizens, starved as much for the need to be heard and counted as for food, accept Menenius' play and respond to it, acting out the roles that he has assigned and defending their position:

1. Cit.	Your belly's answer—what?
	The kingly-crowned head, the vigilant eye,
	The counsellor heart, the arm our soldier,
	Our steed the leg, the tongue our trumpeter,
	With other muniments and petty helps
	In this our fabric, if that they—
Men.	What then?
	'Fore me, this fellow speaks! What then? what then?
	(I. i. 114–20)

Menenius has involved this most vocal member of the citizenry in his play, and the citizen, foiled as he is by the tale's premise, at least speaks in defense and can believe that he is heard.

As a play situation, Menenius' tale has served his purpose admirably. He can persuade both by the form and the content of his discourse that the Senate indeed cares about the body's health; that, despite its seeming parasitism, it is in fact always working for the public good. The play, however, is based on a lie; and Menenius' final assignation of the role of great toe to the vocal citizen is followed by his statement of the clear division that does in fact exist between the Senate and the people:

> But make you ready your stiff bats and clubs,
> Rome and her rats are at the point of battle,
> The one side must have bale. (I. i. 161–63)

It is the patricians, after all, who are the body of Rome, and these citizens merely her rats.[17]

17. Fergusson, *Shakespeare: The Pattern in His Carpet,* 265–66, portrays "wise old Menenius" as "the only character in the play with a disinterested love of Rome and a balanced vision of what the life of the community should be." Only the essential figure of the king is absent from his parable of the belly. Yet Menenius' love of

It is clear in Menenius himself, the most tolerant of the patricians, what the Senate's real views of the populace are. But Coriolanus' first entry leaves the people no doubt at all. Menenius, even though he is contemptuous of the rabble, allows them a situation to act in; Coriolanus never acknowledges their needs at all.[18] Like Henry IV, he lives in an either/or world. Either a patrician or an enemy, either me or not me— there is no space in Coriolanus' mind for the metaphoric ties that unite all humanity. Both plebeians and patricians excuse his divisiveness by allowing his having grown up in war, and no one forms the Player-King's thought—not me may also be me—certainly not Coriolanus, who enters in the rage that characterizes his response to any assault on the integrity of his world. He cannot understand why Menenius, who is part of his world, speaks to the curs, or why the Senate gives them two tribunes:

> He that will give good words to thee will flatter
> Beneath abhorring. What would you have, you curs,
> That like nor peace nor war? The one affrights you,
> The other makes you proud. He that trusts to you,
> Where he should find you lions, finds you hares;
> Where foxes, geese. You are no surer, no,
> Than is the coal of fire upon the ice,
> Or hailstone in the sun. Your virtue is
> To make him worthy whose offense subdues him,
> And curse that justice did it. Who deserves greatness
> Deserves your hate; and your affections are
> A sick man's appetite, who desires most that
> Which would increase his evil. He that depends

Rome does not embrace a love of its citizens, whom he calls rats, and his parable's wisdom does not spring from the desire to instruct those rats in Rome's business. O. J. Campbell, *Shakespeare's Satire* (New York: Oxford University Press, 1943), 204, sees Menenius as "Shakespeare's [buffoonish] mouthpiece." On the other hand, Proser, *The Heroic Image in Five Shakespearean Tragedies*, 156–57, believes that Menenius is misusing the metaphor of the body because he is not, in fact, describing the actual state of Rome—a city where the belly does hoard the food.

18. Campbell, *Shakespeare's Satire*, 202.

Upon your favors swims with fins of lead,
And hews down oaks with rushes. Hang ye! Trust ye?
With every minute you do change a mind,
And call him noble, that was now your hate;
Him vild, that was your garland. What's the matter,
That in these several places of the city
You cry against the noble Senate, who
(Under the gods) keep you in awe, which else
Would feed on one another? What's their seeking?

                    (I. i. 167–88)

Coriolanus' abhorrence of the multitude is rooted in his horror at their changeableness, at their instinct for keeping life in flux, which he judges against his own fixed world with its absolute standard for excellence. In their ephemeral lives, they are merely animals who, if it were not for the government that keeps them submissive, would begin to eat one another. In view of his own experiences, past and to come, Coriolanus' verdict is correct. The plebeians do run away in war; they do hurrah him in and whoop him out of Rome in quick succession. But what Coriolanus accepts as their natures—the nature of beasts—is in fact circumstantial. They cannot adopt the values of a government that starves them to death; they demonstrate their loyalty to no one when no one considers its possibility. In equating their need for change with baseness, Coriolanus destroys the opportunity to learn and teach. Instead of reaching through his isolation in play, which assumes and uses change, he builds around him an even more isolating wall of abuse. He will not even listen to the rabble, for when he wishes to know the purpose of their assembly, he turns to Menenius: "What's their seeking?" Their invasion of his rigid, aristocratic Eden drives him to blind rage, and he uses his tongue as he would like to use his sword: to maim, kill, keep at bay.

This menacing situation within Rome is relieved only by the news of invasion. For the plebeians, war means even further

removal from their own interests; for the patricians, it represents a solution to the domestic crisis. But for Coriolanus, it
means a lifting of the siege on his psyche. Although he attributes to the war the merit of ridding Rome of its "musty su-
perfluity" (I. i. 226), it will also free him from the subtler
threats that words represent: "When blows have made me stay,
I fled from words" (II. ii. 72).[19] In addition, it reunites him with
the lion that he is proud to hunt (I. i. 235–36)—Aufidius, who
helps him perpetuate his ideal world. In war, Coriolanus can
play himself; and he is grateful to Aufidius for providing the
stage.

Aufidius alone inspires Coriolanus to play at being another:

> They have a leader,
> Tullus Aufidius, that will put you to't.
> I sin in envying his nobility;
> And were I any thing but what I am,
> I would wish me only he. (I. i. 228–32)

Yet in choosing to play Aufidius, Coriolanus is demonstrating
that he is, in fact, unwilling to relinquish his own identity. The
Volscian leader is a recognizable image of Coriolanus himself,
Aufidius basing his sense of worth on his prowess in arms and
disdaining the weakness of people who prefer life over honor.[20]
Because Coriolanus is innocent of human nature, never having
allowed the intrusion of undirected experience, he neglects
the area of disharmony that exists between the men who are
respectively first and second in the field of combat. He has
never felt the degradation of loss; an oaken garland has adorned
his brow since his first military engagement. And in identifying himself with the perpetually defeated Aufidius, he has ne-

19. For an excellent discussion of language and the disharmony between words
and feeling in *Coriolanus*, see Carol M. Sicherman, "*Coriolanus*: The Failure of
Words," *English Literary History*, XXXIX (1972), 189–207. On this subject, see also
James L. Calderwood, "*Coriolanus*: Wordless Meanings and Meaningless Words,"
Studies in English Literature, VI (1966), 211–24.

20. Sicherman, "*Coriolanus*," 203–205, explores the differences between Coriolanus and Aufidius.

glected the principle behind play—to become another as the other is, not to assume that the other is oneself. Coriolanus, therefore, never frees himself from his own limited nature; he simply assumes, like Shylock, that all those in his own world—mother, wife, enemy—are one with him, enjoying their supporting roles in his personal play as much as he does the leading part.

In battle before Corioles, where he wins the name that he willingly accepts as part of himself, Coriolanus demonstrates his failure to lead in war as well as in peace. He listens to no dissenting voice; he takes Corioles' insults as directed personally at him, and he determines others' actions with his words. It is his war, this man of single purpose, and even before his army engages the enemy, he has determined their cowardice:

> They fear us not, but issue forth their city.
> Now put your shields before your hearts, and fight
> With hearts more proof than shields. Advance, brave Titus!
> They do disdain us much beyond our thoughts,
> Which makes me sweat with wrath. Come on, my fellows!
> He that retires, I'll take him for a Volsce,
> And he shall feel mine edge. (I. iv. 23–29)

That the Volscians dare to oppose his reputation by not fearing him arouses in Coriolanus the same wrath he felt towards the plebeians when they questioned the Senate's governance. Although he calls the troops "my fellows," he immediately stamps them, not as brothers, but as cowards. He knows the war is his and, never once moving outside the personal gratification that he receives from the prospect of defeating his detractors, communicates that feeling to his men. Before him is the enemy, and behind him is the enemy. The war must be conducted his way, and any man who dares to disagree is as much an enemy as a Volscian.

The physical results of his verbal conduct are inevitable. The Romans retreat before the Volscians, and once more Coriolanus has proof of his first opinion—the proof that he has himself verbally preestablished:[21]

> All the contagion of the south light on you,
> You shames of Rome! you herd of—Biles and plagues
> Plaster you o'er, that you may be abhorr'd
> Farther than seen, and one infect another
> Against the wind a mile! You souls of geese,
> That bear the shapes of men, how have you run
> From slaves that apes would beat! Pluto and hell!
> All hurt behind! backs red, and faces pale
> With flight and agued fear! Mend and charge home,
> Or, by the fires of heaven, I'll leave the foe
> And make my wars on you. Look to't; come on!
> If you'll stand fast, we'll beat them to their wives,
> As they us to our trenches. Follow 's. (I. iv. 30–42)

Coriolanus understands how fear spreads through an army, but he does not understand how to replace it with courage. Courage is *his* attribute, and because he jealously guards it, he cannot communicate it to others. The soldiers are again reduced to a herd of unnamed beasts on whom Coriolanus wishes the boils and plagues that reveal the inner corruption that he assumes is there. Even as he asks for their renewed assault, he presents them with their possible bravery as an *if*, and the results are again immediate. For his isolation, he wins isolation. For the man who believes that he is the only warrior capable of merit, the return is betrayal. Hotspur faced the same problem at Shrewsbury, when not only Glendower but also his own father abandoned him to play the game that he felt he owned.

---

21. Berne, *Games People Play*, 85–87, calls this game "Now I've got you, you son of a bitch." In Berne's analysis of the game's moves and advantages, he touches on many of Coriolanus' behavior patterns:

Moves: (1) Provocation—Accusation. (2) Defense—Accusation. (3) Defense—Punishment.

Advantages: (1) Internal Psychological—justification for rage. (2) External Psychological—avoids confrontation of own deficiencies. (3) Internal Social—NIGYSOB. (4) External Social—they're always out to get you. (5) Biological—belligerent exchanges, usually ipsisexual. (6) Existential—people can't be trusted.

When Coriolanus enters the gates of the enemy city, his troops refuse to follow. In his solitary greatness, Coriolanus succeeds in emerging victorious and reopening the gates through which Titus Lartius will lead the Roman army. But as a leader of men, Coriolanus is a failure.

His handling of the troops before Corioles is immediately contrasted with the more human Cominius' address to his retreating soldiers:

> Breathe you, my friends. Well fought; we are come off
> Like Romans, neither foolish in our stands
> Nor cowardly in retire. Believe me, sirs,
> We shall be charg'd again. (I. vi. 1–4)

His soldiers are "sirs" on whom he depends for valor and sense. He allows them to be Romans, men fighting a battle that is their own. But then Coriolanus arrives on the scene in his natural costume—blood from head to foot. His obsession betrayed by his repeating "Come I too late?" (I. vi. 24, 27), he undercuts the general Cominius' more temperate strategies with his quick judgment: "Are you lords a' th' field? / If not, why cease you till you are so?" (I. vi. 47–48). Coriolanus' eagerness to play his own scene of triumph deflects his will from Cominius as he begs permission to move against Aufidius. Like the plebeians, Cominius is bullied into giving him, in spite of his wounds and blood, the permission to mount beyond human nature.

As Coriolanus turns to address a new group of men, the men Cominius has already included in the war, he speaks in his habitual manner:

> Those [I would choose] are they
> That most are willing. If any such be here
> (As it were sin to doubt) that love this painting
> Wherein you see me smear'd; if any fear
> Lesser his person than an ill report;
> If any think brave death outweighs bad life,
> And that his country's dearer than himself;

Let him alone, or so many so minded,
Wave thus to express his disposition,
And follow Martius. (I. vi. 66–75)

Although he addresses them with kindlier thoughts than he did his former followers in arms, he still places his desire for a brave man in the conditional mood; the syntactic governor of his sentence is *if*. It would be a sin to doubt that such a man exists among his troops, but Coriolanus manifests that doubt in the patterning of his words. In the heat of battle, however, with his sense of glory and triumph exciting him to fevered anticipation, he communicates his own love of war—its bloody signs, its honorable glories, its patriotic motives. In that almost delirious moment, he brings with him the already participating soldiers, who demonstrate their readiness to use Coriolanus by lifting him in their arms as if to use him as their weapon against the Volscians. He has not entered their world; they have recognized him in his: "O, me alone! make you a sword of me?" (I. vi. 76). Instantaneously he is isolated, as he was within Corioles, and stripped of humanity—a man who has become his function. Still, however, his characteristic *if* betrays his fear that no one but himself can live up to his expectations: "If these shows be not outward, which of you / But is four Volsces?" (I. vi. 77–78).

Coriolanus is a symbol of military potential, a man who has transcended his humanity to become part of the force that he symbolizes; but he is no leader either in war or in peace. Moreover, he is an inadequate tool in the hands of anyone else. Like Duke Vincentio at the beginning of his tutelage, Coriolanus will not stage himself to the people's eyes, nor will he allow himself to be staged. When Aufidius and the Volscians are defeated and Cominius strives to bring him out of his self-imposed isolation, Coriolanus foils the attempt. He will neither accept his earned share of the booty nor hear his deeds extolled. Coriolanus, because he is not a player, cannot even understand the need for others to share inspiring experiences:

Lart.   O general!
Here is the steed, we the caparison.
Hadst thou beheld—

Mar.   Pray now, no more. My mother,
Who has a charter to extol her blood,
When she does praise me grieves me. I have done
As you have done—that's what I can; induc'd
As you have been—that's for my country:
He that has but effected his good will
Hath overta'en mine act.

Com.   You shall not be
The grave of your deserving; Rome must know
The value of her own. 'Twere a concealment
Worse than a theft, no less than a traducement,
To hide your doings, and to silence that
Which, to the spire and top of praises vouch'd,
Would seem but modest; therefore I beseech you,
In sign of what you are, not to reward
What you have done, before our army hear me.

                                    (I. ix. 11–27)

Again Coriolanus becomes a symbol—now Titus Lartius'
steed—and again the mystery of a human being's accomplish-
ing such deeds of valor is left unexplored and unextended to
others. It is not merely for Coriolanus that Cominius insists on
publicizing his unimaginable courage. It is also for the soldiers
who have observed him, who need their share in that humanity reinforced; and Coriolanus' refusal to allow Cominius
to use him selfishly denies his deeds to anyone but himself.
When he responds to the army's accolade with a diatribe
against flattery, his seeming modesty is graceless and selfish.
Only the name, Coriolanus, will he accept as tribute—a name
he can embrace as his own because he has won it with his
sword. Not the admiration of others, not the material gains of
war, but a name synonymous with victory brings to his face a
blush of gratitude.

When Coriolanus returns victorious to Rome, he brings with

him the inevitable problems of his nature. From this symbol—
a man who has denied his common share of humanity—the
Senate will seek to frame a leader of state. Coriolanus, whose
nature rebels at public display and whose identity is rendered
inflexible by being strapped to a single definition of human
worth, will move into a society still desperately in need of flexibility and communication. By allowing himself to be per-
suaded to run for Consul, over his own understanding that it
does not fit his nature—"Know, good mother, / I had rather be
their servant in my way / Than sway with them in theirs" (II.
i. 202–204)—he enters the realm of tragedy. He is incapable of
performing the role in which he is cast and unable either to
change himself to suit it or to change it to suit him.

Disguise and the Potential for Change

On the battlefield, Coriolanus can take care of his own
needs. Physical attack eliminates the danger of psychological
invasion, and Coriolanus willingly pays the price in blood for
remaining separate and intact. In peace, however, he trusts to
the people of his own world to sustain him: Menenius, Virgilia, his son Martius, the aristocrats of Rome, and, above all,
Volumnia. From his mother he has learned to be who he is—a
man of focused rage, a mechanically passionate killer. Trained
to anger and pride because they are the emotions of the godlike—a training passed on to his butterfly-tearing son—Coriolanus fails to recognize any other human feelings. He is closed
to the tender emotions so integral to intimacy; Virgilia is not a
woman of his mother's steely cast, nor are his attempts to instruct her in the overtly aggressive family style successful. Because he cannot risk the vulnerability demanded by adult
sexuality, he remains dependent on his mother for guidance
and approbation. It is she who created the world of heroic
combat that he made his own, and he never doubts that she
will continue to collaborate on it with him. Volumnia wants
him to be Consul, and he assumes that she knows what is best.

Rome, however, is larger than he allows. The people's tribunes await him as he returns triumphant even in the eyes of
prattling nurses and reeking kitchen servants. While Volumnia
and Menenius count his wounds like gold, Sicinius and Brutus
number Coriolanus' psychic infirmities. They understand fallen
human nature well. The degree to which Coriolanus rises
above his common humanity is the degree to which they sink
into it. As tribunes, they are not detached enough from humankind to mete justice to their constituents. Menenius comments
on their own brand of pride:

> You know neither me, yourselves, nor any thing. You are ambitious
> for poor knaves' caps and legs. You wear out a good wholesome
> forenoon in hearing a cause between an orange-wife and a forset-
> seller, and then rejourn the controversy of threepence to a second
> day of audience. When you are hearing a matter between party
> and party, if you chance to be pinch'd with the colic, you make
> faces like mummers, set up the bloody flag against all patience,
> and in roaring for a chamber-pot, dismiss the controversy bleed-
> ing, the more entangled by your hearing. All the peace you make
> in their cause is calling both the parties knaves. You are a pair of
> strange ones. (II. i. 67–80)

The just leader is a man who both understands the nature of
infirmity and controls it, a Player-King who has learned his
own share of human vice as a cipher and who then can bring
a community to its best realization, even if momentary, by
playwriting it into awareness. The tribunes know only one part
of the leader's function—the small vices of orange-wives and
forset-sellers; they know enough to call both parties in a dis-
pute knaves, but not enough to make them act like noble
people. Blinded by their own infirmities, limited to the body's
imperfections, quite overthrown by pinches of colic, they are
no prospective Consuls. Their understanding of human nature, however, extends far beyond Coriolanus'; and when he
rejects the role of his community's playwright, they take it
over, much as Pandarus takes over Hector's abandoned func-

tion. They playwrite from self-interest, which is for a time parallel to the people's interest. Coriolanus will destroy both if he is named Consul. And so they lie in wait, knowing that they can at any time force Coriolanus to act himself before Rome:

> He cannot temp'rately transport his honors
> From where he should begin and end, but will
> Lose those he hath won. (II. i. 224–26)

With the scene set for the reengagement of Rome's populace and Rome's aristocracy—a struggle only temporarily put aside during the war with the Volscians—Coriolanus enters the stage. Again he has the chance, if not to stage himself, at least to allow himself to be staged by Cominius, who wishes simultaneously to praise Rome's greatest warrior and to inculcate his virtues in the people. But Coriolanus moves to leave, not—as the people's tribunes believe—because they have driven him away, but because he cannot stand his deeds being made public. When Cominius begins, Coriolanus fulfills his impulse to flee, exiting with the lines:

> I had rather have one scratch my head i' th' sun
> When the alarum were struck than idly sit
> To hear my nothings monster'd. (II. ii. 75–77)

Menenius in turn tries to use Coriolanus' ungracious exit to demonstrate the virtue of modesty, but he too fails. Coriolanus' reluctance to remain and be praised communicates not modesty but arrogance. Menenius again casts himself in the role of impressario, mediating between his temperamental artist and the audience. His playwriting attempts to counter that of the tribunes, but Coriolanus, the supposed leader of Rome, can play only himself. Ultimately, he will fit better into the tribunes' play than into Menenius', although neither is his own. Whereas Cominius speaks the truth about his military history, veering away from direct truth only in his comment that Coriolanus "stopp'd the fliers, / And by his rare example made the coward / Turn terror into sport" (II. ii. 103–105), and proclaims him the Senate's choice for Consul, Coriolanus is not able to play the role required of him before he rises to the position.

To become Consul, he must count Rome's populace human; he must become one of them by shedding his patrician's costume and accepting the gown of humility, a toga so worn that the body is visible beneath. It is his first test of identity because, through it, he will adopt a disguise alien to his own name and stature. Willingly, Henry V cloaks his regality to walk among the common soldiers, learning and teaching as he goes. Willingly, Duke Vincentio hides his ducal power beneath a friar's robe, Hamlet his new awareness beneath the cloak of madness. But for Coriolanus, as for Richard II, divesture is not desired. The act of removing the safe clothing that marks a man's position in society is threatening to a man unsure of who he is as a man beneath the clothing. Coriolanus begs to be released from this obligation:

> I do beseech you,
> Let me o'erleap that custom; for I cannot
> Put on the gown, stand naked, and entreat them
> For my wounds' sake to give their suffrage. Please you
> That I may pass this doing. (II. ii. 135–39)

He is unable to bear his actions becoming subject to the scrutiny of those whom he would exclude from them. He wants to give the commons no share of his wounds—wounds he received for his sake, for Rome's sake as he defines the city, but never for these animals' sakes. For Coriolanus, the donning of the toga is simple prostitution. He is expected to show the wounds as if he received them only to pay for popularity. But the pleading tone of his utterances demonstrates that it is not merely pride that prompts him to ask for release. The fear of being touched, which he never knows in war because he can fight off the assault, moves him to beg to be let off. Without either his armor or his patrician robes, he is vulnerable. His verbal treatment of the people, then, seemingly uncalled-for in its hostility, functions to keep up the wall around his nature even in the disguise of a humble man.

The hostilities do not begin with the citizens. Evaluating his merit in their own way, they reach a noble decision:

> We have power in ourselves to do it [to deny him our voices], but it is a power that we have no power to do; for if he show us his wounds and tell us his deeds, we are to put our tongues into those wounds and speak for them; so, if he tell us his noble deeds, we must also tell him our noble acceptance of them. Ingratitude is monstrous, and for the multitude to be ingrateful were to make a monster of the multitude; of the which we being members, should bring ourselves to be monstrous members. (II. iii. 4–13)

They clearly want to do the right thing: in their discussion, they reach for the only instruction in government that they have been given—Menenius' tale of the belly—and use his metaphor to guide their actions. If Coriolanus shows his wounds, which they figure as dumb mouths, they will become his tongues, which can simultaneously taste and articulate his valor. There is no jealousy in their assessment of Coriolanus' courage, merely a desire to experience it and to give to it in return what it lacks—a voice. The image of tongues in wounds raises again the possibility of cannibalism, but the people's metaphor transforms that suggestion into an image of the highest form of human cooperation, a vision of social reciprocity that, if enacted, would be redemptive play. Knowing that they have the power to vote against him, they wish to choose and enact the nobler course of action.

They have decided, then, before Coriolanus appears, to conduct themselves as befits a self-respecting people, to show themselves worthy of the power newly conferred on them. But Coriolanus himself transforms them into the ungrateful monster they had chosen not to become. They greet him with ingenuous respect and admiration; they leave him degraded and mocked. Where they had looked to be elevated by his godlike presence, they find themselves mired in the base role that he assigns them. Their willingness to play their new selves with him is baffled by Coriolanus' insistence on their remaining true to his opinion of them.

Rather than use the wearing of the gown of humility as an occasion for growth, Coriolanus conducts himself with even more than his usual pride to compensate for it. He blocks his view of the citizens as people with his remembrance of them as cowards and fliers, fating them now as he had before to act basely. With Menenius presenting him to the people and cuing him to his task, and the people insisting on their right to be admitted to his audience in ones, twos, and threes, Coriolanus denies his proper function as human, as hero, as prospective Consul: "I would they would forget me, like the virtues / Which our divines lose by 'em" / (II. iii. 57–58). He assumes that the unwashed animals appearing before him are unteachable, and, in the course of the scene, his assumptions about their nature transform them from many aspiring human beings to one ungrateful monster:

Cor.	You know the cause, sir, of my standing here.
3. Cit.	We do, sir, tell us what hath brought you to't.
Cor.	Mine own desert.
2. Cit.	Your own desert!
Cor.	Ay, not mine own desire.
3. Cit.	How, not your own desire?
Cor.	No, sir, 'twas never my desire yet to trouble the poor with begging.
3. Cit.	You must think, if we give you any thing, we hope to gain by you.
Cor.	Well then, I pray, your price a' th' consulship?
1. Cit.	The price is, to ask it kindly.
Cor.	Kindly, sir, I pray let me ha't. I have wounds to show you, which shall be yours in private. Your good voice, sir, what say you?
2. Cit.	You shall ha't, worthy sir.

Cor.	A match, sir. There's in all two worthy voices begg'd. I have your alms, adieu.
3. *Cit.*	But this is something odd.
2. *Cit.*	And 'twere to give again—but 'tis no matter.

(II. iii. 62–84)

The citizens, in trying to draw him out to speak of his merits, only succeed in releasing Coriolanus' proud refusal to talk of anything except his own desert. Their politics are unsophisticated but sound. When the third citizen tells Coriolanus that, in return for their votes, the people expect to gain, Coriolanus turns the money metaphor into the specific context of price. He expects them to ask to be bribed. But the response clearly shows that he is off the mark. "The price is, to ask it kindly." What the citizens crave is a return on the respect they accord Coriolanus. They ask him merely to treat them in kind, to admit that his kind is their kind, that the gown of humility symbolizes his awareness that he too is human. The price of the consulship is "to ask it kindly"—that is, both courteously and humanly. His refusal to comply with the spirit of the request turns these originally favorable and involved citizens into indifferent and potentially hostile rebels.

With the fourth citizen, who brings up his notorious antagonism to the people, Coriolanus dissertates on flattery and the citizens' blind acceptance of any who flatter them as their friends. On this perfect occasion to teach the populace the nature of true nobility, Coriolanus degrades their intentions and alienates them as human beings. For Coriolanus, to be a leader means merely to have won leadership, not to inculcate virtue in those who are led. By assuming from the onset that they are merely unteachable animals, Coriolanus has distorted and transformed their original humanity into his own image of them as beasts. When Menenius comes to tell him that he has stood his time, all he can think about is getting rid of that ill-fitting gown of humility:

> *Cor.* May I change these garments?
>
> *Sic.*   You may, sir.
>
> *Cor.* That I'll straight do; and, knowing myself again,
>   Repair to th' Senate-house. (II. iii. 146–48)

Even though Brutus and Sicinius are directly responsible for moving the people to turn against Coriolanus, it is Coriolanus who has allowed it to happen. The citizens came as individuals; by refusing to acknowledge them as such, Coriolanus has turned them into a mob. They came with full intention of doing the honorable thing; they left knowing less of what was honorable than before. By refusing them their humanity instead of learning from it, by mocking them instead of teaching them, Coriolanus has handed the people over to the tribunes. The penalty will fall directly on him, but his crime encompasses all—himself, the patricians, the plebeians.

Brutus and Sicinius make short work of bringing Coriolanus' action to its violent conclusion. Simultaneously news of Aufidius in arms reaches Rome. Again civil insurrection and threatened invasion meet to bring confusion instead of harmony. Coriolanus, enamored of the new scene that he will be called upon to act in as himself, is suddenly confronted with the news that the populace is enraged against him. With his military fervor already activated, he loses even the irony that thinly veiled his hatred for the contaminating herd. Despite the Senate's cautions, he reiterates his former grievances over the corn:

> *Men.* Not now, not now.
>
> *1. Sen.*   Not in this heat, sir, now.
>
> *Cor.* Now, as I live, I will.
>   My nobler friends, I crave their pardons.
>   For the mutable, rank-scented meiny, let them
>   Regard me as I do not flatter, and
>   Therein behold themselves. I say again,
>   In soothing them we nourish 'gainst our Senate

> The cockle of rebellion, insolence, sedition,
> Which we ourselves have plough'd for, sow'd, and
>   scatter'd,
> By mingling them with us, the honor'd number,
> Who lack not virtue, no, nor power, but that
> Which they have given to beggars. (III. i. 63–74)

All the pent rage of his forced accommodations explodes as Coriolanus presents the tribunes with his real views of the people. The central issue in the play exposes itself in his setting himself up as a standard against which all others must measure their own inadequacies. Instead of being a magnetic center on which correspondences converge, Coriolanus is a repelling magnet, rejecting instead of embracing, isolating instead of joining. He is one of the "honor'd number," and he defines virtue and power, which in his singleness of mind he equates with the spoils of victory, as commodities that will be lost by sharing. The Player-King knows well that in broadening the base of power and virtue, he increases its store in himself. But for Coriolanus, anything shared is given away, and anything given away is lost. Brutus responds accurately to his setting himself up as a mirror of judgment:

> You speak a' th' people
> As if you were a god, to punish; not
> A man of their infirmity. (III. i. 80–82)

Menenius can no longer keep him in check. The excuse to call his utterances choler Coriolanus rejects out of hand and doubles his accusations, turning them on the Senate who have allowed this "triton of the minnows" (III. i. 89) to speak a peremptory "shall." He betrays the limitations of the military mind, with its either/or alternatives, in asserting that the consulship is sullied by its tie to the plebeian voice:

> and my soul aches
> To know, when two authorities are up,
> Neither supreme, how soon confusion

> May enter 'twixt the gap of both, and take
> The one by th' other. (III. i. 108–12)

In him rests no understanding of a humanly populated state in which each citizen can be responsible for himself and still serve a larger purpose, where each citizen has Adam's choice of good or evil but exercises it in a realm where the harmony of a right choice exerts a palpable influence. Coriolanus moves further and further into the anger that is the only emotion he understands, espousing his narrow, exclusive doctrine of service and his detestation of cowardice. Again he predetermines his end with words, so that when the moment arises and the crows do peck the eagles (III. i. 139), he will be able to congratulate himself on his perspicacity. Finally, the threat that he has made twice before in the drama, once during the rebellion and once during the assault on Corioles, is realized as he acts out his words and draws his sword on Romans—the tribunes, aediles, and people—who, catching his own diseased rage in lieu of his absent guidance, seek to bring him to the Tarpeian rock. Sicinius shouts: "Where is this viper / That would depopulate the city and / Be every man himself?" (III. i. 262–64). He has voiced Coriolanus' ultimate aim.

His momentary escape, engineered by Menenius and the other Senators, is but temporary. It wins him a second chance to wear a costume of humility—this time, according to Volumnia's suggestion, with his hat in his hand; but Coriolanus is too threatened by disguise to learn from it. He has, however, begun to doubt the firmness of the patrician ground on which he always felt secure, to blame the Senate for appeasing the people by giving them corn and tribunes. He has begun, too, to think the patricians are cowards. And now, as the population of his world dwindles, he begins to wonder about Volumnia's silence:

> I muse my mother
> Does not approve me further.

. . . .
Enter VOLUMNIA.
                    I talk of you:
Why did you wish me milder? Would you have me
False to my nature? Rather say, I play
The man I am. (III. ii. 7–8, 13–16)

The beginning of what will be for Coriolanus a fatal schism
occurs in this scene where the mother asks her son not to act
on his understanding of her training. The boy whom she taught
to act out frustrations through rage she is now prompting to
use hypocrisy and deceit. Metaphorically, she has made herself the Roman aristocracy: "I am in this / Your wife, your son,
these senators, the nobles" (III. ii. 64–65). His confusion
mounts as Volumnia instructs him to disobey the dictates of
the heart he had always believed was one with hers. Now his
mother is stage managing him in an alien play, telling him exactly how to bow and scrape before the multitude, hat in hand.

    Not even among those he thought were his own can Corio-
lanus act himself any longer. As Volumnia promises her praise
if he "perform a part / [He has] not done before" (III. ii. 109–
10), he assesses the distance between what he is asked to act
and what he is:

                    Well, I must do't.
Away, my disposition, and possess me
Some harlot's spirit! My throat of war be turn'd,
Which quier'd with my drum, into a pipe
Small as an eunuch, or the virgin voice
That babies lull asleep! The smiles of knaves
Tent in my cheeks, and schoolboys' tears take up
The glasses of my sight! A beggar's tongue
Make motion through my lips, and my arm'd knees,
Who bow'd but in my stirrup, bend like his
That hath receiv'd an alms! I will not do't,
Lest I surcease to honor mine own truth,
And by my body's action teach my mind
A most inherent baseness. (III. ii. 110–23)

The humility of spirit that he is now asked to perform he equates with eunuchs, women, knaves, schoolboys, and beggars. His fear of ceasing to act himself—a fear Richard II experienced upon descending to the base ground—overpowers his desire to please Volumnia. Although conquered momentarily by the pressure of his mother's threat of displeasure, that fear will again overcome him as he faces the scene in which he must play his new part. Brutus and Sicinius have also been stage managing the scene to come, knowing far better than the patricians how impossibly rigid is Coriolanus' definition of himself. With both parties counting on the same actor to deliver himself in their behalf, Coriolanus again enters the public scene, repeating his cue, "mildly" (III. ii. 142).

Although he has picked up the theatrical metaphor from his mother's promptings, Coriolanus has not assimilated the principle of play. Instead of readying himself to *become* a different man, he prepares merely to *act* another man. The pressure, built up by his new uncertainties, his frustrations, and his fears, drives him within moments of his entry to abandon the new role and, with relief, to play himself again. The single word, "traitor" (III. iii. 67), denies him all his accumulated honors; Coriolanus responds by venting his rage and wins, for all his honors, the exile he has prepared for himself from the beginning of his drama. According to Coriolanus, the people have done it, and the Senate has done it in allowing the people that power. Of course, Coriolanus has done it to himself. For the limited man who holds himself up as the limiting standard for everyone else, no ground in his own city remains. Coriolanus, trained in aggression, cannot accept his fate as dictated by anyone but himself. If no one in Rome allows him to be Rome, he will turn the sentence on those who imposed it: "I banish you!" (III. iii. 123):

> Despising,
> For you, the city, thus I turn my back;
> There is a world elsewhere. (III. iii. 133–35)

In his heart, Coriolanus believes himself to be Rome and the only Roman in it. Rome, therefore, lives on in him and he abandons that other city to defeat and slavery. He is to discover, finally, that no world exists elsewhere that is not prepared within.

Exile and the Lesson Not Learned:
"Nor I nor any man . . ."

🦞 Coriolanus' fixed identity in his fixed world, denied by both the people who banished him and the patricians who allowed them to do it, functions in even more limited terms than he has ever known. He has twice appeared in disguise, and on both occasions he has chosen to remain Coriolanus rather than to play towards a fuller humanity. Now, in exile, he is a nameless man, with no external Rome to define him as Coriolanus, no society to send him to his natural scene of battle as the victorious warrior. He is a machine without a defining hand, of no use to himself or to anyone else. Ironically, Coriolanus has delivered himself over to the position of cipher in his world and has finally become in act what he always was in spirit—the world's exile.

Before he leaves, however, he reasserts his understanding of himself before family and friends. To Volumnia, he returns the precepts he learned at her knee: Fortune's blows are the test of a man's true courage. He rises in farewell to the fullness of himself, able to demonstrate his nobility of spirit in the courage of his leavetaking because he has the proper audience. The few remaining faithful whom he is now leaving behind— mother, wife, general, friend—are the last external vestiges of his identity, and even they have been guilty of betrayal in asking him to change from the man he is. While still before them, Coriolanus is capable of playing himself:

> I shall be lov'd when I am lack'd. Nay, mother,
> Resume that spirit when you were wont to say,
> If you had been the wife of Hercules,

> Six of his labors you'ld have done, and sav'd
> Your husband so much sweat. Cominius,
> Droop not, adieu. Farewell, my wife, my mother,
> I'll do well yet. Thou old and true Menenius,
> Thy tears are salter than a younger man's,
> And venomous to thine eyes. My sometime general,
> I have seen thee stern, and thou hast oft beheld
> Heart-hard'ning spectacles; tell these sad women
> 'Tis fond to wail inevitable strokes,
> As 'tis to laugh at 'em. My mother, you wot well
> My hazards still have been your solace, and
> Believe 't not lightly—though I go alone,
> Like to a lonely dragon, that his fen
> Makes fear'd and talk'd of more than seen—your son
> Will or exceed the common or be caught
> With cautelous baits and practice. (IV. i. 15–33)

He addresses them all, but it is to his mother that he begins and ends his discourse. In predicting his vengeance—they will want him when he's gone—Coriolanus again determines the future action. In fact, Rome does not miss him until he forces home his threat by coupling with Aufidius; the city becomes a harmonious working unit after his banishment. But bolstered by the illusion that he will be missed, Coriolanus can play out his courage, which becomes clearly defined as the ability to remain unchanged by external circumstances. He asserts that he is still the center of Rome—although a lonely dragon, his fen will remain the focus of his enemies—and he leaves affirming his singleness of being:

> While I remain above the ground, you shall
> Hear from me still, and never of me aught
> But what is like me formerly. (IV. i. 51–53)

The facts of isolation are quite different, however. Alienated from his source of identity, Coriolanus has two choices: to discover his humanity as a cipher or to find someone to identify him. Wandering cityless is the man who had made himself a tool of the state. Steed without rider, sword without arm, Coriolanus discovers that his exile creates a change that no amount of courage can withstand. He has chosen under far easier circumstances to reject the opportunity to be touched by common humanity; now with solitude aggravating the wound of defeat, he moves again to protect his identity at any cost.[22] Very few stage moments pass before Coriolanus, dressed meanly, *"disguis'd and muffled"* (IV. iv.), makes his way to his last source of affirmation—his defining opposite, Aufidius.

Like Bullingbrook, Coriolanus' unwillingness to learn is negatively demonstrated by the absence of soul-searching soliloquies and by a syntax that falls into the structure of either/or. His desperate need to play the man he is brings him to Aufidius' Antium, there to be released from his most recent gown of humility and to know himself again. His considerations before entering Antium are few. He notes the changes in his world but never moves beyond his wonder to discover the principle of change and how to control it:

> My birthplace hate I, and my love's upon
> This enemy town. I'll enter. If he slay me,
> He does fair justice; if he give me way,
> I'll do his country service. (IV. iv. 23–26)

His either/or simplification of his options makes sense to him. Should Aufidius kill him, he will at least die worthily and honorably; should Aufidius accept him, he can be himself again—a serviceable weapon.

That Coriolanus has not allowed his reduction in state and dress to penetrate the material of his ego is clear from his treatment of Aufidius' servants. Even in a costume that places him below their level, he treats them with the disrespect he accords all common men. From his peremptory "Away!" he

---

22. Katherine Stockholder, "The Other Coriolanus," *Publications of the Modern Language Association*, LXXXV (1970), 229, 231, notes Coriolanus' limitation of himself to type, becoming "so entrapped in his image that he ceases to exist for himself when the mirror is removed."

moves to violence, pushing and finally beating the servant who seeks to eject him. Not before these jackdaws will he unveil himself. He waits for Aufidius, the last reflector of himself, to recognize him and, in the recognition, to raise him to what he is. But Aufidius does not know his opponent without his identifying martial costume:

> Cor. [*Unmuffling.*]   If, Tullus,
> Not yet thou know'st me, and, seeing me, dost not
> Think me for the man I am, necessity
> Commands me name myself.
>
> Auf.   What is thy name?
>
> Cor. A name unmusical to the Volscians' ears,
> And harsh in sound to thine.
>
> Auf.   Say, what's thy name?
> Thou hast a grim appearance, and thy face
> Bears a command in't; though thy tackle's torn,
> Thou show'st a noble vessel. What's thy name?
>
> Cor. Prepare thy brow to frown. Know'st thou me yet?
>
> Auf. I know thee not. Thy name? (IV. v. 54–64)

Coriolanus, dressed like a common man, is not the godlike, seemingly invincible spirit of Mars that Aufidius knows on the battlefield. In his human form he is unrecognizable, although his nobility shines through the torn tackle.

Coriolanus' disappointment is evident; he must be seen through Aufidius' eyes to be the man he is. Aufidius' failure to know Coriolanus, however, places him for the first time in a superior position. When at last Coriolanus announces himself and vents his rage to the only man who would understand him, Aufidius responds with all his own pent emotions. He is allowed for the first time to see his archenemy as a man weak and cast down. Together they play a love scene of great power,

Coriolanus presenting himself as sacrifice or tool to the hand that can use him, Aufidius embracing him like a new wife, telling of the dreams that have brought them together night after night in the combat that so closely resembles the act of love. But in this embrace, both men have mistaken one another. Coriolanus takes Aufidius as a man who is himself— noble and disinterestedly brave. Aufidius receives Coriolanus as a man whom fortune has humbled if not tamed. Aufidius is happy that Coriolanus is no longer a god, and Coriolanus is happy to become godlike again. The anticipations that each has of their relationship will prove false to both and fatal to Coriolanus.

Here in Antium, however, Coriolanus has again managed to slough off humble dress and don the regal robes that befit his usefulness to the state. He has learned nothing in exile except malice and resentment towards all of Rome. Rather than accept his own weaknesses, he leaps to blame others—commoners and nobility are now one in their treachery—and descends to what seems an act of treason. But treason as a word does not account for Coriolanus' need to find a scene for himself—as he sees himself—to move in. Never embracing the art of playing, he rejects the uncomfortable threat of alien clothes and alien lands to find a new home where he can become again what he is—a great warrior who can serve in his own way.

The "New" Role

In Coriolanus' desperate thirst to regain his Rome, he has dissociated the nobility of conquest from the nobility of loyalty. In his search for use, he has severed the last emotional ties that made his utility humanly functional. In his need for a love object, he has substituted the narcissistic image of his alter ego for the former self-reflections of mother, wife, and friend. Coriolanus' rigidity, which fixes him in the either/or mode of warfare, has finally divided his world in two. His feeling life is now locked in a separate cage from his professional life, yet both make demands on his sense of honor. To vent his rage against those whom he calls enemies, he must also destroy those whom he has loved.

Coriolanus' narrowness before the wide range of human possibility has led him from one prison to another, and in both he is his own jailer. His object is to exclude rather than to include, to maintain himself aloof from sullying contacts. Consequently, he has rejected all opportunities to grow. Now he has convinced himself that as a warrior he is Coriolanus still, that only the uniform is different. He fights in Volscian—not Roman—armor, and his blind refusal to see that menacing division of self will lead to his fatal miscalculation of his new position. A Player-King would have sealed the schism before it opened; a self-aware player would have recognized it. But Coriolanus, who has never faced his limitations, believes that he can deny his human origins entirely and, godlike, avenge himself on his human detractors. In assessing his own weaknesses so poorly, he also weighs those of Aufidius inaccurately. The combination at once raises Coriolanus to greatness and degrades him utterly.

Among the Volscians, he is a god. He allows them—because they have taken up his cause as their own—the humanity he denies the Roman populace. And because he has taken up their cause and added to it the luster of his reputation, they allow him the glory they could never accord Aufidius. Cominius observes:

> He is their god; he leads them like a thing
> Made by some other deity than Nature,
> That shapes man better. (IV. vi. 90–92)

The metaphoric illusion that Coriolanus was never able to communicate to his own people he creates for the Volscians. The Romans, as Coriolanus determined in his images of them, act like cornered animals. They begin to prey on one another, each turning the blame for this cataclysmic threat on the other, and all on the tribunes. Coriolanus' influence is again divisive, turning one side to animals, the other to gods. Aufidius hears of his troops' response to their new leader:

> I do not know what witchcraft's in him, but
> Your soldiers use him as the grace 'fore meat,
> Their talk at table, and their thanks at end;
> And you are dark'ned in this action, sir,
> Even by your own. (IV. vii. 2–6)

To the Volscians, it is Mars who has descended to lead them into battle. Coriolanus is no simple human being, nor is he a man like Henry V who detests the ceremony that separates him from his kind. He accepts the nomination to divinity as his due, never assessing the human reactions around him. He is doomed to fall prey to the enemy within, the human enemy lurking in the alter ego.

Like the tribunes, Aufidius understands him. He too can calculate Coriolanus' moods well enough to know that he can move and manipulate them. From a once brave and honorable warrior, Aufidius has become a cunning underground fighter. Coriolanus distorts all those he touches, warping them around his own oversized figure. Aufidius notes the pride of his former opponent, which has exceeded his own estimate:

> yet his nature
> In that's no changeling, and I must excuse
> What cannot be amended. (IV. vii. 10–12)

Despite repeated opportunities, Coriolanus' nature remains unchanged. Aufidius excuses this fault of nature, but he cannot destroy himself by pampering it, even though he alone, of all the characters in the drama, reads Coriolanus accurately and sympathetically:

> Whether 'twas pride,
> Which out of daily fortune ever taints
> The happy man; whether defect of judgment,
> To fail in the disposing of those chances
> Which he was lord of; or whether nature,
> Not to be other than one thing, not moving
> From th' casque to th' cushion, but commanding peace
> Even with the same austerity and garb
> As he controll'd the war; but one of these
> (As he hath spices of them all, not all,
> For I dare so far free him) made him fear'd,
> So hated, and so banish'd; but he has a merit
> To choke it in the utt'rance. (IV. vii. 37–49)

Pride, a defective judgment, an inability to change—Aufidius names all of Coriolanus' fatal weaknesses. All of them, however, are rooted in the same soil—the willful blindness to human nature that forces a person to build walls around himself, walls that not only protect but also immure. Even though his greatness gives the lie to detraction, that greatness rests with "th' interpretation of the time" (IV. vii. 50). It cancels out and is cancelled by the vices that form this proud nature: "One fire drives out one fire; one nail, one nail; / Rights by rights fouler, strengths by strengths do fail" (IV. vii. 54–55). And he, Aufidius, will supplant Coriolanus' fire with his own. Coriolanus' singleness of being cannot for a moment allow equal reign with any man. Once more he locks himself inside the walls of an enemy town, just as he is locked within the prison of himself that makes of all others an enemy.

In this role—no "changeling"—Coriolanus greets Rome. The emotional ties that made him dress in humble robes he has cut off as he relaxes into the role of god. He will not allow Rome to humanize itself before him: he will hear no names, give no private audiences. All ties of love and friendship dissolve before Coriolanus' need to assert his own name in the only way he knows how—by etching it with fire and carving it with sword. Cominius speaks of his interview:

> Yet one time he did call me by my name.
> I urg'd our old acquaintance, and the drops
> That we have bled together. Coriolanus
> He would not answer to; forbade all names;
> He was a kind of nothing, titleless,
> Till he had forg'd himself a name a' th' fire
> Of burning Rome. (V. i. 9–15)

As cipher, he did not passively absorb the patterns of human life into his own; now he denies his old identity, epitomized by the name Coriolanus, only to gain a new one of the same kind but greater. In destroying Rome, Coriolanus would become Romanus just as he became Coriolanus in his defeat of Corioles. Then there would be no question—he would be Rome.

His inability to play has precluded the Player-King's gift of harmony. Coriolanus wills monody instead. Any note that seeks to couple with his own he rejects, and if rejection alone will not still it, he destroys it. Cominius and Menenius, the Romans whom he once considered friends, are simple distractions to his godlike singularity. Menenius, who mistakes Coriolanus' rejection of Cominius for human weakness—he had not dined—who had indeed always been the "book of his good acts" (V. ii. 15), suffers Cominius' fate. Even though Menenius had always tried to humanize his idol at least to the public, Coriolanus remained the divine machine whose wounds were counted, not wept over. To Cominius, Coriolanus denies the name of brother; to Menenius, the name of father. He explains his new position:

> My affairs
> Are servanted to others; though I owe
> My revenge properly, my remission lies
> In Volscian breasts. (V. ii. 82–85)

Coriolanus' ability to turn away even those whom he acknowledged as his own in Rome depends on his self-deluding separation of personal revenge from public service. Nobility of spirit is not vengeful, but revenge in the public service of the state is noble. Only the flimsiest of rationalizations and the sternest of postures support Coriolanus' sense of his own greatness.

Volumnia, who once before demonstrated her understanding of her son in prompting him to an action against his will, is capable of succeeding where Menenius failed. Just as Coriolanus is congratulating himself on his perfect portrayal of constancy, his wife, his son, and his mother enter. As he sees them and their retinue, he feels for the first time that to be truly alone means to deny human nature. Volumnia is the only being to whom Coriolanus bows as before one greater than he, and Virgilia and young Martius complete the chain of ties that extends from past to future. Here before him is everything that made him a man—his human origin in his mother's womb, his human need for love in his chosen wife, his human immortality in his son. To destroy Rome is to destroy these and so to destroy himself:

> Let it be virtuous to be obstinate.
> What is that curtsy worth? or those doves' eyes,
> Which can make gods forsworn? I melt, and am not
> Of stronger earth than others. My mother bows,
> As if Olympus to a molehill should
> In supplication nod; and my young boy
> Hath an aspect of intercession, which
> Great Nature cries, "Deny not." Let the Volsces
> Plough Rome and harrow Italy, I'll never
> Be such a gosling to obey instinct, but stand
> As if a man were author of himself,
> And knew no other kin. (V. iii. 26–37)

He had never recognized this weakness; he had never doubted his ability to detach himself from the natural world and become *sui generis*. His war against Rome is not treachery if he is an avenging deity, but it is petty, vicious, and ignoble if he is a mere human. Prior to the appearance of his humanity's proofs, he could assure himself that he was indeed beyond such frailties. But now he squarely confronts the fact of his nature and so the fact of his schizophrenic division of self:

> Like a dull actor now
> I have forgot my part, and I am out,
> Even to a full disgrace. Best of my flesh,
> Forgive my tyranny; but do not say
> For that, "Forgive our Romans." (V. iii. 40–44)

The role of avenging deity he had never tallied with the natural man who loves his mother, his wife, and his son.[23] If he is a deity, he is the author of himself. If he acknowledges that he is not the author of himself, he is an unnatural man. His mother harps on this unnaturalness, kneeling to him, calling him hard, describing the characteristic either/or position he has placed them in—they must either pray for their country or for him.

As Coriolanus rises to leave, just as he had risen in the past to flee from the words that threatened more than blows, Volumnia delivers her final speech, in which she fingers every tender spot in her son:

> Thou know'st, great son,
> The end of war's uncertain; but this certain,
> That, if thou conquer Rome, the benefit
> Which thou shalt thereby reap is such a name
> Whose repetition will be dogg'd with curses;
> Whose chronicle thus writ: "The man was noble,
> But with his last attempt he wip'd it out,
> Destroy'd his country, and his name remains
> To th' ensuing age abhorr'd." Speak to me, son.
> Thou hast affected the fine strains of honor,
> To imitate the graces of the gods:

23. Fergusson, *Shakespeare: The Pattern in His Carpet,* 270.

> To tear with thunder the wide cheeks a' th' air,
> And yet to charge thy sulphur with a bolt
> That should but rive an oak. Why dost not speak?
> Think'st thou it honorable for a noble man
> Still to remember wrongs? (V. iii. 140–55)

She first destroys his hope of achieving his name and identity as Rome by realistically prophesying his future reputation. Then she raises his worshipped honor only to dash it as wiped out by his last action, in which a man who thought he was honorable committed treason because he felt wronged. She urges Virgilia to speak, and young Martius too, plying Coriolanus with all the debilitating effects of a mother-son tie—the guilts, the accusations, the loyalties that succeed in tying Coriolanus in emotional knots. Because he has not foreseen his own role weakening under the pressure of his human instinct, which he has attributed to a gosling, he is mesmerized by this assault. He does not recognize the part of him now brought to light, which will allay his rage, equivocate with his service, and animate his statued life. Emotion is what Volumnia wields, the human feeling that Coriolanus has separated from himself in his rise to divinity. After the nasty pressure of Volumnia's "Thou hast never in thy life / Show'd thy dear mother any courtesy" (V. iii. 160–61), after her urging of wife and son, she again turns to the justice of her demand:

> Say my request's unjust,
> And spurn me back; but if it be not so,
> Thou art not honest, and the gods will plague thee
> That thou restrain'st from me the duty which
> To a mother's part belongs.—He turns away.
> Down, ladies; let us shame him with our knees.
> . . . .
> Come, let us go.
> This fellow had a Volscian to his mother;
> His wife is in Corioles, and his child
> Like him by chance.—Yet give us our dispatch.

I am hush'd until our city be afire,
And then I'll speak a little. (V. iii. 164–69, 177–82)

She has broken open the crack in Coriolanus' defensive wall. He is a man and not a god. He cannot have been author of himself and, if he is not, he is drawn by the ties of nature. In fact, beneath his hard, defensive wall is the unformed, vulnerable creature he had always striven to protect. The dehumanization of any person can never be total. He can isolate himself, defend himself, and scorn others, but still nature ties him to the feelings of shame and guilt that accompany unnatural acts.

Volumnia, at whose knee he learned honor, has still played the mother's part. She has presented him with a solution that she announces is honorable. But it is her last thrust—the final image she creates of the mother dying in agony amidst the fires her son sets—that breaks down the wall altogether:

O mother, mother!
What have you done? Behold, the heavens do ope,
The gods look down, and this unnatural scene
They laugh at. O my mother, mother! O!
You have won a happy victory to Rome;
But, for your son, believe it—O, believe it—
Most dangerously you have with him prevail'd,
If not most mortal to him. But let it come. (V. iii. 182–89)

No longer looking at the scene from above, trying to leave so that he is not contaminated by human weaknesses, Coriolanus acknowledges his humanity with the reiteration of "mother." Like Hamlet before him, who comes to understand that the readiness is all, Coriolanus can only note the consequences of his penetrated armor and bid them come. But even over his recognition that this knowledge he has been avoiding throughout his life will destroy him, he tries clumsily to draw Aufidius into play:

> Now, good Aufidius,
> Were you in my stead, would you have heard
> A mother less? or granted less, Aufidius? (V. iii. 191–93)

His gesture, however, remains verbal. He does not stop to consider how he would feel were he Aufidius, but simply to force Aufidius to become him for that moment of metaphoric illumination.

Ironically, we hear Menenius explain to Sicinius the seeming alteration of his nature in terms of metamorphoses reaching towards a purer state—from grub to butterfly, from man to dragon:

> The tartness of his face sours ripe grapes. When he walks, he moves like an engine, and the ground shrinks before his treading. He is able to pierce a corslet with his eye, talks like a knell, and his hum is a battery. He sits in his state, as a thing made for Alexander. What he bids be done is finish'd with his bidding. He wants nothing of a god but eternity and a heaven to throne in.
>
> (V. iv. 17–24)

Yet persuasive as is his role of god, like nothing human—engine, sword, knell, battery; not an Alexander but a statue of him from which the ground shrinks—Coriolanus lacks eternity and a heavenly throne. The question repeatedly raised in the course of the drama—is he a god, a man, or a beast?—has already been answered when Menenius chooses divinity for him. Coriolanus has discovered his human vulnerability and its mortal consequences. The harmony he has always disrupted in Rome now coalesces around Volumnia, the only person who could defeat him. She makes Rome's peace, as Aufidius will restore Corioles over the body of Coriolanus.

Aufidius prepares his "pretext" (V. vi. 19) well, accusing Coriolanus of bowing his nature for the first time, of being unable to accept being "joint-servant" (V. vi. 31) to the state, of willfully ignoring the merit that would choke it in the utterance. Thus prepared with the lies that he knows are lies, Au-

fidius gives sway to the destruction of his honor. From
Coriolanus he has caught the rage of spirit, the intolerance of
weakness; and in his mirror, he will show Coriolanus his own
intolerance. Like the tribunes who goad him into delivering
himself, like Volumnia who at last uses him to save her city,
Aufidius plans to make Coriolanus—this symbol of greatness—
of service. In dehumanizing the world around him, Coriolanus
had dehumanized himself. The brutal irony is that Coriolanus
himself reduced the world to the level where the murder of a
man could be excused. He could kill rats, hares, geese; therefore he can be killed as a viper, turned against himself like a
sword, or transformed permanently into spirit like a god. Aufidius is treacherous, but Coriolanus has taught him how.

The ease of Coriolanus' destruction is horrifying; Aufidius
simply has to reverse the polarity of friend-enemy and Coriolanus reacts like a puppet. He begins with accusations, follows
by calling names—"traitor," "boy of tears"—and leaves Coriolanus to kill himself with words:

> Measureless liar, thou hast made my heart
> Too great for what contains it. "Boy"? O slave!
> Pardon me, lords, 'tis the first time that ever
> I was forc'd to scold.
>
> . . . .
>
> Cut me to pieces, Volsces, men and lads,
> Stain all your edges on me. "Boy," false hound!
> If you have writ your annals true, 'tis there
> That, like an eagle in a dove-cote, I
> Flutter'd your Volscians in Corioles.
> Alone I did it. "Boy"! (V. vi. 102–105, 111–16)

Coriolanus turns the Volscians back into hated enemies in as
appallingly brief a time as he turned the Romans against him.
He refuses to be used any longer as a symbol of any other
man's prowess, demanding in his isolation that he be acknowledged a god. Brutally Aufidius puts an end to Coriolanus' mortal life and then, needing fully to emphasize Coriolanus'

mortality and to act out the insatiable need to rise above him, he stands on the body. The act is repulsive to the lords, to the audience, and to Aufidius himself, but he must perform it in his rage—the rage he caught like a disease from Coriolanus.

Coriolanus as a drama is an external event. It includes few soliloquies, few metaphoric flights. It deals with a rigid man, who cannot accept the imperfect or the mutable in life and who wrongly works at keeping himself unchanged. At the heart of the drama's astonishing bareness of adornment is a man who seeks to reduce himself to the superhuman. He cannot play because he will not bend or alter the shape that he depends on for certainty. Always he denies, rejects, and divides; never affirms or unites. Wherever he is, the world is in two. Coriolanus, for all his resemblances to Hamlet, is basically unlike him. His drama does not muddle through flashes of illumination over which the dark closes. There is no darkness in *Coriolanus*, only the light of public display. From within the drama, Coriolanus has shaped his play, bringing release only in death because he has never attached himself to life. He lacks the moral awareness of the habitual player and limits his definition of what is to himself. As a hero, Coriolanus is an obstacle to his world's quest for peaceful wholeness, a man who must die so that others can open the human world to itself again.

CHAPTER VI

The Tempest: Heaven, Earth, and Rainbow

꣠ The Adversary's response to the threat posed by mutability is "Fast bind, fast find": tyrannical, disharmonious force. For the Player-King, who surrenders himself to change until it asserts the principle of change—everything is itself and yet other—force cedes to play, and play teaches the independence yet interrelation of part to part and part to whole. On an island in the sea, yet in communication with all the world's patterns, Prospero dramatizes and corrects the desires of his fallen kind, desires once mounted against him when he was isolated within his community. Like many of Shakespeare's failed Player-Kings, Prospero was deprived of the role he refused to enact. While Duke of Milan, he assumed like Richard II that his power rested in his title; like Coriolanus, he ignored the human need to change. Violently wrenched from his illusions by his brother's treachery, a treachery in which he was not only victim but colluder, he is forced to act out his isolation and become in reality the exile he had been playing. On his island, Prospero's task is to relearn and recreate the principle of human community with the use of his books, his daughter, his spirits, and his thing of darkness. He must of necessity apprentice himself to the study of nature, understand its laws and harmonies, and convert that understanding into enlightened teaching.

This, for twelve years, is Prospero's activity. He begins his residency on the island as a white magician, a master of those arts that will into manifestation the patterns and harmonies allowed by the world's historic origin in oneness. From his study

297

of these connections, a preoccupation that, "but by being so retir'd / O'er-priz'd all popular rate" (I. ii. 91–92), he learned the springs of action, a study fundamental but abstract. Like Duke Vincentio's, his unacted wisdom bred corruption. The study of magic, although visionary, spiritual, and self-disciplinary, is solitary and cannot generate social harmony unless the magician uses it to share his vision with the individual members of that society. Magic and play do share a methodology, forcing pieces of the universe to assume shapes and relationships cast by magician or playwright, and they may share a common goal if the magic is designed to right a previously unharmonious relationship, but they are at root dissimilar. Effective magic requires a strong human will operating on the elements of the world, but the magician's effects are external to human conscience. Play, on the other hand, forces a person to change his nature from within. It moves through outer experience to inner perception, from event to reaction. It can unlock the human potential for love, compassion, and justice by releasing the individual from a restricting self-definition. Magic, therefore, can create the circumstances for Prospero's play, but it cannot of itself redeem anyone. Prospero uses it as stagecraft to create the outer situations for the characters in his play; the results are left to the transformations that individuals undergo within themselves.[1]

It is up to Prospero's understanding of himself and of human nature to effect the changes he desires, and Prospero is a man brutally scarred by his life's experiences. For twelve years, he has not only had the opportunity to enlarge his studies but also to brood over his wounds. *The Tempest*, then, is a test not only

1. In addition, if all magic is suspect because the magician must supplicate finite spirits, as Robert H. West affirms in *Shakespeare and the Outer Mystery*, 93, Prospero would have to leave his study for the sake of his soul: "[Prospero] parts with [magic] and with mysterious Ariel in a way that suggests that whatever the glories and enlargements of such excursions as his into outerness, he must in the end, short of utter destruction, turn back to the world of pathos and the grave."

for his society but for himself as well: which will prevail—his human thirst for vengeance or his equally human yearning for virtue? The Player-King, because he is human and because his world is fallen, faces the trial of his vision as he plays it with others. Prospero is not merely a manipulating, mechanical instigator of events; he is emotional, cynical, cautious, untrusting—a human being changing with the changes he effects. His final success, therefore, raises the estimation of human heroism. He faces his weaknesses as well as his strengths fully, and gradually overcomes the one in the other. His irascibility and his tyrannical bearing are the signs of his conflict as he moves to bring to repentance those whom he has the power to destroy.[2]

Tempest—Rebellion and Control

Before reconstruction is possible, destruction must first take place. The old society of Prospero's land sails within his range of power, and Prospero creates a tempest—the storm that dissolves the surface of role and function and cuts the social ties among the men struggling for life. Through Ariel, Prospero has enacted the metaphor of chaos: earth vanishes, winds mount, fire breaks out, water surges. In the breakdown of the natural world, the men on board see the occasion for social unrule. Self-love dominates as each human atom returns to its initial state, unyoked to any other. The boatswain declares all titles nullified before the storm—"What cares these roarers for the name of king?" (I. i. 16–17)—and asserts the

2. John Dover Wilson, *The Meaning of "The Tempest"* (Newcastle upon Tyne: Literary and Philosophical Society, 1936), and Egan, *Drama within Drama*, 100, both see Prospero starting the play as a tyrannical figure. Egan interprets Prospero's plan as intending "to eliminate, by force if necessary, all elements of humanity that will not conform to his vision." Frank Kermode in his introduction to the new Arden edition of *The Tempest* (Cambridge: Harvard University Press, 1958), xlviii, l, explains Prospero's predicament more accurately as his need to control his own passions before he can rule others and cast away his magic. Kermode points out that Prospero's fall, like Adam's, was the result of his excessive pursuit of knowledge.

principle of self: "None [are on board] that I more love than myself" (I. i. 20). Sebastian and Antonio busy themselves with cursing what they cannot control; the king himself prays below deck, recognizing in the tempest a power greater than his own. Only Gonzalo, who once before faced the upheaval of order with a firm sense of rightness, affirms the now disintegrating unity of social governance. Amidst chaos, he proclaims law against the boatswain. In creating the tempest, Prospero has subjected his enemies to what they imagine was his own fate, and they metaphorically become him as they play the experience of sudden death at sea, as they will later play his miraculous salvation. Prospero has rendered each one a cipher as name and title vanish before the storm. Civilization has ended in shipwreck, as the Adversary's principle of self-seeking, planted by the rulers' example and released by the specter of death, usurps order.

But metaphors extend outward in concentric circles. In order to release his subjects from their disguised social state of seeming order, Prospero had to create for them an image of total destruction. That image resonates in his own world as he meets his three children—first Miranda, then Ariel, and finally Caliban. Rebellion, which not only creates but also is created of chaos, is in the air. Prospero has taken a risk, and now the results of his tempest begin to move on his island. In the drama's first act, we find the magician under the strain of keeping his world intact in the face of the powerful opposing metaphor that he put into play. In order to create the magic that will lead his enemies to act out their human sins, he must keep his own characters carefully in check. From the moment he creates the tempest, Prospero must control every movement and every experience in the drama. His object is to bring to each person his own virtue, a virtue more viable than magic because it can confront opposition and remain whole. He can effect this metamorphosis only by using his knowledge to make each character act himself out in a controlled play, face his deficiencies, and emerge cleansed and self-aware.

The first rebellion he faces is from his daughter, Miranda, whom he alone has raised and educated to young adulthood. She is respectful and cautious when she addresses him, yet her ability to accuse him, although tactfully, of causing needless suffering demonstrates her independence. She is not merely Prospero's puppet; he has allowed her tenderness and mercy to grow uninhibited by the bitterness that his story could evoke. Now, uneducated in duplicity and the subtleties of civilized sin, Miranda sees the shipwreck as her father's willful cruelty, and, like Ariel later, she feels it her duty to communicate to him her deep feeling of sympathy for the sufferers:

> If by your art, my dearest father, you have
> Put the wild waters in this roar, allay them.
> The sky it seems would pour down stinking pitch
> But that the sea, mounting to th' welkin's cheek,
> Dashes the fire out. O! I have suffered
> With those that I saw suffer. A brave vessel
> (Who had, no doubt, some noble creature in her)
> Dash'd all to pieces! O, the cry did knock
> Against my very heart. Poor souls, they perish'd.
> Had I been any god of power, I would
> Have sunk the sea within the earth or ere
> It should the good ship so have swallow'd, and
> The fraughting souls within her. (I. ii. 1–13)

Miranda's goodness manifests itself in the spontaneous leap of her feelings to any given situation, here for the noble creatures perishing and, a few moments later, for her father in his ancient distress. Her sympathetic instinct for play is as pure as a child's. When Prospero tells her of their original journey to the island, she feels less for the viciousness of her uncle's treachery than for her father's plight: "Alack, what trouble / Was I then to you!" (I. ii. 151–52).

In the course of her life, she has experienced only Caliban's lust, and now she witnesses the seeming destruction of a ship of men and hears of her own and her father's narrow escape from the same fate. Her first lesson in worldly truth she tempers with her unswerving confidence in the soundness of the whole: "What foul play had we, that we came from thence? / Or blessed was't we did?" (I. ii. 60–61). Because her training has been true to the virtuous fabric of her innocence, she absorbs these events without bitterness. The experience was hers only in dim memory; Prospero questions her closely on that issue. It is important for him to know how much of their history rests within her, what residue of memory remains that might transform her wonder into untimely resentment. Prospero's task with Miranda is to teach her the necessary amount of doubt to live in the world that he is designing for her. His story alone, however, does not reach that goal. She can only, after his tale is over, reiterate her query about the ship "still ... beating in [her] mind" (I. ii. 176). Her rebellion is stilled, but Prospero has not made his lesson affective.

Telling his tale does, however, give him the opportunity to pore over his feelings once more, for the first time publicly, to submit them to light, and to search out his own motives with care. He knows now what he had failed to recognize when he was Duke of Milan—that a ruler cannot withdraw into private studies, that such withdrawal allows evil to flourish, that a person can only act out a role for so long without wanting to become it:

> To have no screen between this part he play'd
> And him he play'd it for, he needs will be
> Absolute Milan. (I. ii. 107–109)

Yet despite his recognition of his own guilty part in his brother's crime, his rancor remains. The experience lives strongly in his memory, a memory never to be erased, only tempered by a wider sense of justice. And now Miranda challenges his motives for creating the wreck, not knowing that it is the first act of his play, the opening devoted to creating a metaphoric bond between him and his would-be assassins. And as she questions his motives, he must review them.

To tell his story, he removes the magic cape that covers the man beneath and exposes himself to Miranda's judgment. The relationship between the man and the magician he must keep healthy or risk denying his human wisdom by using his magical power to act out vengeance. Before Miranda he is not merely father but a man sinned against, trying to convince an innocent goodness that he is not returning the sin. For this reason he is anxious for her understanding. Her mind still beats on the wreck and the suffering souls, and he must plant within it the means to grasp its significance without exposing his entire plan to her. For she too is an actress in his play and cannot know its full scope without losing her pure reactions to it. His constant accusations that she is not attending do not necessarily expose a tyrannical nature but rather one too anxious for understanding; he must assure himself that she is at least balancing her preoccupation with the new shipwreck with his tale of their earlier shipwreck. It is the first part of his training in the art of judgment. Satisfied that he has at least planted the seeds of healthy doubt in her too-willingly merciful sympathy, he assures her that he must fulfill the moment of his fortune and gives her over to sleep.

But the metaphor of rebellion continues to affect Prospero as Ariel checks back to his master, proudly asserting the perfect enactment of his orders. Again Prospero must regain control as Ariel reminds him of his promise to free him after his toil, and again Prospero makes use of memory to still the re-

bellion, needing once more the resurrection of the past to rec-
tify the future. As Miranda is the innocent human player,
spontaneously putting herself in the position of those she sees,
so Ariel is the innocent play spirit, desiring uncontrolled liberty. His servitude to Prospero, who has human designs in creating this play, is mere toil to him. All that holds him to the
human scene is gratitude and loyalty to Prospero. Sycorax, the
witch, ruled the island tyrannically; she was devoted to the
disharmony of black magic, acting out on the island the quality
of evil that brought Prospero to ruin.[3] Ariel, the spirit of play, is
antithetical to the pursuit of power, and his refusal to obey
Sycorax imprisoned him and the virtue of his being until Prospero freed him. His search for liberty, for total freedom from
the human scene of will and desire, is natural to him, yet he is
moved by love and gratitude to attend Prospero and play for
him.

Ariel, an ascending spirit associated with the air that he
blows into storms and the fire he creates on board the ship, is
being aided by Prospero to become himself by gradually attaining his liberty—moving from total imprisonment in the
cloven pine, to controlled freedom under Prospero, to absolute
freedom. Like the magic he serves, Ariel is Prospero's tool to
arouse sympathy and to bring play to human society. And with
Ariel, Prospero lays bare more of his plan than he had with
Miranda, who would not be able to understand that the cleansing of a human mind necessitates the pain of separation from
habitual mental process, that it requires the psychic expansion
of madness:

> *Pros.* Who was so firm, so constant, that this coil
>   Would not infect his reason?

3. Kermode, *The Tempest*, xlvii–xlviii, assigns to Sycorax the power of natural
magic, to Prospero the power of holy magic. West, however, in *Shakespeare and the
Outer Mystery*, 86, believes that even holy magic was a suspect study.

Ari.   Not a soul
But felt a fever of the mad, and play'd
Some tricks of desperation. (I. ii. 207–10)

Prospero has again kept control over his own actors by appeal-
ing to the best in their natures, but again his control is only
temporary. He must use his power to give each individual actor
his own share of control before the moment of his metaphor
passes by.

Sycorax's son, Caliban, Prospero's third rebel, whom he had
adopted and tried to teach, chooses this moment of chaos to
press home his claim to the island. In this legal claim to power
over earth, Caliban reflects the Adversary's nature. His desires
are material, as is his amphibious nature, apparently part human and part fish. Composed of earth and water, he is all that
descends by its essential heaviness. The ascendant elements
that allow glimpses of the spirit and that temper lust—for sex,
power, ownership—seem absent from Caliban's makeup.
Through experience of his nature, Prospero has decided that
Caliban is unteachable, a being who must be controlled by the
threat of physical punishment and not by the promise of reward. And so Prospero uses magic to control him, having failed
with formal teaching to inculcate in him love, respect, or gratitude. Only Prospero's magic now keeps him in awe, although
Caliban claims to have once loved Prospero when Prospero
loved him. Caliban's attempted rape of Miranda separated
them, each believing the other from that point an enemy. But
the play that Prospero is enacting for the benefit of Miranda
and the community that she will rule will also change Caliban.
It is not that Caliban is ineducable; Prospero has not taught
him well.[4]

4. Egan, *Drama within Drama*, 95, refers to Caliban as "the amoral, appetitive,
suffering Self in all of us, ever in search of freedom to satisfy all its hungers—vis-
ceral, sexual, and emotional." Kermode, *The Tempest*, xliii, xlvi, in establishing the

By the time Prospero has pulled together his own children,
handling each according to his or her own nature, he is ready
to proceed with the education of the shipwrecked souls. He is
not, at the beginning of his drama, an omnipotent being. He is
a powerful magician; yet magic is a strained control over nature, with each of nature's elements—Ariel's air and fire and
Caliban's earth and water—willing its individual freedom. Were
he to create harmony through magic alone, it would last as
long as his powers and no longer. And the created order, per-
force temporary, would be a direct reflection of the character
of the magician. Sycorax's former rule illustrates the limitations of magic's quality and duration. Prospero must, therefore,
take his current opportunity to give his characters the experiences that will restore each to his own virtue. In the form of
personal responsibility, virtue lives on to create harmonies beyond an individual's life. Yet Prospero must face, too, his own
strong desire to punish his enemies. In creating for them a
metaphoric reenactment of his own experiences, he is prey to
feeling them again himself. As Player-King, he must keep
separate in his mind the two elements of metaphor that he is
creating for them. He must not make Hamlet's mistake of becoming engulfed by the past. For this day, he must be the isolated creator of illusion, the controller of experience, the
magician-playwright who will effect permanent metamorphosis with his play.

Magic: The Mirror of Desire

Through the tempest, Prospero has separated the actors of
three distinct plays. The most important in terms of the future

---

opposition of Art, represented by Prospero, and Nature, represented by Caliban, as the
play's theme, focuses on Caliban's state as the touchstone for value in the play. He
asserts that Caliban is unteachable, that, in fact, his education was harmful as well as
useless because he can only abuse the language he was taught. Yet Kermode also
posits a hint that Caliban "gains a new spiritual dimension from his glimpse of the
'brave spirits.'" Caliban is perhaps more complex than the natural man on whom nur-
ture will not stick.

is Ferdinand, who must meet and love Miranda. The most important in terms of the past are Alonso, Sebastian, and Antonio, who must do penance for their crimes and, if possible, emerge as new men. The third set of actors forms incidentally—Stephano, Trinculo, and Caliban—yet they too will emerge from their experiences changed. Throughout the drama, Prospero remains disguised, sometimes under his magic cloak, sometimes invisible, sometimes playing a role. He is simultaneously staging three plays, each with different terms and different ends. In each play, however, the actors will face their desires clearly mirrored to them and, like Portia's suitors, discover themselves by reaching out for them.

Prospero's first play begins with Ferdinand, Miranda's destined husband. He must somehow transform this young man's grief and despair into fruitful love. But under no circumstances can he simply make this love, around which the new harmonies will be formed, the result of a magic spell. Instead he uses magic to create the suggestion of love. Ariel draws him towards Prospero and Miranda with the harmonies of music, singing:

> Come unto these yellow sands,
>   And then take hands:
> Curtsied when you have, and kiss'd,
>   The wild waves whist:
> Foot it featly here and there,
> And, sweet sprites, the burthen bear. (I. ii. 375–80)

As yet, Ferdinand has no indication that any human being except himself exists on these shores, but he hears and is drawn by the powerful suggestion of music, the careful relationship of part to part that is the symbol in Shakespeare's comedies of both play and love. The music has allayed the storm without and the grief within, and Ferdinand assumes that it is attached to a god of the island. The suggestion of love draws him, yet he remembers his father. Ariel therefore continues:

Full fadom five thy father lies,
  Of his bones are coral made:
Those are pearls that were his eyes:
  Nothing of him that doth fade,
But doth suffer a sea-change
Into something rich and strange.
Sea-nymphs hourly ring his knell:
              Burthen [*within*]. Ding-dong.
Hark now I hear them—ding-dong bell.
                    (I. ii. 397–405)

The lesson that Miranda clearly voiced when she saw that her
and her father's coming to the island was not simply foul but
also blessed play now penetrates Ferdinand's mind. The mortal, erring father made of bone and eye is now metamorphosed
by the sea into coral and pearl, a change rich in both physical
and spiritual terms and strange in its unearthliness.

The song foreshadows the series of metamorphoses that will
take each person from himself and then return him richer than
before.[5] It prepares Ferdinand to accept the terms of the island,
rich with illusion, its air laden with magical harmonies:

The ditty does remember my drown'd father.
This is no mortal business, nor no sound
That the earth owes. (I. ii. 406–408)

He is prepared to abandon the worldly passion of grief and
give way to the flight of his imagination taking him out of the
realm of the mortal. Prospero reaches Ferdinand not by spell
but by suggestion, and then he allows the atmosphere of the
island and the natural attraction of a young man and a young
woman to do the rest. All he need do is bring Miranda, the
image of Ferdinand's desire, to the spot where he was led and
let love take hold. Their first meeting goes even better than

5. Reuben Brower traces the images of change as "the blending of states of
being" in his essay on *The Tempest* in *The Fields of Light: An Experiment in Critical
Reading* (New York: Oxford University Press, 1951), 116.

Prospero had expected. Miranda, exhilarated by the news that he is not a spirit but a man, leaps to thinking him a god; he in turn cannot believe she is simply a maid and addresses her as "the goddess / On whom these airs attend!" (I. ii. 422–23).

But this is a love that must last through worldly trials, must keep the forces of disharmony in check, and, although their instantaneous feeling of love for one another is potent, it is untried, like Portia's and Bassanio's in Belmont. Prospero disguises himself as the tyrant of the island in order to teach both to bear crosses and to test Ferdinand's patience and fortitude:

> They are both in either's pow'rs; but this swift business
> I must uneasy make, lest too light winning
> Make the prize light. (I. ii. 451–53)

He paralyzes Ferdinand, then chains his body to the task of bearing logs in order to emphasize by contrast the nature of true freedom—a lesson that Ferdinand quickly experiences:

> My spirits, as in a dream, are all bound up.
> My father's loss, the weakness which I feel,
> The wrack of all my friends, nor this man's threats,
> To whom I am subdu'd, are but light to me,
> Might I but through my prison once a day
> Behold this maid. All corners else o' th' earth
> Let liberty make use of; space enough
> Have I in such a prison. (I. ii. 487–94)

Gratified at the ease with which love takes hold, Prospero, the controlling center, breathes in an aside, "It works" (I. ii. 494).

Far more complex, however, is his task with his own generation. Between him and them lie the knife of guilt and the poison of injury. All the vices that accompany lust for power belong to Antonio, the core of wickedness; Alonso, his former accomplice; and Sebastian, his new gull. Ego-bound, with a lust to make the world reflect him, Antonio writes his own play based on his personal metaphors. He could not rest until he had usurped the power that he had borrowed as surrogate duke, and for that privilege he enslaved Milan to Naples and Alonso. Now he can use his success as a model for another younger brother. Antonio has the Adversary's psychology. His plays are always designed to enhance himself, just as he intends this new plot to result in his shaking off the debt to Alonso and simultaneously indebting the new King of Naples, Sebastian, to him. His psychology is not altered by the experience of the tempest. He remains power-hungry, self-aggrandizing, and materialistic.

As the good Gonzalo tries to console the king for his seeming loss of Ferdinand, Sebastian mocks him, the vision of goodness that he sees in the island, and the grief that he tries to allay. Sebastian's natural form of play is gambling: "Which, of he or Adrian, for a good wager, first begins to crow?" (II. i. 28–29). Life is an opportunity to win material goods for a few risks. Unlike Ferdinand and Gonzalo, both imaginative men, he denies the overtly strange occurrences, answering Gonzalo's remarks on the freshness of their clothing with flippant sarcasm: "If but one of his pockets could speak, would it not say he lies?" (II. i. 66–67). He enjoys catching errors and improprieties—widow Dido—and will not allow the truth of an imagination that sees Carthage at Tunis: "His word is more than the miraculous harp. . . . What impossible matter will he make easy next?" (II. i. 87, 89–90). In his lack of any but material vision, the kind that measures and weighs the ephemera of the world, he is in the company of Bullingbrook, of Shylock, of Pandarus, committed to transforming his world by plot into a mirror of his own desires. Mystery does not frighten him; spiritual truth has no power over him. Alonso, grief-stricken over the loss of Ferdinand, falls into the despair of the guilty; Antonio merely plots the way to use his weakness. Given the chance to show signs of redemption in his opportunity to become a new man, he reasserts his old self, demonstrating the

Adversary's tenacious hold over the tangible and the manipulable. The magical harmonies of the island that put others to sleep have no effect on him. Prospero, rendering inactive those characters unnecessary to the action, gives Antonio the opportunity to confront his mirror and play himself again as he tempts a slow but willing Sebastian to repeat his successful treachery.

At this point, Prospero could leap to his own desire to destroy the Adversary and return the governance of civilization to the worthy and the penitent. Yet he does not. He again works through suggestion, now Ariel's song in Gonzalo's ear, to awaken the good and let them deal with the situation before them. Antonio is temporarily thwarted by Gonzalo's awakening, but, despite the corroborating evidence of Sebastian's story of wild beasts, the seeds of doubt are planted and the court party decides not to sleep again. Prospero knows that his brother, his other half with whom he had once shared the governance of Milan, is the enemy he must disarm, but he knows too that he must disarm him permanently by creating in the others the viable virtues that will recognize and contain him. Again play is the answer, not magic.

The headiness of Antonio's power lust becomes an entirely tangible commodity—liquor—in the third set of actors. Stephano, a butler, and Trinculo, a fool, are released from their former servitude as they wander about the island, and they too begin to dream of becoming as great as their desires. Caliban sees his opportunity for revenging himself on Prospero; for the first time he can act out his dream of asserting himself over his master. The three form a comical yet troublesome new plot for Prospero, who must keep his eye on them because they alone know of his existence on the island. The desire to transcend physical limit appears in Ferdinand as love, in Antonio and Sebastian as power, in Stephano and Caliban as drunkenness. Spirits take the place of spirit. To balance the new love of his

daughter and Ferdinand, Prospero must teach them how to
control their desires and prepare their love to meet worldly
difficulties. It is a lesson at this point only half taught. He must
convince Antonio that his plans to achieve full power will always be checked by circumstances. With the butler, the fool,
and the monster-servant, he must demonstrate the ultimate
failure of bottled flight. For the time of his drama, Prospero
alone can guide the natural human desire to ascend into a balanced equilibrium where the heavens and the earth touch in
the human mind and body.

Stephano, entering the stage, sings his version of a love
song:

> "The master, the swabber, the boatswain, and I,
>   The gunner and his mate,
> Lov'd Mall, Meg, and Marian, and Margery,
>   But none of us car'd for Kate;
>   For she had a tongue with a tang,
>   Would cry to a sailor, 'Go hang!'
> She lov'd not the savor of tar nor of pitch,
> Yet a tailor might scratch her where e'er she did itch.
>   Then to sea, boys, and let her go hang!"
> This is a scurvy tune too; but here's my comfort.
>   (II. ii. 46–55)

Within him is the thirst for the harmonies of music and of love,
but all he can produce is a scurvy tune, in the realization of
which he turns to his bottle where all frustrations are temporarily comforted. Caliban, too, searches for a power that he
cannot manage and, in his desire to attain it, takes Stephano
for a god and his liquor for true spirits. Trinculo recognizes the
absurdity of this marriage of desires, but moves with them for
the liquor and the fun. Together, the three go merrily off on a
drunken illusion of fulfillment, where each is free from his
bondage. As long as the liquor holds out, they can avoid recognizing their own inability to handle liberty:

'Ban, 'Ban, Ca-Caliban
Has a new master, get a new man.
Freedom, high-day! high-day, freedom! freedom, high-day,
freedom! (II. ii. 184–87)

The first part of Prospero's play is well under way. He has created the tempest, isolated the human atoms of his civilization, and returned each man to his fundamental desires. He has given the guilty the sympathetic experience of living through his torment. Now as each pursues the quest proper to his nature, Prospero forms the scenes and manipulates the actors, not by magic, which he uses like stage machinery to create illusions and plant suggestions, but by play, where each character can act himself out and find the inevitable end of his desires. For Ferdinand, the end will be the harmony of love which he and Miranda, like the heroes and heroines of the comedies, can bring to their society. For Antonio, the end will be the natural containment of his Adversary's disruptive need for self-aggrandizement and self-reflection, a containment he must recognize as inevitable where people seek the bonds of harmony. For Alonso, the end will be freedom from guilt by his becoming his own victim. For Caliban, Stephano, and Trinculo, the end will be the recognition that they are limited to their functions as servants, unable to transcend—except in a dream suddenly made real by liquor—the material signs of power and wealth.

Three Plays

As the love between Ferdinand and Miranda moves to their mutual exchange of bondage, each to be the other's master or mistress and servant, and as Caliban's plot to free himself by killing Prospero leads him further into slavery, Prospero prepares his art for the trio of his old enemies. Fatigue and hunger work on their bodies, creating despair in Alonso, desperate hope in his predators. Their sense of isolation is increased, their reliance on themselves total. At that moment, Prospero enters amidst his music, invisible and removed. Only Gonzalo and Alonso react to its sound, they alone responsive to the harmonies of the spirit. Prospero first spreads a table in this wilderness, like the devil when he tempted Christ in the desert. The sight of physical satisfaction moves them all, but the strangeness of the servers distresses them. They start to believe in strange shapes, in the creatures that travelers have cited as living in strange lands. The force of the imagination takes hold of all, even Sebastian and Antonio, who would not allow Gonzalo to build Carthage at Tunis. The offering of food is ambivalent. The food satisfies a physical hunger, yet it is offered by strange and unknown beings. It is a test for them— will they gratify their hunger or will they prefer to keep their spirits spare? Sebastian is the first to choose to satisfy his hunger rather than nourish his doubt: "They have left their viands behind; for we have stomachs. / Will't please you taste of what is here?" (III. iii. 41–42). Alonso at first rejects it, demonstrating his closeness to redemption in that decision alone, yet Gonzalo—the perpetual optimist who in his age is like Miranda in her youth, seeing goodness everywhere—persuades him to take the offering at face value. Gonzalo does not see the devil's banquet, but the table set by God before him in the presence of his enemies. The good man sees his reflection everywhere; the sinful man doubts the actions of people and nature; the evil man takes what he can, believing that he can manipulate it once he has it to gratify his needs and desires.

As each again acts out the man within him, Prospero moves to the next scene of this play. Ariel, in the disguise of the ancient symbol of rapacious greed—the harpy, who soiled what she did not eat—causes the banquet to vanish. Their own desires are concretized in this creature, the pure image of a cunning and vicious predator. Their actions have, through

Prospero's magic, created the true picture of themselves which they now confront. It is their first correction—the hand reaching out to grab what it can take is paralyzed in midair as what it was reaching for vanishes—as all material things vanish before time. The visual lesson is further expounded by Ariel's words:

> You are three men of sin, whom Destiny,
> That hath to instrument this lower world
> And what is in't, the never-surfeited sea
> Hath caus'd to belch up you; and on this island
> Where man doth not inhabit—you 'mongst men
> Being most unfit to live. I have made you mad;
> And even with such-like valor men hang and drown
> Their proper selves. (III. iii. 53–60)

What Ariel speaks is not the truth: the island is inhabited by a man, Prospero, and it is he, not Destiny, who has caused nature to reject them. But at this point Prospero cannot appear. He must convince these men that evil meets its inevitable punishment at the hands of Destiny, the organizing principle for the "lower world," the world of material nature. In addition, Ariel suggests to them the suicide of madness—not the literal self-murder that the harpy seeks, but the sea change that transforms the body into the eternal and beautiful things of the spirit. He is there to snatch away their souls so that they may be reborn in virtue.

They cannot, however, accept this plot, denying as it does the signs of their power. To demonstrate that power again, they draw swords on Ariel, giving him the opportunity to correct them and clarify the cause of this retributive justice:

>   You fools! I and my fellows
> Are ministers of Fate. The elements,
> Of whom your swords are temper'd, may as well
> Wound the loud winds, or with bemock'd-at stabs
> Kill the still-closing waters, as diminish

> One dowle that's in my plume. My fellow ministers
> Are like invulnerable. If you could hurt,
> Your swords are now too massy for your strengths,
> And will not be uplifted. But remember
> (For that's my business to you) that you three
> From Milan did supplant good Prospero,
> Expos'd unto the sea (which hath requit it)
> Him, and his innocent child; for which foul deed
> The pow'rs, delaying (not forgetting), have
> Incens'd the seas and shores—yea, all the creatures,
> Against your peace. Thee of thy son, Alonso,
> They have bereft; and do pronounce by me
> Ling'ring perdition (worse than any death
> Can be at once) shall step by step attend
> You and your ways, whose wraths to guard you from—
> Which here, in this most desolate isle, else falls
> Upon your heads—is nothing but heart's sorrow,
> And a clear life ensuing. (III. iii. 60–82)

Thus the devourers are devoured by the spirit of their lust.
The source of their power is removed as they cannot use—and
then by spell cannot lift—their weapons of destruction. They
meet face to face the judgment of the powers they worship,
the simple eye-for-an-eye justice that deprives a father of a son
in return for depriving a father of a daughter. As cruel and merciless as Alonso, Antonio, and Sebastian were to Prospero, so
cruel and merciless are the powers that Prospero's play presents to them as their judges. Ariel's speech is true metaphorically if not literally. But for the material man, the literal must
be understood before the greater mysteries of the spirit can be
approached. Ferdinand and Miranda are indeed lost to their
fathers, but are to be found again in each other and the powers
of harmony that their love bestows.

In this banquet play, Prospero begins to correct the mistake
of the literal and the material by removing all such comforts,
by sending his enemies into the madness that will destroy

their old selves. And, just as important, he himself acts out his desire for revenge, knowing it to be only a step in the process of purgation, but a step that he can take with them.[6] He has finally relieved himself of the need to exact vengeance by placing the vengeance in the context of a final virtue. Alonso is stricken immediately by the portrait of his sin. He feels for the first time that he is living through the experiences to which he had condemned Prospero. Sebastian and Antonio, however, cling tenaciously to their material hold on the world:

> Seb.   But one fiend at a time,
> I'll fight their legions o'er.
>
> Ant.   I'll be thy second. (III. iii. 102–103)

Having purged himself of the poisonous need for revenge, Prospero returns to Ferdinand and Miranda calmer and more loving. Ferdinand has already passed the tests that Prospero set up for him, and now he can be given the prize. Yet the final lesson in control is still to be taught; Prospero reminds him that the body's desire must never precede the spirit's rituals. For the earthbound only the sorrow of evanescence awaits. The spirit and the flesh must recognize and respect one another. Nor can the virtuous man be complacent; Prospero warns Ferdinand against the powers that the flesh has even over the strongest will:

> do not give dalliance
> Too much the rein. The strongest oaths are straw
> To th' fire i' th' blood. Be more abstenious,
> Or else good night your vow! (IV. i. 51–54)

---

6. Fergusson, *Shakespeare: The Pattern in His Carpet*, 309, notes the parallel between this situation in Shakespeare and the Greek and Christian (notably present in Dante) view of wisdom: "The growing soul resuffers its mistaken or evil motives in the light of truth, in order to free itself from them." This idea was also present in *The True Declaration*, a moralizing report on the state of the Virginia colony, in the form of "*Quae videtur paena, est medicina.*" See Kermode, *The Tempest*, xxviii–xxix.

To demonstrate the lesson fully and to create for the couple the full metaphoric harmony of life, Prospero stages a second play. He has caused the elements to rebel and rip apart the fabric of social ties; now he must recreate them around this center of love. The masque is a wish transformed to promise by play. Iris, the rainbow, enters. Echoing the biblical covenant between God and man after the Flood, she appears as the sign of cosmic peace between the spirit and the flesh. Awesome yet elusive, without clear beginning or end yet beginning in the sky and ending on the earth, she unifies in her form the many colors of life, serving as a visible mediator between pure light and limited vision.

As the messenger of the gods—like Mercury to whom Vernon compares Hal—Iris links the two aspects of human nature, not in opposition but in conjunction. In Prospero's play, she appears to summon Ceres, the powerful goddess of the earth whose province extends over phenomenal nature—the flowers, the crops, the vines, the cattle. Although she presides, too, over human fruition, she clearly dissociates herself from Venus and Cupid, who were responsible for uniting Persephone to Dis, the youth of spring to the dark regions of the dead. Lust, the separation of love from the spirit, fulfills itself by force and treachery, and its personification, Venus, must be far away from these proceedings. Although they had intended to work their power on this couple, they have been disarmed by the total harmony of Ferdinand's and Miranda's love. When Juno enters, the cosmic scene is complete. Present on the stage are heaven, earth, and the rainbow that mediates between them.

As Juno and Ceres bless the couple appropriately, Ferdinand responds to the image's magnificence and wisdom:

> This is a most majestic vision, and
> Harmonious charmingly.
> . . . .

> Let me live here ever;
> So rare a wond'red father and a wise
> Makes this place Paradise. (IV. i. 118–19, 122–24)

Prospero has indeed presented in his play the full harmonies of Eden, where the interaction of the elements was pure and purposeful. Yet Ferdinand, transported by this harmony, mistakes the case. The vision is indeed harmonious charmingly—that is, by charms. Eden no longer exists, and even though a wise ruler can bring the notes together again, he cannot maintain it by himself forever. The vision must be given to others, who must pursue it in themselves and in their world.

The strain is apparent in Prospero: "Hush and be mute, / Or else our spell is marr'd" (IV. i. 126–27). Reaper and nymphs, men and spirits, couple in a dance, but within moments the vision vanishes before Prospero's recollection of yet another group of characters who must be checked. The tension within him mounts as his moments become precious. He gives his final lesson hurriedly, as he must:

> You do look, my son, in a mov'd sort,
> As if you were dismay'd; be cheerful, sir.
> Our revels now are ended. These our actors
> (As I foretold you) were all spirits, and
> Are melted into air, into thin air,
> And like the baseless fabric of this vision,
> The cloud-capp'd tow'rs, the gorgeous palaces,
> The solemn temples, the great globe itself,
> Yea, all which it inherit, shall dissolve,
> And like this insubstantial pageant faded
> Leave not a rack behind. We are such stuff
> As dreams are made on; and our little life
> Is rounded with a sleep. (IV. i. 146–58)

Ferdinand's desire to live forever in the harmony of Prospero's charms must be corrected. The fabric of the vision, its actors, its scenes, its movements, like the concrete forms that humans

build to realize their dreams, are all ephemeral. The permanent harmony of Eden does not exist. What does remain is the
dream itself, the dream that is human life struggling to become
greater than its natural limits, struggling too to find its form.
Prospero speaks in terms of play to explain the limitations of
life. The Player-King can build towers, palaces, temples, globes,
but he must be aware that all his building is doomed to destruction, for he builds from himself, and he is mortal, out of
the earth's materials, and they are mortal. The sleep that rounds
life also rounds the actions of the characters within the play.
Life is play; play is life. The forms fade and vanish, but the
imagination that creates them transcends the realm of the mortal. Prospero forces Ferdinand to confront the real limits of human nature; he cannot allow his future son-in-law, civilization's
future king, to repeat his own error.

Nor will Prospero repeat it. He cannot ignore the threat
posed by the trio of drunkards, who have lost their bottles in
the scummy pool. For them he stages a simple play, its purpose to catch and to punish them. He has despaired of teaching Caliban anything, believing that his kindnesses have been
"all, all lost, quite lost" (IV. i. 190). And those who cannot be
instructed must be checked. Before his protected grove, he has
Ariel place the rich clothing that befits a king. Prospero knows
from bitter experience that the accouterments of power bestow
the feeling of power. Only Caliban has enough sense to realize
that the appearance is not enough. Prospero's tutoring has not
been entirely in vain. Stephano and Trinculo play royalty:

> *Trin.* O King Stephano! O peer! O worthy Stephano!
> look what a wardrobe here is for thee!
> *Cal.* Let it alone, thou fool, it is but trash.
> *Trin.* O, ho, monster! we know what belongs to a frip-
> pery. O King Stephano! (IV. i. 222–26)

Unlike Antonio, who desires power for its own sake, these servants are satisfied with the simple reflection of power, the ma-

terial signs of wealth and position. For such gross physicality, Prospero provides gross physical punishment. Like the beasts they imitate in their spiritual blindness, they are driven off and hunted.

Prospero has devised for each set of characters the play appropriate to its needs for education. The blatantly material servants' desires are fulfilled and then the desire itself corrected through pain. The Adversary's company, more sophisticated in their use of earthly possessions and therefore more dangerous, are driven mad—a psychological pain—their habitual patterns of response disrupted and their sins, resulting from these patterns, realized before them and punished according to their own standards. The lovers, Ferdinand and Miranda, are trained to accept human limit and to persevere, to understand the flight of their love as mysterious and beautiful but not necessarily permanently viable. To the heavenly, Prospero brings earth; to the earthly, heaven. Now, with his enemies within his control, Prospero can begin to move towards balancing the two, towards the rainbow. ✓

Charms O'erthrown

⚔ Like the magician of the tarot pack's major arcana, Prospero has stood with his right hand grasping the wand of wisdom upraised towards heaven, his left hand pointing to the earth—the ultimate symbol of the individual forming a bridge between the divine and the mortal. From the heavens he derives power because he individuates the human desire for perfection. He has grasped the mysterious harmonies among the elements, which he can control to bring his vision to manifestation. Prospero as Player-King is the figure of the rainbow, an open circuit on which the human spirit rises to fulfillment and divinity manifests itself in separate consciousnesses. Even though Prospero has attained the mysterious wisdom of the occult, he must know that his personal vision can guide the human imagination only temporarily, for he is mortal and he is old. He must prepare, therefore, to bestow his gifts on his descendants by disseminating his wisdom. He must posit within each consciousness that can achieve it the vision of harmony between the earthly and the heavenly. The earthly—sexual lust, power hunger—can be controlled by the soul's vision of freedom from the body—Ariel's desire for liberation from labor. The heavenly must be tempered by the earthly facts of a fallen world—the recalcitrant brutishness of Caliban. Ferdinand must know that he cannot live on the island forever, Paradise though it seems.

Magic has been for Prospero the stagecraft of his play. He has been able through the transcendent Ariel to disrupt the elements and bring them back to harmonious interaction; he has been able to use the elemental spirits as actors in his plays. But his aim is to transmit his own knowledge to the civilization that he had abandoned and that had in turn banished him—an end unaccomplishable anywhere but in the individual person. Now all his enemies lie within his power; his temptation to turn his power to destruction is strong. But he knows that he must complete his plays, stage their last scene, which is a drawing together of all that has been separated—the world's recreation from chaos—and return to his own mortality.

He enters dressed in his magic robes, the sign of his continuing elemental control, to hear Ariel's description of his enemies' madness:

> Ari.   Your charm so strongly works 'em
> That if you now beheld them, your affections
> Would become tender.
>
> Pros.   Dost thou think so, spirit?
>
> Ari.. Mine would, sir, were I human.
>
> Pros.   And mine shall.
> Hast thou, which art but air, a touch, a feeling
> Of their afflictions, and shall not myself,

> One of their kind, that relish all as sharply
> Passion as they, be kindlier mov'd than thou art?
> Though with their high wrongs I am strook to th'
> quick,
>
> Yet, with my nobler reason, 'gainst my fury
> Do I take part. The rarer action is
> In virtue than in vengeance. They being penitent,
> The sole drift of my purpose doth extend
> Not a frown further. Go, release them, Ariel.
> My charms I'll break, their senses I'll restore,
> And they shall be themselves. (V. i. 17–32)

In spite of Ariel's fixed desire to be himself in returning to the
elements, he has been woven into Prospero's design and af-
fected by the plays he has acted in, just as all actors' experiences in play enlarge their beings. And Prospero is moved at
this moment to shake off the bitter taste of the wrongs done
him, surprised by his play's extension as far as Ariel and gratified by the magnitude of his success. He puts aside fury for
reason, vengeance for virtue, helped by his own servant's education to put through his plan as he had conceived it. For his
purpose was always to act out his own passions and so to release them solely to make his enemies penitent. With Alonso,
Antonio, and Sebastian on the way under Ariel's charge, Prospero moves towards the renunciation of his power.

All the spirits that have helped in his "rough magic" (V. i.
50), those "weak masters" (V. i. 41) of the elemental world, he
calls together to announce his abdication from power. Not
their natural power but his will has made the tempest, and
now, as he must, he resigns his will, asking merely for the solemn music that will return the mad to sanity within his
charmed circle:

> But this rough magic
> I here abjure; and when I have requir'd
> Some heavenly music (which even now I do)
> To work mine end upon their senses that

This airy charm is for, I'll break my staff,
Bury it certain fadoms in the earth,
And deeper than did ever plummet sound
I'll drown my book. (V. i. 50–57)

Prospero resigns to the elements his power over them, ready
to cancel all spells and face the results of his play. He stands
or falls now by human will—his own and those of the beings
whom he has tutored.

His first confrontation, however, is not direct. Prospero must
allow both himself and his former countrymen to bring their
actions to a halt. They, charmed out of their senses, commun-
ing only with the inner stings that now torment them, stand
stricken while he addresses each one, moving from Gonzalo,
to whom he promises reward for virtue, to Alonso and Sebastian, who are punished for their sins against him and Miranda—Sebastian doubly because of his renewed villainy
against his brother. Antonio, Prospero's Adversary, he greets
last, understanding that he cannot cure his destructive materialism, but knowing that he must forgive him and encompass
him in order to bring a fragmented, polarized world together
again. His magic, like the spirits in his play before Ferdinand
and Miranda, vanishes heavily. The tightly coiled power that
produced Prospero's strain unwinds itself. The staff, the book,
and the robes now belong to a past role, and he must become
himself again—the Duke of Milan and a man. He accepts the
transformation by calling for his former garb. He must not face
his enemies as the potent minister of their punishment; he
must greet them, live among them, as a man. Only Ariel remains to obey his last commands, and that from loyalty and
gratitude, not from fear or submission to potent magic.

Upon awakening to the real vision of Prospero, Alonso, who
has been brought from rationalized memory to personal reenactment by Prospero's play, begs forgiveness. His movement

from king to beggar has completed itself successfully. But Sebastian and Antonio remain silent, recognizing Prospero as an end to their ambitions, both as their original victim and as their precedent for further conquest of power. Returning from madness, they have not brought with them the fruits of repentance but merely a recognition of power that supersedes their own. Prospero recognizes their state and governs them, who still cannot govern themselves from within, with the threat of exposure. Since experience has trained him in human limit, he knows that he must check those he cannot redeem. Blackmail must be within his real powers:

> *Pros.*   But you, my brace of lords, were I so minded,
> I here could pluck his Highness' frown upon you
> And justify you traitors. At this time
> I will tell no tales.
>
> *Seb.*   [*Aside.*] The devil speaks in him.
>   (V. i. 126–29)

From Antonio no word issues. Yet as Iris saved the harpies from death, so Prospero will include these creatures in his new world because, as Player-King, he assimilates rather than destroys, deals in virtue rather than vengeance. They cannot partake in the harmonies of the upraised spirit, but they can be silenced.[7] Their only further words in the play manifest their steadfast materialism. Upon viewing Stephano, Trinculo, and Caliban, Sebastian, turning exclusively to Antonio, renews his mocking queries:

---

7. See Kermode's discussion in *The Tempest*, liv, lxii, of Antonio as an example of Machiavellian *virtu* rather than Christian virtue. He sees him as Prospero's failure because Antonio will not choose the good. Kermode continues: "A world without Antonio is a world without freedom; Prospero's shipwreck cannot restore him if he desires not to be restored, to life. The gods chalk out a tragicomic way, but enforce only disaster. The rest is voluntary" (p. lxii). Prospero allows Antonio's participation in the universal harmony to be voluntary, but he will not allow him to destroy that harmony.

Seb.   Ha, ha!
What things are these, my Lord Antonio?
Will money buy 'em?

Ant.   Very like; one of them
Is a plain fish, and no doubt marketable.

(V. i. 263–66)

Their experience in the mysterious forces of human aspiration
and human limit has left them untouched, and they remain as
they were, enamored of earth.

But with Alonso, who has become a true brother in the likeness of their experiences, Prospero can share a final lesson.
Even the dearest gift that a person is given by the world, a
child, must be lost, but for that loss the increase is twofold.
Prospero's wish that Ferdinand and Miranda be King and
Queen of Naples he can now trust to Alonso, who has learned
how to see clearly by having his senses dimmed:

O heavens, that they were living both in Naples,
The King and Queen there! That they were, I wish
Myself were mudded in that oozy bed
Where my son lies. (V. i. 149–52)

Relinquishing in his wish the earthly crown he had so coveted
that he sought to extend it to Milan, Alonso has undergone his
final sea change.

At seeing his play effect true human feeling in Alonso, Prospero can reveal to him and all the company his son and future
daughter, the vision of wholeness they now deserve. The two
are behind a curtain, a play in themselves as they play at chess.
They, the two heirs of two opposing worlds, have become one
in the game that symbolizes human conflict from pawn to king.
As they manipulate the pieces, they play their functions as the
world's future; they have accepted their roles as Player-King
and Player-Queen. And even in conflict, they turn to each

other with love, each abandoning his or her right to the other as the other in turn gives it back, just as both had placed themselves in servitude to the other:

> *Mir.*   Sweet lord, you play me false.
>
> *Fer.*   No, my dearest love,
>   I would not for the world.
>
> *Mir.*   Yes, for a score of kingdoms you should wrangle,
>   And I would call it fair play. (V. i. 172–75)

Miranda, in play, recognizes potential falsehood and Ferdinand, in play, negates ambition. Male and female, old and new, worldly and innocent—the principle of duality has met and united in Ferdinand and Miranda, neither now desirous of remaining in Paradise forever but accepting conflict and limit within the embrace of their love.[8] Alonso's reaction to the vision is at first suspicion, but on hearing that Miranda is Prospero's daughter and his son's chosen wife, he regresses temporarily into the pain of guilt:

> *Alon.*   I am hers.
>   But O, how oddly will it sound that I
>   Must ask my child forgiveness!
>
> *Pros.*   There, sir, stop.
>   Let us not burthen our remembrances with
>   A heaviness that's gone. (V. i. 196–200)

In the new world, with all sins, all injustices acted out and released, there must be no turning back to the past. To remember too keenly is to negate the promise of the rainbow.

The good old man, Gonzalo, who has witnessed in the innocence of a virtuous heart the play before him, gives voice to

---

8. Holland, *The Shakespearean Imagination*, 318, interprets the chess game as the transmutation of conflict into game.

the mysterious, paradoxical beauty of the scene. He brings together the two seemingly opposing experiences that form the
drama's center:

> Was Milan thrust from Milan, that his issue
> Should become kings of Naples? O, rejoice
> Beyond a common joy, and set it down
> With gold on lasting pillars: in one voyage
> Did Claribel her husband find at Tunis,
> And Ferdinand, her brother, found a wife
> Where he himself was lost; Prospero, his dukedom
> In a poor isle; and all of us, ourselves,
> When no man was his own. (V. i. 205–13)

In his innocence, Gonzalo believes that the uncommon joy
that has pervaded the isle can be set down for all time if it is
written in gold on lasting pillars. Prospero's lesson, however—
that all the towers, the palaces, the temples, the globe itself
shall fade into nothingness—has at least been planted in the
minds of the new king and queen. Gonzalo's naïveté in desiring this experience of loss and return to be rendered immortal
contrasts sharply with Prospero's attitude. For the innocent
good man, whose goodness was insufficient to bar the will of
evil, it seems possible to save this moment forever in the gran-
deur of the world. But for Prospero, who knows that goodness
must be viable, that the spirit alone takes the imprint of experience, the moment can exist only in the human desire to
keep it whole by continuing to act it out. To Miranda's excla-
mation of joy at the brave new world she sees, Prospero has
added simply: " 'Tis new to thee" (V. i. 184). In a fallen world,
innocence is not enough to prevent evil. Paradise is no more,
and all that humans can do is to will it to action through play,
whose effects, however ephemeral, will live on within the
mind.

But even Prospero's limits are expounded as Caliban,
pinched and stinking, enters the stage to observe the after-

math of the scene. The brutish, unteachable son of Sycorax sees his master in a new light. He, too, has learned from experience what Prospero could never teach him from the book. After observing how fine Prospero is in his duke's robes and hearing Prospero acknowledge "this thing of darkness" (V. i. 275) as his own, Caliban takes his orders to prepare the cell for company with a new spirit:

> Ay, that I will; and I'll be wise hereafter,
> And seek for grace. What a thrice-double ass
> Was I to take this drunkard for a god,
> And worship this dull fool! (V. i. 295–98)

He could worship false masters again; he is moved by the brave new spirits whom he sees in Prospero's company. But his blind—because vengeful—love of any person who he thinks will free him from servitude is over. Prospero's boots are finer to lick than Stephano's, and through his experiences Caliban has recognized his own limit. Their relationship, which started in false expectations, renews itself in mutual recognition. Even though Prospero's play was intended for the human world, its harmonies reach above and below it to move Ariel to compassion and Caliban to repentance. Both are accidental reverberations that testify to the strength of Prospero's play: since both Ariel and Caliban knew Prospero's powers as a magician, it is not magic that moved them, but the play in which they acted and discovered themselves.

Not Prospero, however, but the audience is the last actor in the play. Coming before those who have witnessed the entire drama from his point of view, Prospero—not magician, but actor—pleads for release from his own bondage:

> Now my charms are all o'erthrown,
> And what strength I have's mine own,
> Which is most faint. Now 'tis true,
> I must be here confin'd by you,

Or sent to Naples. Let me not,
Since I have my dukedom got,
And pardon'd the deceiver, dwell
In this bare island by your spell,
But release me from my bands
With the help of your good hands.
Gentle breath of yours my sails
Must fill, or else my project fails,
Which was to please. Now I want
Spirits to enforce, art to enchant,
And my ending is despair,
Unless I be reliev'd by prayer,
Which pierces so, that it assaults
Mercy itself, and frees all faults.
        As you from crimes would pardon'd be,
        Let your indulgence set me free. (Epilogue)

The lessons of the play are all put finally before the audience. Ferdinand has learned; Alonso has learned; Prospero has learned. But their learning is a play which, to succeed, must reach out to those they represent. To extend the harmonious reverberations outward and make the true magic, which is play, to create an Eden again, no matter how ephemeral, the audience must adopt and act out the spirit of forgiveness, for that is true freedom.[9] Applause is its expression, a magical clap-

---

9. Fergusson, *Shakespeare: The Pattern in His Carpet*, 310, in assigning this speech to the "real world where only 'mercy' itself, not poetry or ceremony, however beautiful, can provide the freedom we need and seek," is ignoring the play's poetry and ceremony as the medium for teaching that mercy. As Prospero has given it, so should we return it. The real world, as Prospero has demonstrated, is difficult to distinguish from the world of illusion. The two blend so that a play's teaching can be inculcated in the audience. John Russell Brown, *Shakespeare and His Comedies* (London: Methuen, 1957), 249–50, emphasizes the play's instruction as contrived by Prospero and sees this last speech as revealing the imperfection of any human performance, even the wisest. Egan, *Drama within Drama*, 117, notes that while the play's termination in the Epilogue breaks down the barriers between play and reality, the "triumphant mergence of our world with that of the play" is a possibility rather than a fact. Prospero, like Henry V, does not violate free will.

The vision of Prospero as poet and director, a type of Shakespeare himself, is a general one. Fergusson, p. 307, sees Prospero (and Duke Vincentio) plotting behind

ping together of two hands to create a sound that, multiplied over a community, brings together play and audience, player and spectator, obliterating the distinction between the players within the play and the players outside it.

---

the scenes to "test and enlighten [his] subjects." They illustrate Shakespeare's notion of the analogy between the world of the theater ruled by a poet-director and the world of the human community ruled by a king. Holland, *The Shakespearean Imagination*, 319, 321, also sees Prospero as a teacher and dramatist, and *The Tempest* as a "play about plays, playing plays and playing chess, and the way play can work transformations; turn greed for political power into political responsibility; transform lust into love and, ultimately, marriage." He understands that the dramatist Prospero's manipulation of his island as theater is godlike, extending Fergusson's analogy of Prospero as king to Prospero as god, who "manipulates all nature, the theater of this world, to tutor man into the newness and freshness of Paradise." Egan, p. 119, rightly places Prospero's art with Shakespeare's, in the human world: "[Shakespeare's] ultimate definition of his own dramatic artistry—of its aims, problems, and possibilities in our world—thus culminates in the anticipation of a communal ceremony of affirmation, one in which playwright, actors, and audience can unite in a recognition, acceptance, and celebration of our shared humanity." See, too, Harriett Hawkins, "Fabulous Counterfeits: Dramatic Construction and Dramatic Perspectives in *The Spanish Tragedy, A Midsummer Night's Dream*, and *The Tempest*," *Shakespeare Studies*, VI (1970), 51–65.

CHAPTER VII

"Many Persons—and None"

There was no one in him; behind his face (which even in the poor paintings of the period is unlike any other) and his words, which were copious, imaginative, and emotional, there was nothing but a little chill, a dream not dreamed by anyone. . . .

The story goes that, before or after he died, he found himself before God and he said: "I, who have been so many men in vain, want to be one man: myself." The voice of God replied from a whirlwind: "Neither am I one self; I dreamed the world as you dreamed your work, my Shakespeare, and among the shapes of my dream are you, who, like me, are many persons—and none."[1]

None of the players that Shakespeare created in his works equals his or her own creator. Yet in exposing the player in himself through the players within the play, Shakespeare makes his audience and his readers aware of that "little chill" at the human center. The unimpeded communication between the playwright, who gives his characters the will to create their own plays within the universe governed by his words, and the audience, who receives these plays as testament to its play faculty, is akin to the communication believed in the Christian tradition to exist between God, the creator and audience, and humanity, the chief reflector of the Word and testament to the goodness of the plan.

Shakespeare's Player-Kings enact the plan. Once they abandon their fixed places in the world, whether marked by name, title, occupation, or kinship, they become conscious actors. As

1. Jorge Luis Borges, *Dreamtigers*, trans. Mildred Boyer and Harold Morland (New York: Dutton, 1970), 46–47.

actors, ciphers to which any number can be added, they can play the history of humanity. If they then add the act that fulfills their education and use themselves as media to teach others the way, they make the experience infinitely repeatable. The mystery surrounding them—Henry V's omniscience, Portia's power over the sea and Antonio's ships, Duke Vincentio's grace, Prospero's magic—merely intensifies the feeling that such harmony is now a special event, incomprehensible in rational terms.

The Adversaries deny the plan. Bullingbrook says one thing and means another; Shylock cannibalizes his world; Angelo decides that only his pleasure has meaning; Claudius divides *seeming* from *being* in Denmark. In turning all their love inward rather than outward, they undermine the natural movement of word into act. Their efforts are ultimately futile in a world governed by the Logos, but only a Player-King can frustrate their efforts within the dramas. When none exists or when one fails to mature—*Troilus and Cressida, Hamlet, Coriolanus*—the world of the drama is ceded to tragedy.

Shakespeare's "all the world's a stage," therefore, is the nexus for an intricate pattern of ideas and assumptions. The perfect harmony depicted in Genesis of the one Creation sounding in the many was shattered with the Fall. In the postlapsarian world, the human function is to seek the metaphors that reveal the harmonic system and then to return it to wholeness by acting them out. It is to remember Eden in play, which in this sense becomes a form of worship, an experience of bringing to birth the inherent pattern of Creation. Shakespeare, forming his drama so that actors and audience alike discover their true selves as players, restores infinite possibility to human limit and makes Creation, for a brief time, whole again.

Sources Cited

Primary Sources

Borges, Jorge Luis. *Dreamtigers.* Translated by Mildred Boyer and Harold Morland. New York: Dutton, 1970.

Evans, G. Blakemore, ed. *The Riverside Shakespeare.* Boston: Houghton Mifflin, 1974.

Feuillerat, Albert, ed. *The Prose Works of Sir Philip Sidney.* Vol. III. Cambridge: Cambridge University Press, 1923.

Gosson, Stephen. *The Schoole of Abuse.* 1579. Reprint. New York: Garland, 1973.

Herford, C. H., Percy and Evelyn Simpson, eds. *Ben Jonson.* Vol. VIII. Oxford: Clarendon Press, 1954.

Heywood, Thomas. *An Apology for Actors.* 1612. Reprint. New York: Garland, 1973.

Marston, John. *Antonio and Mellida.* Edited by G. K. Hunter. Lincoln: University of Nebraska Press, 1965.

Northbrooke, John. *A Treatise wherein Dicing, Dauncing, Vaine playes, or Enterluds . . . are reproved.* ?1577. Reprint. New York: Garland, 1974.

Prynne, William. *Histriomastix.* 1633. Reprint. New York: Garland, 1974.

Waterhouse, Osborn, ed. *The Non-Cycle Mystery Plays.* Early English Text Society, extra series, CIV. London: Kegan Paul, Trench, Trübner, 1909.

Whitelocke, Sir James. *Liber Famelicus.* Edited by John Bruce. Westminster: The Camden Society, 1858.

Secondary Sources: Books

Axline, Virginia M. *Dibs in Search of Self: Personality Development in Play Therapy.* Boston: Houghton Mifflin, 1964.

Bache, William B. *"Measure for Measure" as Dialectical Art.* Lafayette, Ind.: Purdue University Press, 1969.

Baldwin, T. W. *William Shakspere's Small Latine and Lesse Greeke.* Vol. I. Urbana: University of Illinois Press, 1944.

Barber, C. L. *Shakespeare's Festive Comedy.* Princeton: Princeton University Press, 1959.

Beckerman, Bernard. *Shakespeare at the Globe, 1599–1609.* New York: Macmillan, 1962.

Bennett, Josephine Waters. *"Measure for Measure" as Royal Entertainment.* New York: Columbia University Press, 1966.

Bergeron, David M. *English Civic Pageantry, 1558–1642.* Columbia: University of South Carolina Press, 1971.

Berne, Eric. *Games People Play: The Psychology of Human Relationships.* New York: Grove, 1964.

Brower, Reuben. *The Fields of Light: An Experiment in Critical Reading.* New York: Oxford University Press, 1951.

Brown, John Russell. *Shakespeare and His Comedies.* London: Methuen, 1957.

Burke, Kenneth. *The Philosophy of Literary Form: Studies in Symbolic Action.* New York: Vintage Books, 1957.

Calderwood, James. *Shakespearean Metadrama.* Minneapolis: University of Minnesota Press, 1971.

Campbell, O. J. *Shakespeare's Satire.* New York: Oxford University Press, 1943.

Chambers, E. K. *The Elizabethan Stage.* Oxford: Clarendon Press, 1923.

Clemen, Wolfgang. *The Development of Shakespeare's Imagery.* Cambridge: Harvard University Press, 1951.

Cope, Jackson I. *The Theater and the Dream: From Metaphor to Form in Renaissance Drama.* Baltimore: Johns Hopkins University Press, 1973.

Doran, Madeleine. *Endeavors of Art: A Study of Form in Elizabethan Drama.* Madison: University of Wisconsin Press, 1964.

Dowden, Edward. *Shakspere: A Critical Study of His Mind and Art.* Rev. ed. London: Kegan Paul, Trench, Trübner, 1892.

Egan, Robert. *Drama within Drama: Shakespeare's Sense of His Art.* New York: Columbia University Press, 1972.

Farrell, Kirby. *Shakespeare's Creation: The Language of Magic and Play.* Amherst: University of Massachusetts Press, 1975.

Fergusson, Francis. *The Idea of a Theater*. Princeton: Princeton University Press, 1949.

———. *Shakespeare: The Pattern in His Carpet*. New York: Delacorte, 1970.

Fisch, Harold. *"Hamlet" and the Word: The Covenant Pattern in Shakespeare*. New York: Frederick Ungar, 1971.

Gardner, Helen. *The Business of Criticism*. Oxford: Clarendon Press, 1959.

Hartley, Ruth E., Lawrence K. Frank, and Robert M. Goldenson. *Understanding Children's Play*. New York: Columbia University Press, 1952.

Holland, Norman N. *The Shakespearean Imagination*. Bloomington: Indiana University Press, 1964.

Holloway, John. *The Story of the Night: Studies in Shakespeare's Major Tragedies*. Lincoln: University of Nebraska Press, 1961.

Huizinga, Johan. *Homo Ludens*. Boston: Beacon Press, 1950.

Jones, Ernest. *Hamlet and Oedipus*. New York: Norton, 1949.

Kantorowicz, Ernst H. *The King's Two Bodies*. Princeton: Princeton University Press, 1957.

Knight, G. Wilson. *The Wheel of Fire*. Rev. ed. London: Oxford University Press, 1957.

Levin, Harry. *The Question of "Hamlet"*. New York: Oxford University Press, 1959.

Mack, Maynard. *Killing the King: Three Studies in Shakespeare's Tragic Structure*. New Haven: Yale University Press, 1973.

McFarland, Thomas. *Tragic Meanings in Shakespeare*. New York: Random House, 1966.

Motter, T. H. Vail. *The School Drama in England*. 1929. Reprint. Port Washington, N.Y.: Kennikat Press, 1968.

Nelson, Robert J. *Play Within a Play: The Dramatist's Conception of His Art*. New Haven: Yale University Press, 1958.

Palmer, John. *Political and Comic Characters of Shakespeare*. London: Macmillan, 1961.

Prior, Moody E. *The Drama of Power: Studies in Shakespeare's History Plays*. Evanston: Northwestern University Press, 1973.

Proser, Matthew N. *The Heroic Image in Five Shakespearean Tragedies*. Princeton: Princeton University Press, 1965.

Prosser, Eleanor A. *Hamlet and Revenge*. Rev. ed. Stanford: Stanford University Press, 1971.

Ribner, Irving. *Patterns in Shakespearian Tragedy*. London: Methuen, 1960.

Righter, Anne. *Shakespeare and the Idea of the Play*. London: Chatto & Windus, 1962.

Sanford, Wendy Coppedge. *Theater as Metaphor in "Hamlet"*. Cambridge: Harvard University Press, 1967.

Spencer, Theodore. *Shakespeare and the Nature of Man*. New York: Macmillan, 1942.

Tillyard, E. M. W. *Shakespeare's History Plays*. London: Chatto & Windus, 1944.

Traversi, Derek. *An Approach to Shakespeare*. Vol. I. Garden City, N.Y.: Anchor Books, 1969.

———. *Shakespeare from "Richard II" to "Henry V"*. Stanford: Stanford University Press, 1957.

Ure, Peter. *Shakespeare: The Problem Plays*. London: Longmans, Green, 1961.

Van Doren, Mark. *Shakespeare*. New York: Holt, 1939.

West, Robert H. *Shakespeare and the Outer Mystery*. Lexington: University of Kentucky Press, 1968.

Wickham, Glynne. *Early English Stages, 1300–1660*. London and New York: Routledge and Kegan Paul and Columbia University Press, 1963.

Wilson, John Dover. *The Fortunes of Falstaff*. Cambridge: Cambridge University Press, 1943.

———. *The Meaning of "The Tempest"*. Newcastle upon Tyne: Literary and Philosophical Society, 1936.

Wind, Edgar. *Pagan Mysteries in the Renaissance*. New York: Norton, 1968.

Winny, James. *The Player King: A Theme of Shakespeare's Histories*. New York: Barnes & Noble, 1968.

Secondary Sources: Articles

Berger, Harry, Jr. "*Troilus and Cressida*: The Observer as Basilisk." *Comparative Drama*, II (1968), 122–36.

Blanpied, John W. " 'Unfathered heirs and loathly births of nature':

Bringing History to Crisis in *2 Henry IV*." *English Literary Renaissance*, V (1975), 212–31.

Calderwood, James L. "*1 Henry IV*: Art's Gilded Lie." *English Literary Renaissance*, III (1973), 131–44.

———. "*Coriolanus*: Wordless Meanings and Meaningless Words." *Studies in English Literature*, VI (1966), 211–24.

Danson, Lawrence N. "Metonymy and *Coriolanus*." *Philological Quarterly*, LXII (1973), 30–42.

Davis, Jo Ann. "Henry IV: From Satirist to Satiric Butt." *Aeolian Harps*. Edited by Donna G. Fricke and Douglas C. Fricke. Bowling Green, Ohio: Bowling Green University Press, 1976.

Dean, Leonard F. "*Richard II*: The State and the Image of the Theater." *Publications of the Modern Language Association*, LXVII (1952), 211–18.

Dorius, R. J. "A Little More Than a Little." *Shakespeare Quarterly*, XI (1960), 13–26.

Elton, W. R. "Shakespeare's Ulysses and the Problem of Value." *Shakespeare Studies*, II (1967), 95–111.

Faber, M. D. "Falstaff Behind the Arras." *American Imago*, XXVII (1970), 197–225.

Fergusson, Francis. "Philosophy and Theatre in *Measure for Measure*." *Kenyon Review*, XIV (1952), 103–20.

Fink, Eugen. "The Oasis of Happiness: Toward an Ontology of Play." *Game, Play, Literature*. New Haven: Eastern Press, 1968.

Forker, Charles R. "Shakespeare's Theatrical Symbolism and Its Function in *Hamlet*." *Shakespeare Quarterly*, XIV (1963), 215–29.

Freud, Sigmund. "The 'Uncanny.'" Translated by Alix Strachey. *On Creativity and the Unconscious*. New York: Harper & Row, 1958.

Frye, Northrop. "The Argument of Comedy." *English Institute Essays, 1948* (1949), 58–73.

Gottschalk, Paul A. "Hal and the 'Play Extempore' in *1 Henry IV*." *Texas Studies in Literature and Language*, XV (1974), 605–14.

Hawkins, Harriett. "Fabulous Counterfeits: Dramatic Construction and Dramatic Perspectives in *The Spanish Tragedy, A Midsummer Night's Dream*, and *The Tempest*." *Shakespeare Studies*, VI (1970), 51–65.

Hawkins, Sherman H. "Virtue and Kingship in Shakespeare's *Henry*

IV." English Literary Renaissance, V (1975), 313–43.

Homan, Sidney R. "Iago's Aesthetics: *Othello* and Shakespeare's Portrait of an Artist." *Shakespeare Studies*, V (1969), 141–48.

Kermode, Frank. "Introduction." *The Tempest*. New Arden Edition. Cambridge: Harvard University Press, 1958.

Kris, Ernst. "Prince Hal's Conflict." *Psychoanalytic Quarterly*, XVII (1948), 487–506.

Marsh, Derick R. C. "Interpretation and Misinterpretation: The Problem of *Troilus and Cressida*." *Shakespeare Studies*, I (1965), 182–98.

McGuire, Richard L. "The Play-within-the-play in *1 Henry IV*." *Shakespeare Quarterly*, XVIII (1967), 47–52.

McNeir, Waldo F. "Structure and Theme in the First Tavern Scene of *Henry IV, Part One*." *Essays on Shakespeare*. Edited by Gordon Ross Smith. University Park: Pennsylvania State University Press, 1965.

Mehl, Dieter. "Forms and Functions of the Play within a Play." *Renaissance Drama*, VIII (1965), 41–62.

Quinn, Michael. " 'The King Is Not Himself': The Personal Tragedy of Richard II." *Studies in Philology*, LVI (1959), 169–86.

Rabkin, Norman. *"Troilus and Cressida*: The Uses of the Double Plot." *Shakespeare Studies*, I (1965), 265–82.

Reiman, Donald. "Appearance, Reality, and Moral Order in *Richard II*." *Modern Language Quarterly*, XXV (1964), 34–45.

Rose, Mark. *"Hamlet* and the Shape of Revenge." *English Literary Renaissance*, I (1971), 132–43.

Shuchter, J. D. "Prince Hal and Francis: The Imitation of an Action." *Shakespeare Studies*, III (1967), 129–37.

Sicherman, Carol M. *"Coriolanus*: The Failure of Words." *English Literary History*, XXXIX (1972), 189–207.

Siemon, James E. *"The Merchant of Venice*: Act V as Ritual Reiteration." *Studies in Philology*, LXVII (1970), 201–209.

Sisk, John P. "Bondage and Release in *The Merchant of Venice*." *Shakespeare Quarterly*, XX (1969), 217–23.

Stockholder, Katherine. "The Other Coriolanus." *Publications of the Modern Language Association*, LXXXV (1970), 228–36.

Wertheim, Albert. "The Treatment of Shylock and Thematic Integrity in *The Merchant of Venice.*" *Shakespeare Studies*, VI (1970), 75–87.

Wilson, Harold S. "Action and Symbol in *Measure for Measure* and *The Tempest.*" *Shakespeare Quarterly*, IV (1953), 375–84.

Zimbardo, Rose A. "The Formalism of *Henry V.*" *Shakespeare Encomium.* Edited by Anne Paolucci. New York: City College, 1964.

Index

References to the minor characters are grouped under the title of the play; references to the major characters are grouped under the name of the character.